AF693172

NEXT-GEN

NLP

FOR BUSINESS

From Core Concepts to Scalable AI Solutions

By

Dr. Hesham Mohamed Elsherif

ABOUT THE AUTHOR

Dr. Hesham Mohamed Elsherif stands at the forefront of library management, research, and the practical implementation of Artificial Intelligence (AI) in educational and library systems. With over 22 years of dedicated service in the field, he brings a wealth of expertise that bridges the worlds of technology, organizational leadership, and scholarship.

Dr. Elsherif's academic credentials are as diverse as they are impressive. He holds two doctoral degrees—one in **Management and Organizational Leadership** and the other in **Information Systems and Technology**. This dual specialization has equipped him with a holistic perspective on how institutions can effectively integrate emerging technologies, particularly AI, to optimize resource allocation, streamline operational processes, and enrich learning experiences.

A recognized authority in **empirical research methodology**, Dr. Elsherif specializes in **qualitative approaches** and **action research**. His mastery of these methodologies has not only bolstered his own scholarly work but has also allowed him to pioneer new ways of investigating and implementing AI-driven solutions in school, academic, and public libraries. Whether he is designing user-centric AI tools or conducting in-depth studies on technology adoption, Dr.

Elsherif's methodical and data-driven approach consistently yields impactful, real-world results.

Over the years, he has made significant strides in shaping the academic community - not just as a **professional researcher**, but also as an **Adjunct Professor**. In the classroom, Dr. Elsherif has a remarkable ability to translate complex theories into accessible insights, thereby training a new generation of thought leaders and specialists in both library science and technology. This multifaceted role, spanning teaching, research, and practice, has cemented his status as a **pioneer** whose influence extends well beyond traditional academic boundaries.

Dr. Elsherif's expertise and passion are truly global in scope. He has served as a **consultant to numerous educational institutions worldwide**, offering guidance on best practices, AI integration strategies, and effective management models. His international collaborations speak to the versatility of his knowledge, which is informed by a deep understanding of how AI can enhance resource discovery, user engagement, and scholarly communication across cultural and institutional contexts.

Central to Dr. Elsherif's mission is the belief that **innovative technologies**, including AI, must be harnessed responsibly and ethically. This commitment is evident in his approach to library management and educational technology, where he advocates for solutions that are inclusive, data-secure, and aligned with the core values of academic freedom and public service. By focusing on ethical implementation, he ensures that advancements in AI serve learners, educators, and researchers effectively and fairly.

Today, Dr. Elsherif continues to break new ground in **library innovation**, **academic research**, and **technology leadership**. Combining a passion for education with an unparalleled depth of knowledge, he remains a guiding force - **inspiring, educating, and leading** in library systems, educational institutions, and beyond.

Through his work, he illuminates the path toward a future where AI seamlessly complements human expertise, thereby enriching the academic and public spheres for generations to come.

PREFACE

It is with great enthusiasm that we present the *Next-Gen NLP for Business: From Core Concepts to Scalable AI Solutions.* As both a practical manual and a strategic resource, this book is designed to bridge classical linguistic approaches with cutting-edge machine learning and deep learning techniques, reflecting how NLP has become a cornerstone in modern, data-driven enterprises.

Over the past few decades, NLP has evolved from a niche research topic to a mission-critical asset across diverse industries. With the exponential rise in unstructured text data—ranging from customer feedback and corporate documents to social media discussions—organizations are increasingly leveraging NLP solutions to gain competitive advantages and fuel data-centric decision-making. From optimizing customer engagement to detecting fraud and managing large-scale operational workflows, NLP empowers businesses to transform text data into actionable insights.

This transformation necessitates a holistic approach. While corporate leaders require strategic guidance to align AI investments with organizational objectives, data scientists and software engineers must remain well-versed in the latest architectures and deployment methodologies. Furthermore, the need for responsible AI has never been more urgent. Issues of bias, transparency, and regulatory compliance are now fundamental considerations in every NLP project life cycle.

Given these factors, we have structured the *NLP* to serve as a comprehensive, end-to-end guide:

1. **Strategic Foundations** – We begin with a thorough overview of NLP's origins, key milestones, and the foundational linguistic concepts that underpin modern techniques. This segment underscores the strategic relevance of NLP initiatives in the

corporate world, helping decision-makers identify clear business cases and ROI pathways.

2. **Core Techniques** – The heart of NLP lies in text processing, feature engineering, and the foundational statistical methods that paved the way for more advanced solutions. Classical approaches such as Bag-of-Words, TF-IDF, and Hidden Markov Models are explored in detail, highlighting the critical role they continue to play in many industry applications.
3. **Deep Learning Paradigms** – Recent advancements in neural networks, attention mechanisms, and Transformer-based architectures have redefined the NLP landscape. By demystifying the underlying concepts and providing practical fine-tuning strategies, we empower readers to elevate their NLP initiatives with next-generation solutions like BERT, GPT, and others.
4. **Special Topics and Emerging Frontiers** – As organizations expand globally, topics such as multilingual NLP, conversational AI, and specialized industry applications are no longer optional considerations. Ethical and compliance-focused discussions underscore the importance of responsible AI and model explainability - essentials in today's regulatory environment.
5. **Enterprise Deployment and Future Outlook** – This book culminates in a detailed examination of enterprise-grade deployment, covering infrastructure choices, CI/CD best practices, and scalability strategies. We also explore upcoming frontiers, offering insights into how NLP will evolve and integrate with other AI disciplines.

Our goal is to cater to a diverse readership encompassing C-suite executives, product managers, data scientists, software engineers, and academics. Each chapter is carefully crafted to provide a balance of theoretical depth, practical guidance, and strategic insights. Whether you are orchestrating large-scale NLP deployments, conducting research on state-of-the-art algorithms, or exploring how text analytics can optimize day-to-day operations, this *NLP Bible* offers clear, authoritative direction.

Above all, we seek to instill a sense of ongoing innovation. While NLP technology has made unprecedented strides, continuous learning and adaptation remain paramount. We hope this guide serves not only as a reference for current practices, but also as a catalyst for envisioning future breakthroughs. The synergy between business imperatives and robust engineering will foster a fertile environment for creative applications that reshape how enterprises interface with the written word.

It is our sincere hope that this comprehensive resource empowers you to harness NLP's transformative potential. By combining tradition and proven frameworks with forward-thinking perspectives, we endeavor to equip you with the knowledge and inspiration required to excel in this rapidly evolving field.

Welcome to the *Next-Gen NLP for Business: From Core Concepts to Scalable AI Solutions*. Let us begin this journey together toward building a more insightful, efficient, and innovative future.

Table of Contents

Part I: Foundations And Strategic Overview

Chapter 1: Introduction to NLP

Defining NLP and Its Strategic Importance

Natural Language Processing (NLP) can be defined as the interdisciplinary field that empowers machines to interpret, analyze, generate, and manipulate human language. By merging computational linguistics, data science, and artificial intelligence (AI), NLP solutions unlock the latent value embedded in textual and verbal data. From email exchanges and social media comments to corporate reports and call center transcripts, NLP algorithms transform unstructured language into structured insights - generating actionable intelligence for enterprise decision-making.

Over the years, traditional rule-based systems have evolved into machine learning (ML)–driven models, and more recently, deep learning architectures. This progression reflects the industry's increasing emphasis on automation, scalability, and enhanced accuracy. As organizations move toward more digital-centric operations, NLP becomes a pivotal strategic differentiator, enabling them to:

1. **Improve Operational Efficiency**

- **Automation of Repetitive Tasks**: Automated text classification or sentiment detection can fast-track tasks that would otherwise consume considerable human effort (e.g., triaging customer support tickets).
- **Scalable Text Analysis**: NLP solutions ingest, parse, and process high volumes of text data in seconds, empowering analysts and knowledge workers to focus on higher-value activities.

2. **Enhance Customer Engagement**

- **Personalized Interactions**: Next-generation chatbots and voice-driven assistants leverage NLP to deliver tailored user experiences, boosting customer satisfaction and loyalty.
- **Real-Time Feedback Loops**: By mining feedback from surveys, social media, and user forums, enterprises can rapidly adapt product roadmaps and service offerings.

3. **Derive Business Intelligence**

- **Predictive Insights**: Advanced NLP models, coupled with predictive analytics, inform corporate strategy through trend analysis and market sentiment monitoring.
- **Data-Driven Innovation**: Continuous ingestion and analysis of natural language content fosters a culture of perpetual learning and innovation.

4. **Ensure Compliance and Reduce Risk**

- **Regulatory Monitoring**: Automated document scanning and contract analysis ensure adherence to industry-specific regulations (e.g., HIPAA, GDPR) and internal governance.
- **Fraud Detection and Security**: NLP-based anomaly detection identifies suspicious language patterns in emails and other communications that may indicate fraudulent activity.

Through these vectors, NLP plays a vital strategic role in helping organizations stay competitive in a marketplace defined by exponential data growth and evolving consumer expectations. When integrated effectively, NLP initiatives drive operational optimization, advance enterprise-wide digital transformation goals, and solidify an organization's market position.

Illustrative Example: Simple NLP Workflow in Python

While enterprises often employ comprehensive platforms (such as proprietary or cloud-based AI suites), the following illustrative code snippet demonstrates a simplified NLP workflow using Python's **spaCy** library. This example tokenizes text, assigns part-of-speech tags, and performs named entity recognition (NER). In a corporate setting, these steps often form the foundation of advanced use cases - like compliance checks or automated customer support routing.

```
# Install spaCy (if not already installed):

# !pip install spacy

# Download a spaCy language model (e.g., English):

# !python -m spacy download en_core_web_sm

import spacy

# Load the spaCy language model

nlp = spacy.load("en_core_web_sm")

# Example text that might come from an email or a customer
feedback form

text_data = """

Hello Team,

I am writing to request more information about the new
product launch in Germany.

Regards,

Alex Johnson

"""
```

```
# Process the text data
doc = nlp(text_data)
# Tokenization and Part-of-Speech (POS) Tags
print("Tokens and POS Tags:")
for token in doc:
    print(f"{token.text:<15} {token.pos_}")
# Named Entity Recognition (NER)
print("\nNamed Entities:")
for ent in doc.ents:
    print(f"{ent.text:<15} {ent.label_}")
```

1. **Tokenization and POS Tagging**

- The script breaks text into individual tokens and assigns parts of speech (e.g., verbs, nouns, adjectives). This information is crucial for understanding grammatical structures and providing context for downstream tasks such as text classification.

2. **Named Entity Recognition (NER)**

- Entities like *Person*, *Location*, or *Organization* are identified and categorized, which can be critical in legal document processing, customer sentiment analysis, and compliance checks.

Although this simplified demonstration may not showcase enterprise-level optimization (such as distributed processing or advanced Transformer-based methods), it underscores fundamental NLP processes that underpin more sophisticated workflows. At scale, enterprises typically incorporate robust data pipeline architectures, model versioning, real-time monitoring, and alignment with security protocols to ensure reliability and compliance.

Key Milestones in NLP Development

A Chronological Journey

The evolution of Natural Language Processing (NLP) is marked by a series of groundbreaking milestones, each reflecting the industry's shift from rule-based systems to sophisticated machine learning models.

Early Beginnings: Rule-Based Methods (1950s–1980s)

In the nascent stages of NLP, researchers primarily relied on **rule-based methods**. These early systems were constructed on hand-crafted rules and heuristics to process and interpret human language. Pioneering work in machine translation and syntactic parsing during this era laid the foundation for more advanced methods. Key characteristics included:

- **Deterministic Processing:** Rule-based systems operated on explicitly defined grammars and dictionaries, ensuring predictable outcomes.
- **Limited Scalability:** Although effective in narrowly defined contexts, these systems struggled with the inherent ambiguities of natural language, leading to limited adaptability in diverse, real-world scenarios.

Example: A simple rule-based tokenization using Python's regular expressions:

```
import re

# Simple rule-based tokenization using regular expressions

text = "Welcome to the NLP evolution: from rule-based systems to machine learning!"

tokens = re.findall(r'\b\w+\b', text)

print("Tokens:", tokens)
```

This snippet exemplifies how early NLP systems parsed text by matching word boundaries, a rudimentary yet crucial step in linguistic analysis.

The Statistical Revolution: Emergence of Machine Learning (1990s–2000s)

The advent of the **statistical paradigm** in the 1990s marked a significant departure from deterministic rule-based methods. This period saw the introduction of data-driven techniques that leveraged probability models to handle language ambiguity more effectively. Key advancements included:

- **N-gram Models:** Statistical models that estimated the probability of word sequences, significantly improving tasks like speech recognition and text prediction.
- **Hidden Markov Models (HMMs) and Conditional Random Fields (CRFs):** These probabilistic models enhanced capabilities in part-of-speech tagging and named entity recognition, enabling systems to learn from large corpora rather than relying solely on pre-defined rules.

Illustrative Example: Training a simple text classifier using n-gram features with scikit-learn:

```
from sklearn.feature_extraction.text import CountVectorizer

from sklearn.naive_bayes import MultinomialNB

from sklearn.pipeline import make_pipeline

# Sample dataset: short documents with binary labels

texts = [

    "Machine learning is revolutionizing NLP.",

    "Rule-based systems were the initial approach.",
```

```
    "Statistical methods brought probabilistic reasoning.",
    "Deep learning has transformed language models."
]
labels = [1, 0, 0, 1]  # 1: Modern approaches, 0: Early methods
# Create a pipeline that vectorizes text using n-grams and trains a classifier
model = make_pipeline(CountVectorizer(ngram_range=(1, 2)), MultinomialNB())
model.fit(texts, labels)
# Predicting on a new text sample
sample_text = ["Advancements in NLP include both statistical and deep learning methods."]
prediction = model.predict(sample_text)
print("Prediction:", "Modern approach" if prediction[0] == 1 else "Early method")
```

In this example, the classifier leverages bigram features to differentiate between texts that describe modern versus early NLP approaches. This reflects the statistical shift where models learned linguistic patterns from data rather than relying on rigid rules.

Deep Learning and Transformer Era (2010s–Present)

The 2010s ushered in an era of **deep learning**, further revolutionizing NLP. Neural networks, particularly deep architectures such as LSTMs and, later, Transformer models, introduced unparalleled levels of performance and adaptability. Key milestones include:

- **Word Embeddings:** Techniques like Word2Vec, GloVe, and FastText enabled dense vector representations of words, capturing intricate semantic relationships.
- **Recurrent Neural Networks (RNNs) and LSTMs:** These models improved the handling of sequential data, making them ideal for language modeling and machine translation.
- **Attention Mechanisms and Transformers:** The introduction of the Transformer architecture (e.g., BERT, GPT series) transformed NLP by enabling parallel processing of text and facilitating the training of large-scale, contextualized language models. This era emphasizes transfer learning, where pretrained models are fine-tuned to specific enterprise tasks.

This phase is characterized by a dramatic increase in model complexity and performance, driving enterprise applications in areas such as conversational AI, sentiment analysis, and predictive analytics.

Strategic Implications for Modern Enterprises

Understanding this evolutionary journey is crucial for contemporary enterprises, as it illuminates several strategic imperatives:

- **Scalability and Flexibility:** Modern NLP solutions built on deep learning and Transformers are highly scalable, adapting seamlessly to diverse and evolving business needs.
- **Data-Driven Decision Making:** The shift from rule-based to statistical and neural approaches has enabled organizations to harness vast amounts of unstructured data, transforming it into actionable insights.
- **Future-Proofing Investments:** Recognizing the historical trajectory of NLP helps businesses anticipate future trends, ensuring that investments in NLP infrastructure remain robust in the face of rapid technological change.

By integrating lessons from both the early rule-based systems and the subsequent machine learning breakthroughs, enterprises can craft a comprehensive NLP strategy that leverages historical wisdom while embracing cutting-edge innovations.

NLP in the Corporate Ecosystem

Driving Business Value

In today's rapidly digitizing marketplace, NLP is not merely a technological pursuit but a strategic business enabler. It plays a pivotal role in converting unstructured text data into actionable insights, directly impacting operational efficiency, customer engagement, and ultimately, the bottom line.

Business Use Cases

1. **Customer Experience and Engagement**

- **Chatbots and Virtual Assistants:** NLP-driven chatbots streamline customer service by providing instant responses and 24/7 support, reducing the workload on human agents.
- **Sentiment Analysis:** By analyzing customer feedback across various channels (social media, surveys, emails), NLP models help businesses understand customer sentiment, enabling timely interventions and enhancing customer satisfaction.
- **Personalization:** Tailored recommendations and personalized marketing campaigns are made possible by NLP systems that analyze customer preferences and behavior patterns.

2. **Operational Efficiency and Automation**

- **Document Management:** NLP facilitates the automated classification and indexing of vast volumes of documents, significantly reducing manual processing time.

- **Compliance and Risk Management:** By scanning contracts, legal documents, and communications, NLP tools help ensure compliance with industry regulations (e.g., GDPR, HIPAA) and flag potential risks such as fraudulent activities.
- **Knowledge Management:** NLP-powered search engines and document summarization tools enhance internal knowledge sharing and decision-making processes.

3. **Business Intelligence and Analytics**

- **Trend Analysis:** NLP systems can process and analyze news articles, research papers, and financial reports to forecast market trends and provide competitive intelligence.
- **Predictive Analytics:** When combined with traditional data analytics, NLP insights help predict consumer behavior, optimize pricing strategies, and guide product development.
- **Operational Analytics:** Monitoring operational communications and reports in real time allows companies to identify inefficiencies and optimize internal workflows.

Stakeholder Considerations

Implementing NLP solutions in a corporate setting requires careful alignment with various stakeholder needs:

- **Executive Leadership:**
  Decision-makers focus on how NLP can drive strategic initiatives, boost operational efficiency, and generate competitive advantage. Clear metrics on ROI, cost reduction, and revenue growth are paramount for securing executive sponsorship.
- **Data Science and IT Teams:**
  These groups are responsible for the technical deployment and maintenance of NLP solutions. They require robust, scalable architectures, integration with existing data pipelines, and

continuous support for model updates and performance monitoring.

- **Operational Units:**
  End-users such as customer service teams, compliance officers, and marketing professionals must see tangible benefits from NLP applications. User-friendly interfaces, actionable dashboards, and minimal disruption to existing workflows are critical to adoption and sustained usage.

- **Legal and Compliance Departments:**
  With data privacy and regulatory compliance as top priorities, these stakeholders ensure that NLP solutions adhere to legal standards and incorporate mechanisms for data protection and auditability.

High-Level Return on Investment (ROI)

The ROI from NLP investments can be evaluated across multiple dimensions:

- **Cost Savings:**
  Automation of repetitive tasks and reduction in manual labor result in significant cost reductions. For example, automating customer support through NLP-driven chatbots can lower operational costs while improving service response times.

- **Revenue Growth:**
  Enhanced customer engagement and personalized marketing strategies directly translate into higher customer retention and increased sales. Furthermore, advanced analytics and trend forecasting enable proactive market positioning and informed business decisions.

- **Risk Mitigation:**
  Automated compliance checks and fraud detection reduce legal and operational risks. This proactive approach not only

safeguards the business but also minimizes potential penalties and reputational damage.

- **Operational Efficiency:**
  Streamlining document management and knowledge extraction processes enhances overall productivity. By enabling employees to focus on high-value tasks rather than manual data processing, organizations can achieve more agile and efficient operations.

Illustrative Example: Sentiment Analysis for Customer Feedback

To demonstrate the tangible benefits of NLP in enhancing customer engagement, consider a scenario where an organization deploys a sentiment analysis model to process customer feedback. The following example leverages the Hugging Face Transformers library to classify customer comments as positive, neutral, or negative - an essential metric for measuring customer satisfaction and guiding strategic initiatives.

```
# Install required libraries (if not already installed):

# !pip install transformers torch

from transformers import pipeline

# Initialize a sentiment-analysis pipeline using a pretrained model

sentiment_analyzer = pipeline("sentiment-analysis")

# Example customer feedback data

feedback_samples = [

    "The new product is amazing! I've never been happier with my purchase.",

    "The service was okay, but I expected more attention to detail.",
```

```
    "I'm extremely disappointed. The product quality is subpar and the support is unresponsive."
]

# Analyze sentiment for each feedback sample
results = sentiment_analyzer(feedback_samples)

# Display the analysis results
for sample, result in zip(feedback_samples, results):
    print(f"Feedback: {sample}\nSentiment: {result['label']}, Confidence: {result['score']:.2f}\n")
```

Explanation:

- **Pipeline Initialization:**
  A sentiment analysis pipeline is set up using a pretrained model, enabling rapid deployment with minimal configuration.
- **Feedback Processing:**
  Customer feedback is processed to extract sentiment labels and confidence scores, providing a quantifiable measure of customer satisfaction.
- **Actionable Insights:**
  These insights enable marketing and product teams to identify strengths, address weaknesses, and adjust strategies in real time, thus directly influencing revenue and operational efficiency.

Conclusion

Integrating NLP into the corporate ecosystem offers a multi-faceted value proposition - improving customer experience, streamlining operations, and generating actionable business intelligence. With careful consideration of stakeholder needs and a focus on measurable ROI, enterprises can leverage NLP to drive strategic innovation and maintain a competitive edge in today's data-centric environment. This comprehensive approach not only fosters operational excellence but also paves the way for sustained growth and market leadership.

Chapter 2: Theoretical Underpinnings of Linguistics

Theoretical Underpinnings of Linguistics

Linguistic Fundamentals

A robust understanding of linguistic fundamentals is essential for designing NLP systems that can accurately interpret, generate, and manipulate human language.

Syntax: Structure and Grammatical Rules

Definition:
Syntax refers to the arrangement of words and phrases to create well-formed sentences according to a language's grammatical rules. In NLP, syntax is crucial for tasks such as parsing, machine translation, and information extraction, as it helps systems understand the structural relationships within sentences.

Relevance to NLP:

- **Parsing and Dependency Analysis:** NLP systems rely on syntactic parsing to build tree structures that reveal grammatical relationships (e.g., subject-verb-object relationships).
- **Disambiguation:** Accurate syntactic analysis helps resolve ambiguities in sentences, such as identifying the correct attachment of prepositional phrases.

Illustrative Example: Dependency Parsing with spaCy

Below is a Python code snippet demonstrating how to perform dependency parsing using spaCy, a popular NLP library:

```
import spacy

# Load the spaCy English language model

nlp = spacy.load("en_core_web_sm")
```

```
# Example sentence for syntactic analysis
sentence = "The quick brown fox jumps over the lazy dog."
# Process the sentence to obtain a parsed document
doc = nlp(sentence)
print("Dependency Parsing Output:")
for token in doc:
    # Display token text, its dependency relation, and its head token
    print(f"{token.text:<10} {token.dep_:<10} {token.head.text}")
```

Explanation:

- **Tokenization and Parsing:** The text is tokenized into individual words, and each token is annotated with its dependency relation to other tokens (e.g., subject, object).
- **Structural Insights:** This structured output aids in developing algorithms that understand sentence construction, thereby improving downstream tasks like semantic role labeling and question answering.

Semantics: Meaning and Interpretation

Definition:
Semantics involves the study of meaning in language. It focuses on how words, phrases, and sentences convey meaning, and how this meaning can vary with context. In NLP, semantic analysis is fundamental for tasks such as sentiment analysis, machine translation, and question answering.

Relevance to NLP:

- **Word Sense Disambiguation:** Systems must determine the correct meaning of words that have multiple interpretations depending on the context.
- **Semantic Similarity:** By quantifying semantic similarity, NLP applications can perform tasks such as document clustering, information retrieval, and recommendation systems.
- **Knowledge Graphs and Ontologies:** These structures represent semantic relationships and enable more advanced reasoning over text data.

Illustrative Example: Semantic Similarity using Word Embeddings

Below is an example of computing semantic similarity using the spaCy library's built-in word vectors:

```
# Example words to compare

word1 = nlp("bank")

word2 = nlp("financial institution")

word3 = nlp("river")

# Compute similarity scores

similarity_1_2 = word1.similarity(word2)

similarity_1_3 = word1.similarity(word3)

print(f"Similarity between 'bank' and 'financial institution': {similarity_1_2:.2f}")

print(f"Similarity between 'bank' and 'river': {similarity_1_3:.2f}")
```

Explanation:

- **Word Embeddings:** This code leverages distributed representations (word embeddings) to calculate the semantic closeness of terms, which is pivotal in applications like recommendation engines and semantic search.
- **Contextual Relevance:** By understanding semantic relationships, enterprises can design NLP systems that better capture the nuances of language, leading to more precise interpretations and responses.

Pragmatics: Contextual and Situational Use

Definition:
Pragmatics examines how context influences the interpretation of meaning. It considers factors such as the speaker's intent, the situational context, and the conversational dynamics that shape language use. Pragmatic analysis is vital in ensuring that NLP systems do not just process language mechanically but also grasp the underlying communicative intent.

Relevance to NLP:

- **Context-Aware Systems:** Pragmatic considerations enable the development of chatbots and virtual assistants that tailor responses based on user context and interaction history.
- **Discourse Analysis:** Understanding pragmatic cues improves the performance of dialogue systems and enhances the quality of conversational AI.
- **Sarcasm and Irony Detection:** Capturing pragmatic subtleties aids in accurately identifying sarcasm, humor, or other non-literal language, which is crucial for sentiment analysis and social media monitoring.

Illustrative Example: Contextual Analysis in Dialogue Systems

While pragmatic analysis is inherently complex and context-dependent, a simplified approach might involve tracking conversation context. Below is a conceptual example using Python to maintain dialogue context in a chatbot:

```
class Chatbot:
    def __init__(self):
        self.context = []
    def update_context(self, message):
        self.context.append(message)
    def generate_response(self, current_message):
        # For demonstration, a simplistic approach based on
accumulated context
        if "help" in current_message.lower():
            return "How can I assist you further?"
        elif self.context and "previous" in self.context[-1].lower():
            return "Let's continue from where we left off."
        else:
            return "Tell me more about your inquiry."
    def interact(self, message):
        self.update_context(message)
        response = self.generate_response(message)
        return response
# Instantiate the chatbot and simulate a conversation
```

```
chatbot = Chatbot()
print(chatbot.interact("I need some help with my account."))
print(chatbot.interact("I'm not sure how to proceed."))
```

Explanation:

- **Context Tracking:** This simplified code demonstrates how context can be preserved across interactions to generate more relevant responses.
- **Enhanced User Experience:** By incorporating pragmatic principles, the system can adjust its behavior to better meet the user's needs, thereby improving engagement and satisfaction.

Integrating Linguistic Fundamentals into NLP System Design

Strategic Relevance:

- **Holistic Understanding:** Incorporating syntax, semantics, and pragmatics into NLP models results in systems that are not only technically robust but also contextually intelligent.
- **Improved Accuracy:** Systems designed with linguistic fundamentals in mind exhibit enhanced accuracy in tasks such as machine translation, sentiment analysis, and conversational AI.
- **Competitive Advantage:** Enterprises that leverage these principles can create solutions that adapt more effectively to the nuances of human language, thereby gaining a strategic edge in their respective markets.

In Summary, understanding and applying linguistic fundamentals - syntax, semantics, and pragmatics - enables the development of advanced NLP systems that mimic human-like understanding of language. This approach bridges the gap between theoretical linguistics and practical application, ensuring that NLP solutions are both accurate and contextually aware, ultimately driving superior business outcomes.

Through careful integration of these linguistic principles, organizations can build more resilient, adaptable, and effective NLP systems, paving the way for enhanced operational efficiency and competitive differentiation in the digital landscape.

Linguistic Resources and Corpora

Enabling Data-Driven Linguistic Analysis

A cornerstone of modern NLP system design is the utilization of robust linguistic resources and corpora. These datasets, which consist of curated collections of texts and annotations, underpin the development, training, and evaluation of NLP models. By selecting and leveraging appropriate corpora, enterprises can significantly enhance the accuracy, scalability, and contextual understanding of their language processing systems.

Commonly Used Language Datasets and Corpora

1. **General-Purpose Corpora:**

- **Wikipedia Dumps:**
  Large-scale, multilingual data providing a wealth of information on diverse topics. Wikipedia's structured nature and hyperlinks offer opportunities for tasks like entity linking and topic modeling.
- **Common Crawl:**
  A vast repository of web-crawled data, ideal for training large language models and exploring emerging linguistic patterns across the internet.
- **News Corpora (e.g., Reuters, BBC):**
  Texts from reputable news sources serve as high-quality datasets

for tasks such as named entity recognition (NER), summarization, and sentiment analysis.

2. **Domain-Specific Corpora:**

- **Medical and Clinical Texts (e.g., MIMIC-III):** Curated datasets that provide insights into specialized terminologies and clinical narratives, crucial for building models in the healthcare domain.
- **Legal Corpora (e.g., Case Law, Contracts):** Collections of legal documents and contracts facilitate the development of applications in compliance, contract analysis, and legal research.

3. **Annotated Corpora:**

- **Penn Treebank:** Provides richly annotated syntactic and semantic structures, making it an essential resource for training and evaluating parsing algorithms.
- **CoNLL Datasets:** Frequently used for benchmarking NER, dependency parsing, and other sequence-labeling tasks, these datasets are annotated by expert linguists to ensure quality and consistency.
- **SQuAD (Stanford Question Answering Dataset):** A widely adopted dataset for training and evaluating question-answering systems, offering a rich collection of context-answer pairs.

Best Practices for Corpus Selection

Selecting the appropriate corpus for NLP projects is a strategic decision that can dramatically influence model performance and deployment success. Here are key best practices to consider:

1. **Relevance and Domain Specificity:**

- **Contextual Alignment:**
  Ensure the selected corpus aligns with the target domain or application. For instance, clinical NLP applications should leverage medical texts to capture the specialized vocabulary and context unique to healthcare.
- **Cultural and Linguistic Diversity:**
  Incorporate datasets that represent the language, dialects, and cultural contexts relevant to your user base to enhance model generalization and reduce bias.

2. **Data Quality and Annotation Standards:**

- **Accuracy and Consistency:**
  Prioritize corpora that are well-annotated, with established guidelines and high inter-annotator agreement. High-quality annotations are critical for training reliable models.
- **Data Cleanliness:**
  Use corpora that have been preprocessed to remove noise, irrelevant information, and formatting issues, ensuring that the dataset is ready for immediate integration into your NLP pipeline.

3. **Scalability and Accessibility:**

- **Size and Coverage:**
  Select corpora that provide sufficient data volume and variety to train deep learning models effectively. Larger datasets generally lead to better model performance but may require significant computational resources.
- **Licensing and Accessibility:**
  Ensure that the data is legally and ethically available for use. Open-source and publicly accessible corpora are preferred, as they facilitate transparency and reproducibility in research and enterprise applications.

Illustrative Example: Exploring a Corpus with NLTK

To demonstrate the practical aspect of working with linguistic corpora, consider the example of exploring the Gutenberg Corpus using Python's Natural Language Toolkit (NLTK). The Gutenberg Corpus is a collection of literary texts that can be used for various NLP tasks, including language modeling and syntactic analysis.

```
import nltk

from nltk.corpus import gutenberg

# Download the Gutenberg Corpus if not already available

nltk.download('gutenberg')

# List available texts in the Gutenberg Corpus

print("Available texts in the Gutenberg Corpus:")

print(gutenberg.fileids())

# Load a specific text, e.g., "Emma" by Jane Austen

emma_text = gutenberg.raw('austen-emma.txt')

# Basic text processing: Tokenize into words

tokens = nltk.word_tokenize(emma_text)

print(f"\nNumber of tokens in 'Emma': {len(tokens)}")

# Calculate frequency distribution of words

fdist = nltk.FreqDist(tokens)

print("\nMost common words:")

for word, frequency in fdist.most_common(10):

    print(f"{word}: {frequency}")
```

Explanation:

- **Corpus Exploration:**
  The code lists the texts available in the Gutenberg Corpus and selects one for detailed analysis.

- **Tokenization and Frequency Analysis:**
  Tokenization breaks the text into individual words, while frequency distribution helps identify the most common terms—insights that are valuable for tasks like stop-word filtering and vocabulary development.

- **Scalability of Techniques:**
  Although this example uses a literary corpus, similar methods can be applied to larger, domain-specific corpora to extract valuable linguistic features.

In summary, linguistic resources and corpora are foundational to the success of any NLP initiative. By judiciously selecting high-quality, domain-relevant datasets and following best practices in data management and annotation, enterprises can build NLP systems that are both robust and contextually aware. This strategic approach ensures that the underlying linguistic models not only capture the intricacies of human language but also deliver actionable insights that drive business value and competitive advantage.

Morphology and Language Models

Word Formation and its Impact on NLP Strategies

Understanding the way words are formed – morphology - is essential in designing NLP models that accurately capture linguistic nuances. Morphology examines the structure of words, including prefixes, suffixes, roots, and inflections, providing insights into both the syntax and semantics of language. These insights directly inform the development of language models, which are the backbone of many NLP applications.

Morphological Analysis

Definition:

Morphology is the study of the internal structure of words. It involves the identification of morphemes, the smallest units of meaning, and understanding how they combine to form words. For example, in the word *"unbelievable"*, the prefix "un-", the root "believe", and the suffix "-able" each contribute to the overall meaning.

Relevance to NLP:

- **Handling Inflection and Derivation:**
  NLP systems need to normalize words to their base forms (lemmatization) or reduce them to their stems (stemming) to handle variations in language effectively.

- **Subword Tokenization:**
  Advanced language models (e.g., BERT, GPT) use subword tokenization (e.g., Byte-Pair Encoding, WordPiece) to manage out-of-vocabulary words and capture nuanced morphological patterns.

- **Semantic Enrichment:**
  Morphological features can enhance semantic understanding by distinguishing between different word forms and their contextual uses.

Illustrative Example: Morphological Analysis with spaCy

The following Python code demonstrates how to perform morphological analysis using spaCy. The example highlights how spaCy can extract morphological features from words, aiding in the understanding of their structure and formation.

```
import spacy

# Load the spaCy English language model

nlp = spacy.load("en_core_web_sm")

# Example sentence demonstrating morphological complexity

text = "The organization's unprecedented growth was truly unbelievable."

# Process the text

doc = nlp(text)

print("Morphological Analysis:")

for token in doc:

    # Print token text along with its lemma, part-of-speech tag, and morphological features

    print(f"Token: {token.text:<15} Lemma: {token.lemma_:<15} POS: {token.pos_:<10} Morph: {token.morph}")
```

Explanation:

- **Tokenization and Lemmatization:**
  The script tokenizes the sentence and extracts the base forms (lemmas) of the words, helping normalize variations (e.g., "growth" remains "growth").
- **Part-of-Speech and Morphological Features:**
  Each token's part-of-speech tag and additional morphological features (e.g., tense, number, case) are displayed. These features contribute to a richer understanding of language structure, essential for tasks such as syntactic parsing and semantic analysis.

Language Models and Morphological Information

Integration of Morphology in Language Models:
Modern language models leverage morphological insights to improve performance and robustness. Key strategies include:

- **Subword Tokenization:**
  Techniques like Byte-Pair Encoding (BPE) and WordPiece break down words into subword units. This approach helps manage rare or unseen words and captures meaningful morphemes, ensuring that the model can generalize better across various linguistic contexts.
- **Contextual Embeddings:**
  Language models generate dynamic embeddings that account for the morphology of words in context. This leads to more accurate representations of word meaning and better performance in downstream tasks such as sentiment analysis, machine translation, and information retrieval.

Illustrative Example: Subword Tokenization with Hugging Face's Transformers

Below is a code snippet that demonstrates how subword tokenization is performed using the Hugging Face Transformers library. This process is crucial for handling morphological variations in large-scale language models.

```
from transformers import AutoTokenizer

# Load a pretrained tokenizer (e.g., BERT tokenizer)

tokenizer = AutoTokenizer.from_pretrained("bert-base-
uncased")

# Example word with morphological complexity

word = "unbelievable"
```

```
# Perform subword tokenization
subword_tokens = tokenizer.tokenize(word)
print(f"Subword tokens for '{word}': {subword_tokens}")
# Convert subword tokens to input IDs
input_ids = tokenizer.encode(word, add_special_tokens=True)
print(f"Input IDs: {input_ids}")
```

Explanation:

- **Subword Tokenization:**
  The tokenizer breaks the complex word "unbelievable" into smaller subword units (e.g., "un", "##believ", "##able"), capturing the morphological structure.
- **Input IDs:**
  The tokens are converted to numerical IDs, which are then used as input for deep learning models. This process ensures that the language model can process and learn from the nuanced morphological patterns inherent in human language.

Strategic Implications for Enterprises

Integrating morphological analysis and leveraging language models that incorporate these insights provide several strategic advantages:

- **Enhanced Model Robustness:**
  By effectively handling word variations and unseen terms, models exhibit improved generalization and resilience in diverse real-world applications.
- **Increased Accuracy:**
  Detailed morphological features contribute to better syntactic and semantic understanding, leading to more precise outcomes in tasks such as sentiment analysis, machine translation, and information extraction.

- **Scalable Solutions:**
  The use of subword tokenization and dynamic contextual embeddings ensures that NLP systems remain scalable and efficient, even as linguistic data grows in complexity and volume.

Conclusion

A deep understanding of morphology and its integration into language models is fundamental for designing state-of-the-art NLP systems. By leveraging advanced morphological analysis and incorporating subword tokenization techniques, enterprises can develop robust and accurate models that capture the full spectrum of linguistic phenomena. This comprehensive approach not only enriches the model's semantic capabilities but also drives operational excellence and competitive advantage in an increasingly data-driven corporate landscape.

Chapter 3: Data and Resource Management

Data Collection Techniques

Sourcing Multilingual, Large-Scale Text Data with Compliance and Governance

In the era of big data, the cornerstone of robust NLP applications is access to high-quality, diverse, and multilingual datasets. Effective data collection is not only about volume but also about adherence to regulatory standards and corporate governance.

Multilingual Data Sourcing

Overview:
Enterprises today operate in a globalized market, necessitating the collection of text data in multiple languages to support diverse customer bases and international operations. Sourcing multilingual data enables NLP systems to understand regional dialects, cultural nuances, and linguistic variations. This is pivotal for tasks such as translation, sentiment analysis, and customer service automation.

Key Strategies:

- **Leveraging Public Datasets:**
  Utilize established multilingual corpora (e.g., Wikipedia dumps, Common Crawl) that offer broad coverage of languages and topics.

- **Web Scraping and APIs:**
  Employ web scraping techniques and APIs (e.g., Twitter API, news aggregators) to collect current, domain-specific content across different languages.

- **Collaboration with Local Partners:**
  Partner with regional entities and data providers to access localized datasets, ensuring cultural and contextual relevance.

Large-Scale Data Collection

Overview:
Large-scale data collection requires scalable infrastructure and automated pipelines to efficiently process vast amounts of text data. This involves robust data ingestion mechanisms, storage solutions, and processing frameworks that can handle high throughput without compromising data quality.

Key Strategies:

- **Distributed Data Pipelines:**
  Utilize tools such as Apache Kafka for real-time data ingestion and Apache Spark for distributed processing. This ensures that data flows smoothly from multiple sources into centralized data lakes.

- **Cloud Infrastructure:**
  Leverage cloud services (e.g., AWS, Azure, Google Cloud) for scalable storage, compute power, and data analytics, enabling enterprises to manage large datasets without significant upfront investment in hardware.

- **Automation and Monitoring:**
  Implement CI/CD pipelines and automated monitoring tools to maintain data quality and ensure that data collection processes are both efficient and resilient.

Compliance and Governance

Overview:
Incorporating compliance and governance into data collection practices is non-negotiable. Enterprises must navigate complex legal landscapes such as GDPR, CCPA, and other local data protection regulations. This requires a thorough understanding of data privacy laws and the implementation of stringent data governance policies.

Key Considerations:

- **Data Anonymization:**
  Ensure that personally identifiable information (PII) is anonymized or pseudonymized in accordance with privacy regulations.
- **Consent Management:**
  Maintain transparent consent protocols when collecting data directly from users, including clear disclosures and opt-out mechanisms.
- **Audit Trails and Documentation:**
  Implement robust logging and documentation practices to maintain audit trails of data collection activities, ensuring accountability and traceability.
- **Data Security:**
  Apply state-of-the-art encryption and access control measures to protect data integrity and prevent unauthorized access.

Illustrative Example: Multilingual Web Scraping with Compliance Considerations

The following Python code snippet demonstrates a simplified approach to web scraping that collects multilingual text data from a website, while incorporating basic compliance measures such as language detection and logging for audit purposes.

```
import requests

from bs4 import BeautifulSoup

from langdetect import detect

import logging

# Setup logging for compliance and audit trails
```

```
logging.basicConfig(filename='data_collection_audit.log',
level=logging.INFO,
                    format='%(asctime)s:%(levelname)s:%(message)s')
def fetch_page(url):
    """
    Fetch a web page's content while handling HTTP errors.
    """
    try:
        response = requests.get(url, timeout=10)
        response.raise_for_status()  # Ensure HTTP errors are
caught
        logging.info(f"Successfully fetched {url}")
        return response.text
    except requests.RequestException as e:
        logging.error(f"Error fetching {url}: {e}")
        return None
def extract_text(html):
    """
    Extract text content from HTML while filtering out non-text
elements.
    """
    soup = BeautifulSoup(html, 'html.parser')
    # Remove script and style elements
```

```
    for element in soup(["script", "style"]):
        element.extract()
    text = soup.get_text(separator=" ", strip=True)
    return text
def is_valid_language(text, target_lang="en"):
    """
    Check if the text is in the target language.
    """
    try:
        language = detect(text)
        return language == target_lang
    except Exception as e:
        logging.warning(f"Language detection failed: {e}")
        return False
# Example URL for multilingual content (Replace with a real target URL)
url = "https://www.example.com/multilingual-content"
# Fetch and process the page
html_content = fetch_page(url)
if html_content:
    text_content = extract_text(html_content)
    if is_valid_language(text_content, target_lang="en"):
        logging.info("Text is in the target language (English).")
```

```
        # Save or process text content as needed (e.g., store in a data lake)
        print("Extracted Text:", text_content[:500])  # Print first 500 characters for brevity
    else:
        logging.info("Text is not in the target language. Skipping.")
```

Explanation:

- **Web Page Retrieval:**
  The fetch_page function retrieves the web page content with error handling and logs success or failure events.
- **Content Extraction:**
  The extract_text function cleans the HTML by removing non-text elements (e.g., scripts, styles) and extracts the main text content.
- **Language Detection:**
  The is_valid_language function uses the langdetect library to ensure that the text is in the target language (English in this case), ensuring that data collection aligns with project requirements.
- **Compliance Logging:**
  Logging is integrated throughout the process to create an audit trail, aiding in compliance and governance.

In summary, effective data collection techniques are foundational to building high-performing NLP systems. By sourcing multilingual, large-scale text data through scalable and automated pipelines, and by embedding rigorous compliance and governance protocols into every step, enterprises can ensure that their NLP initiatives are both robust and legally sound. This strategic approach not only enhances data quality and operational efficiency but also secures the enterprise against potential regulatory risks, ultimately driving sustained competitive advantage in an increasingly global marketplace.

Data Quality and Preprocessing

Ensuring Clean, Consistent, and Reliable Data in Corporate NLP

In enterprise environments, the value of an NLP system is closely tied to the quality of the data it processes. Data collected from diverse sources can be noisy, inconsistent, and unstructured. Therefore, robust preprocessing is essential to clean, normalize, and assure the quality of data before it is used to train models or derive insights.

Importance of Data Quality

- **Accuracy:**
  High-quality data reduces errors and improves model performance. Inaccurate or unclean data can lead to poor predictions, misinterpretations, and faulty business decisions.
- **Consistency:**
  Consistent preprocessing ensures that the data follows a uniform format across multiple sources, which is critical for integrating data from different systems or regions.
- **Reliability:**
  Rigorous quality assurance protocols help to maintain the integrity of data over time, ensuring that models remain robust as new data is collected.
- **Scalability:**
  Clean and normalized data is easier to manage and scale. This is essential in corporate environments where data volume may grow exponentially.

Approaches to Data Cleaning and Normalization

1. **Data Cleaning:**

- **Noise Removal:**
  Remove irrelevant characters, HTML tags, and formatting issues that can distort text analysis.
- **Stop Word Filtering:**
  Eliminate common words that do not contribute significant meaning (e.g., "the," "and," "but").
- **Handling Missing Data:**
  Identify and either remove or impute missing values to ensure a complete dataset.
- **Spelling Correction:**
  Standardize spellings to reduce variation and improve matching accuracy.

2. **Data Normalization:**

- **Lowercasing:**
  Convert all text to lowercase to ensure uniformity.
- **Stemming and Lemmatization:**
  Reduce words to their base or root forms to consolidate variations.
- **Tokenization:**
  Break down text into manageable units (words, phrases, or subwords) for further processing.
- **Standardization:**
  Normalize dates, numbers, and other special entities to a common format.

3. **Quality Assurance:**

   - **Automated Quality Checks:**
     Implement validation rules and statistical checks (e.g., distribution analysis) to identify anomalies.

   - **Manual Review:**
     Periodically conduct manual audits of preprocessed data to ensure that automated processes are functioning correctly.

   - **Versioning and Auditing:**
     Maintain version-controlled pipelines and logging to ensure traceability and compliance with corporate governance policies.

Illustrative Example: Data Preprocessing Pipeline in Python

The following Python code snippet demonstrates a simple data preprocessing pipeline that cleans and normalizes text data. This example leverages common libraries such as re, nltk, and spacy to illustrate the key steps.

```
import re

import nltk

from nltk.corpus import stopwords

from nltk.tokenize import word_tokenize

import spacy

# Ensure necessary resources are downloaded

nltk.download('punkt')

nltk.download('stopwords')

# Load spaCy's English model for lemmatization

nlp = spacy.load("en_core_web_sm")
```

```
def clean_text(text):
    """
    Clean the input text by removing HTML tags, non-alphanumeric characters,
    and extra whitespace.
    """
    # Remove HTML tags using regex
    text = re.sub(r'<[^>]+>', ' ', text)
    # Remove non-alphanumeric characters (retain spaces)
    text = re.sub(r'[^a-zA-Z0-9\s]', '', text)
    # Normalize whitespace
    text = re.sub(r'\s+', ' ', text).strip()
    return text
def normalize_text(text):
    """
    Normalize text by lowercasing, tokenizing, removing stop words,
    and lemmatizing.
    """
    # Convert to lowercase
    text = text.lower()
    # Tokenize the text
    tokens = word_tokenize(text)
```

```
    # Remove stop words
    filtered_tokens = [token for token in tokens if token not in stopwords.words('english')]
        # Lemmatize tokens using spaCy
    doc = nlp(" ".join(filtered_tokens))
    lemmatized_tokens = [token.lemma_ for token in doc]
        # Reconstruct the text from tokens
    normalized_text = " ".join(lemmatized_tokens)
    return normalized_text
# Example raw text data
raw_text = """
<html>
<head><title>Sample Data</title></head>
<body>
<p>This is an example of raw text data! It contains HTML tags, punctuation, and stop words.
Data preprocessing is essential for NLP systems.</p>
</body>
</html>
"""
# Data Preprocessing Pipeline
print("Original Text:\n", raw_text)
# Step 1: Clean the text
```

```
cleaned_text = clean_text(raw_text)
print("\nCleaned Text:\n", cleaned_text)
# Step 2: Normalize the text
normalized_text = normalize_text(cleaned_text)
print("\nNormalized Text:\n", normalized_text)
```

Explanation:

- **Cleaning Process:**
  - The clean_text function removes HTML tags, non-alphanumeric characters, and redundant whitespace using regular expressions.
- **Normalization Process:**
  - The text is converted to lowercase to maintain consistency.
  - The word_tokenize function splits the text into individual words.
  - Stop words are filtered out using NLTK's predefined list.
  - The remaining tokens are lemmatized using spaCy to convert words to their base forms.
- **Pipeline Outcome:**
  - The cleaned and normalized text is now more consistent and ready for further NLP tasks such as model training or sentiment analysis.

In summary, in corporate environments, high-quality data is the bedrock of successful NLP initiatives. Implementing comprehensive data cleaning and normalization processes ensures that textual data is accurate, consistent, and reliable. By integrating rigorous quality assurance protocols into the data preprocessing pipeline, organizations can significantly enhance the performance of their NLP systems, reduce the risk of errors, and drive better business outcomes. This strategic approach to data quality not only supports robust analytics and modeling but also aligns with broader corporate governance and compliance requirements.

Infrastructure and Tooling

Enabling Scalable and Robust Enterprise NLP Deployments

In the enterprise landscape, the success of advanced NLP systems is inextricably linked to a robust infrastructure that supports scalable storage, high-performance computing, and seamless integration with third-party solutions. Strategic investment in infrastructure and tooling ensures that NLP solutions not only deliver superior performance but also align with organizational goals for efficiency, cost-effectiveness, and security.

Storage Solutions

Overview:
Storing vast amounts of unstructured text data and model artifacts requires scalable, secure, and accessible storage solutions. Enterprises often deploy a mix of:

- **Data Lakes and Warehouses:**
  These centralized repositories (e.g., Amazon S3, Google Cloud Storage, Azure Data Lake) facilitate the consolidation of raw data and structured datasets, making them readily available for preprocessing and model training.
- **Distributed File Systems:**
  Systems such as Hadoop Distributed File System (HDFS) support large-scale storage and parallel data processing, essential for training complex NLP models.

Strategic Considerations:

- **Data Governance:** Implement stringent access controls, encryption, and compliance measures to safeguard sensitive information.
- **Scalability:** Opt for solutions that can seamlessly expand storage capacity as data volumes increase.

Computing Resources

Overview:
NLP applications, particularly those leveraging deep learning and transformer architectures, demand significant computational power. Enterprises must strategically select between:

- **On-Premises Solutions:**
  High-performance servers and GPU clusters offer complete control over hardware and data security, often preferred by organizations with strict compliance or data sovereignty requirements.
- **Cloud-Based Computing:**
  Cloud platforms (e.g., AWS, Azure, Google Cloud) provide elastic compute resources, enabling rapid scaling and cost-efficient model training and inference. These solutions support pay-as-you-go models, which reduce capital expenditure and accelerate time-to-market.

Strategic Considerations:

- **Performance vs. Cost:** Balance the need for high-performance compute with the cost benefits of cloud scalability.
- **Flexibility:** Leverage hybrid models that integrate on-premises and cloud-based resources to optimize performance while maintaining control over critical data.

Third-Party Solutions and Tooling

Overview:
A comprehensive NLP ecosystem is supported by an array of third-party tools and frameworks that streamline development, deployment, and monitoring. Key components include:

- **Containerization and Orchestration:**
  Tools like Docker and Kubernetes enable consistent, scalable deployments of NLP models across diverse environments. Containerization ensures that models and dependencies are packaged together, while orchestration tools manage scaling, load balancing, and high availability.

- **Model Management and Monitoring:**
  Platforms such as MLflow, Kubeflow, or proprietary solutions provide model versioning, deployment tracking, and performance monitoring. This is critical for ensuring that NLP systems remain efficient, secure, and up-to-date in production environments.

- **Integration Platforms:**
  APIs and microservices facilitate the integration of NLP capabilities into existing enterprise workflows, ensuring seamless interoperability with other business systems.

Strategic Considerations:

- **Vendor Ecosystem:** Choose tools that integrate well with existing corporate systems and meet enterprise security standards.

- **Operational Efficiency:** Invest in automated CI/CD pipelines and monitoring solutions to streamline the model lifecycle and ensure rapid incident response.

Illustrative Example: Deploying an NLP Model with Docker and Kubernetes

Below is a simplified example illustrating how to containerize an NLP application using Docker, along with a Kubernetes deployment configuration. This approach provides a blueprint for deploying scalable, enterprise-grade NLP solutions.

<u>Dockerfile</u>

```
# Use an official Python runtime as a parent image

FROM python:3.9-slim

# Set the working directory in the container

WORKDIR /app

# Copy the current directory contents into the container at
/app

COPY . /app

# Install any needed packages specified in requirements.txt

RUN pip install --no-cache-dir -r requirements.txt

# Expose the port the app runs on

EXPOSE 8080

# Define environment variable for production

ENV ENVIRONMENT production

# Run the application

CMD ["python", "app.py"]
```

Kubernetes Deployment YAML


```yaml
apiVersion: apps/v1
kind: Deployment
metadata:
  name: nlp-model-deployment
spec:
  replicas: 3
  selector:
    matchLabels:
      app: nlp-model
  template:
    metadata:
      labels:
        app: nlp-model
    spec:
      containers:
      - name: nlp-model-container
        image: your-docker-registry/nlp-model:latest
        ports:
        - containerPort: 8080
        resources:
          limits:
```

```
        memory: "4Gi"
        cpu: "2"
      requests:
        memory: "2Gi"
        cpu: "1"
    env:
    - name: ENVIRONMENT
      value: "production"
---
apiVersion: v1
kind: Service
metadata:
  name: nlp-model-service
spec:
  selector:
    app: nlp-model
  ports:
  - protocol: TCP
    port: 80
    targetPort: 8080
  type: LoadBalancer
```

Explanation:

- **Dockerfile:**
  This file creates a Docker image that packages the NLP application along with its dependencies. The container is configured to run on port 8080 and includes environment variables to differentiate between production and development environments.

- **Kubernetes Deployment YAML:**
  This configuration defines a deployment with three replicas of the NLP model container, ensuring high availability and load balancing. It also specifies resource limits to manage performance and a service configuration that exposes the application via a load balancer.

Conclusion

Robust infrastructure and advanced tooling are critical to the success of enterprise-level NLP deployments. By strategically investing in scalable storage, high-performance computing resources, and modern containerization/orchestration technologies, organizations can ensure that their NLP systems are resilient, secure, and ready to handle the demands of large-scale production environments. This integrated approach not only supports efficient model training and deployment but also drives operational excellence and sustained competitive advantage in a rapidly evolving digital landscape.

Part II: Core NLP Techniques and Processes
Chapter 4: Text Processing and Feature Engineering

Tokenization and Text Normalization

In the realm of NLP, tokenization and text normalization form the bedrock of effective text processing and feature engineering. These techniques transform raw textual data into structured, analyzable units, enabling downstream models to perform with greater accuracy and efficiency. In today's competitive business environment, leveraging state-of-the-art tokenization methods - such as Byte-Pair Encoding (BPE) and WordPiece - has become indispensable for achieving superior performance in tasks ranging from sentiment analysis to conversational AI.

Tokenization: Breaking Down Language for Enhanced Analysis

Overview:
Tokenization is the process of segmenting text into smaller components, known as tokens. These tokens might be words, subwords, or even characters, depending on the chosen approach. Advanced tokenization methods have evolved to address challenges such as out-of-vocabulary (OOV) words and morphological variations.

State-of-the-Art Techniques:

- **Byte-Pair Encoding (BPE):**
  BPE iteratively replaces the most frequent pair of bytes or characters with a single, new token. This method efficiently captures common subword units, reducing vocabulary size while preserving semantic information.
- **WordPiece:**
  Similar to BPE, WordPiece breaks down words into subwords

and is used prominently in models like BERT. It is particularly effective in handling rare and compound words by representing them as combinations of common subword tokens.

- **SentencePiece:**
  This approach treats the input text as a raw sequence of characters and applies subword segmentation, which is useful in multilingual settings and in scenarios where traditional whitespace tokenization fails.

Business Impact:

- **Enhanced Model Robustness:**
  By capturing subword-level information, these tokenization methods improve model generalization, allowing for better handling of unseen or rare words.
- **Reduced Vocabulary Size:**
  Smaller, more efficient vocabularies lead to decreased model complexity, which in turn reduces training time and operational costs.
- **Improved Semantic Understanding:**
  Fine-grained tokenization enables models to better capture the nuances of language, leading to improved performance in sentiment analysis, recommendation systems, and other data-driven business applications.

Text Normalization: Standardizing Input for Consistency

Overview:
Text normalization involves converting text to a standardized form to eliminate inconsistencies. Common steps include lowercasing, removing punctuation, handling contractions, and stripping extraneous whitespace. This preprocessing ensures that the NLP pipeline treats semantically equivalent inputs in a uniform manner.

Key Steps:

- **Lowercasing:**
  Standardizes text to a single case, ensuring that "Apple" and "apple" are treated equivalently.
- **Punctuation Removal:**
  Eliminates punctuation that can introduce noise into the analysis.
- **Handling Contractions and Special Characters:**
  Expands contractions (e.g., "can't" to "cannot") and removes or standardizes special characters to reduce variability.
- **Whitespace Normalization:**
  Ensures consistent spacing across the dataset to facilitate accurate tokenization.

Business Impact:

- **Consistency in Data Processing:**
  Normalization reduces variability in input data, leading to more consistent and reliable model outcomes.
- **Enhanced Data Quality:**
  Clean, standardized text improves the accuracy of feature extraction, ultimately supporting more informed business decisions.
- **Operational Efficiency:**
  Streamlined preprocessing pipelines lead to faster training times and reduced computational overhead, directly impacting the bottom line.

Illustrative Example: Tokenization with Hugging Face Transformers

Below is a Python example that demonstrates tokenization using the BERT WordPiece tokenizer. This snippet highlights how state-of-the-art tokenization methods can be seamlessly integrated into an NLP pipeline.

```
from transformers import BertTokenizer

# Initialize the BERT WordPiece tokenizer

tokenizer = BertTokenizer.from_pretrained("bert-base-uncased")

# Example input text

input_text = "The company's unprecedented growth was truly unbelievable!"

# Tokenize the input text using the tokenizer

tokens = tokenizer.tokenize(input_text)

print("Tokens:", tokens)

# Convert tokens to input IDs for model processing

input_ids = tokenizer.encode(input_text, add_special_tokens=True)

print("Input IDs:", input_ids)

# Decode the input IDs back to text to verify the process

decoded_text = tokenizer.decode(input_ids)

print("Decoded Text:", decoded_text)
```

Explanation:

- **Tokenization Process:**
  The BertTokenizer tokenizes the input text into WordPiece tokens, effectively handling complex words by breaking them down into meaningful subword units.

- **Input IDs Conversion:**
  The tokenizer converts tokens into numerical input IDs required by downstream models. This numerical representation is essential for model training and inference.

- **Decoding Verification:**
  Finally, decoding the input IDs back into text verifies that the tokenization process preserves the semantic content of the original text.

In summary, integrating advanced tokenization and text normalization techniques into the NLP workflow is critical for building robust, scalable, and high-performing models in enterprise environments. By utilizing state-of-the-art methods such as Byte-Pair Encoding and WordPiece, businesses can enhance model accuracy, reduce operational costs, and deliver actionable insights that drive competitive advantage. This strategic focus on text processing and feature engineering not only optimizes data pipelines but also underpins successful digital transformation initiatives across industries.

Stemming and Lemmatization

Classic Approaches and Their Corporate Applications

Stemming and lemmatization are foundational text preprocessing techniques in NLP, employed to reduce words to their base or root forms. These methods not only help in managing linguistic variability but also enhance feature consistency across large-scale textual datasets - a critical factor for successful enterprise analytics and decision-making.

Stemming

Overview:
Stemming algorithms, such as the Porter Stemmer and Snowball Stemmer, apply heuristic rules to strip suffixes from words. The

resulting "stem" may not be a valid word but captures the essential semantic component. This approach is computationally efficient and works well for tasks where fine-grained morphological distinctions are less critical.

Corporate Applications:

- **Search and Information Retrieval:**
  By reducing words to a common stem, search systems can match queries with documents that use varied forms of a word, thereby enhancing recall.
- **Sentiment Analysis:**
  Stemming minimizes noise by consolidating word variants, leading to more robust sentiment classification across customer feedback.
- **Text Clustering:**
  In clustering algorithms, stemming reduces dimensionality, allowing for better grouping of documents by their underlying themes.

Illustrative Example: Stemming with NLTK

```
import nltk

from nltk.stem import PorterStemmer

from nltk.tokenize import word_tokenize

# Ensure required resources are downloaded

nltk.download('punkt')

# Initialize the Porter Stemmer

stemmer = PorterStemmer()

# Example text data
```

```
text = "The company's operational activities were operationally efficient and efficiently managed."

# Tokenize the text

tokens = word_tokenize(text)

# Apply stemming to each token

stems = [stemmer.stem(token) for token in tokens]

print("Original Tokens:", tokens)

print("Stemmed Tokens:", stems)
```

Explanation:

- The code tokenizes a sample corporate sentence and applies the Porter Stemmer to each token.
- The resulting stems help in normalizing word forms, thus enhancing the performance of search and clustering systems.

Lemmatization

Overview:
Lemmatization takes a more sophisticated approach by reducing words to their dictionary form, or lemma, using linguistic knowledge. Unlike stemming, lemmatization considers the context and part-of-speech tags, ensuring that the resulting form is a valid word. This method is especially valuable when semantic precision is critical.

Corporate Applications:

- **Document Summarization:**
  Lemmatization aids in generating concise summaries by ensuring that semantically similar words are aggregated.
- **Customer Feedback Analysis:**
  By normalizing textual variations, lemmatization enables more

accurate sentiment analysis and topic modeling, thereby providing clear insights into customer opinions.

- **Machine Translation and Chatbots:**
  High-quality lemmatization supports better language understanding and generation, leading to more natural interactions in multilingual environments.

Illustrative Example: Lemmatization with NLTK's WordNetLemmatizer

```
import nltk

from nltk.stem import WordNetLemmatizer

from nltk.tokenize import word_tokenize

from nltk.corpus import wordnet

# Ensure required resources are downloaded

nltk.download('punkt')

nltk.download('wordnet')

nltk.download('averaged_perceptron_tagger')

# Function to map POS tag to wordnet tag for lemmatization

def get_wordnet_pos(treebank_tag):

    if treebank_tag.startswith('J'):

        return wordnet.ADJ

    elif treebank_tag.startswith('V'):

        return wordnet.VERB

    elif treebank_tag.startswith('N'):

        return wordnet.NOUN
```

```
    elif treebank_tag.startswith('R'):
        return wordnet.ADV
    else:
        return wordnet.NOUN
# Initialize the WordNet Lemmatizer
lemmatizer = WordNetLemmatizer()
# Example text data
text = "The company's operational activities were operationally efficient and efficiently managed."
# Tokenize the text
tokens = word_tokenize(text)
# Tag tokens with part-of-speech tags
pos_tags = nltk.pos_tag(tokens)
# Apply lemmatization using POS tags
lemmas = [lemmatizer.lemmatize(token, get_wordnet_pos(pos)) for token, pos in pos_tags]
print("Original Tokens:", tokens)
print("Lemmatized Tokens:", lemmas)
```

Explanation:

- This code demonstrates lemmatization by tokenizing text, assigning part-of-speech tags, and mapping these tags to WordNet categories.

- The resulting lemmas are semantically correct, ensuring that words like "managed" and "operationally" are reduced to their appropriate base forms (e.g., "manage," "operational").
- The improved semantic consistency is invaluable for tasks such as document summarization and customer sentiment analysis.

In summary, classic text preprocessing techniques like stemming and lemmatization remain vital in corporate NLP pipelines. Their ability to reduce dimensionality, improve feature consistency, and enhance semantic clarity supports a wide range of applications—from search engines and sentiment analysis to machine translation and document clustering. By carefully selecting and applying these techniques, enterprises can ensure that their NLP systems are robust, efficient, and aligned with strategic business objectives, ultimately driving better data-driven decision-making.

Feature Extraction

Bag-of-Words, TF-IDF, and n-gram Models for Downstream NLP Pipelines

Feature extraction is a crucial step in NLP pipelines, transforming raw text into structured representations that machine learning models can process. In enterprise applications, effective feature extraction is key to building robust downstream pipelines for tasks such as classification, clustering, and recommendation systems. Three foundational techniques for feature extraction are the Bag-of-Words (BoW) model, Term Frequency-Inverse Document Frequency (TF-IDF), and n-gram models.

1. Bag-of-Words (BoW) Model

Overview:
The Bag-of-Words model is one of the simplest approaches to text representation. It transforms text into a fixed-length vector by counting the occurrences of each word in the vocabulary,

disregarding grammar and word order. Despite its simplicity, BoW is widely used for its ease of implementation and effectiveness in many scenarios.

Business Applications:

- **Document Classification:**
  BoW is effective for categorizing documents such as emails, customer reviews, or support tickets.
- **Search and Information Retrieval:**
  A BoW representation enables fast retrieval of documents based on keyword matching.

Illustrative Code Example (Using scikit-learn):

```
from sklearn.feature_extraction.text import CountVectorizer

# Sample text corpus

corpus = [

    "The company's revenue grew significantly last quarter.",

    "Customer satisfaction and loyalty increased due to the new product.",

    "The quarterly report shows improved operational efficiency."

]

# Initialize the Bag-of-Words vectorizer

vectorizer = CountVectorizer()

# Fit the vectorizer and transform the corpus into a BoW representation

bow_features = vectorizer.fit_transform(corpus)
```

```
# Display the feature names and the BoW representation
print("Feature Names:", vectorizer.get_feature_names_out())
print("BoW Feature Matrix:\n", bow_features.toarray())
```

2. Term Frequency-Inverse Document Frequency (TF-IDF)

Overview:

TF-IDF builds upon the BoW approach by weighing words according to their importance. The term frequency (TF) measures how often a word appears in a document, while the inverse document frequency (IDF) scales down the weight of common words across the corpus. This method emphasizes words that are more unique to each document.

Business Applications:

- **Sentiment Analysis:**
  TF-IDF helps highlight distinguishing words that contribute to sentiment, filtering out common terms that may not carry meaningful information.
- **Topic Modeling:**
  By emphasizing significant terms, TF-IDF improves the performance of clustering and topic extraction algorithms.

Illustrative Code Example (Using scikit-learn):

```
from sklearn.feature_extraction.text import TfidfVectorizer
# Initialize the TF-IDF vectorizer
tfidf_vectorizer = TfidfVectorizer()
# Fit the vectorizer and transform the corpus into a TF-IDF
representation
```

```
tfidf_features = tfidf_vectorizer.fit_transform(corpus)

# Display the feature names and the TF-IDF representation

print("Feature Names:",
tfidf_vectorizer.get_feature_names_out())

print("TF-IDF Feature Matrix:\n", tfidf_features.toarray())
```

3. n-gram Models

Overview:
n-gram models extend the basic BoW approach by considering contiguous sequences of words (n-grams). While unigrams (n=1) capture individual words, bigrams (n=2) and trigrams (n=3) capture context and word order, which are often critical for understanding meaning in text.

Business Applications:

- **Language Modeling:**
  n-gram models can capture contextual relationships, improving the performance of predictive text and auto-completion systems.
- **Sentiment and Intent Analysis:**
  By considering word pairs or triples, n-gram features can capture idiomatic expressions or common phrases, leading to improved sentiment or intent classification.

Illustrative Code Example (Using scikit-learn):

```
# Initialize a vectorizer with n-gram range (e.g., unigrams and
bigrams)

ngram_vectorizer = CountVectorizer(ngram_range=(1, 2))

# Fit the vectorizer and transform the corpus into an n-gram
representation

ngram_features = ngram_vectorizer.fit_transform(corpus)
```

```
# Display the feature names and the n-gram representation

print("Feature Names (Unigrams and Bigrams):", ngram_vectorizer.get_feature_names_out())

print("n-gram Feature Matrix:\n", ngram_features.toarray())
```

Integrating Feature Extraction into Downstream Pipelines:

In enterprise-level NLP deployments, these feature extraction techniques serve as the foundation for a variety of downstream tasks:

- **Classification Pipelines:**
  Feature matrices generated from BoW, TF-IDF, or n-gram models can be used as input to classifiers (e.g., logistic regression, SVM) for tasks like spam detection or sentiment analysis.
- **Clustering and Topic Modeling:**
  Representations derived from TF-IDF and n-grams can be used in unsupervised learning methods to group similar documents or discover hidden topics.
- **Recommendation Systems:**
  By quantifying textual content, these models enable the recommendation of similar documents or products based on content similarity.

Conclusion

Feature extraction through BoW, TF-IDF, and n-gram models is central to transforming raw text into actionable insights. These techniques allow enterprises to build efficient, scalable NLP pipelines that support a broad range of applications - from customer sentiment analysis to automated document classification. Leveraging these methods enables organizations to harness the power of text data, driving better business outcomes and facilitating data-driven decision-making across various corporate contexts.

Chapter 5: Statistical and Machine Learning Approaches

Classical NLP Algorithms

In the realm of NLP, classical statistical and machine learning algorithms remain a cornerstone for tasks such as document classification and sentiment analysis. While deep learning architectures have surged in popularity, classical methods like Naive Bayes, Logistic Regression, and Support Vector Machines (SVM) continue to offer robust, interpretable, and computationally efficient solutions for many enterprise applications. These algorithms form the bedrock of many NLP systems, delivering reliable performance, especially when labeled data is limited or rapid deployment is essential.

1. Naive Bayes

Overview:
Naive Bayes classifiers are based on applying Bayes' theorem with strong independence assumptions between features. Despite these simplifications, Naive Bayes models perform exceptionally well in text classification tasks due to the high dimensionality and sparsity of textual data. Their simplicity, speed, and ease of implementation make them a popular choice for initial model baselines and production-level sentiment analysis.

Business Applications:

- **Spam Detection:** Efficiently classifies emails or messages as spam or non-spam.
- **Sentiment Analysis:** Quickly identifies the sentiment in customer reviews or social media comments.

Illustrative Code Example (Using scikit-learn):

```
from sklearn.feature_extraction.text import CountVectorizer
```

```
from sklearn.naive_bayes import MultinomialNB

from sklearn.pipeline import make_pipeline

from sklearn.model_selection import train_test_split

from sklearn.metrics import accuracy_score,
classification_report

# Sample dataset: Documents and corresponding sentiment
labels (1: Positive, 0: Negative)

documents = [

    "I love the new product, it is amazing!",

    "The service was disappointing and the staff was rude.",

    "An excellent experience, highly recommend!",

    "The quality is poor and I am not satisfied.",

    "A truly outstanding performance by the team.",

    "I will never buy from here again, very bad experience."

]

labels = [1, 0, 1, 0, 1, 0]

# Create a train-test split

X_train, X_test, y_train, y_test = train_test_split(documents,
labels, test_size=0.33, random_state=42)

# Build a pipeline: CountVectorizer converts text to token
counts and MultinomialNB performs classification

nb_pipeline = make_pipeline(CountVectorizer(),
MultinomialNB())

# Train the Naive Bayes classifier
```

```
nb_pipeline.fit(X_train, y_train)

# Predict sentiment on the test set

y_pred_nb = nb_pipeline.predict(X_test)

print("Naive Bayes Accuracy:", accuracy_score(y_test,
y_pred_nb))

print("Classification Report:\n", classification_report(y_test,
y_pred_nb))
```

2. Logistic Regression

Overview:

Logistic Regression is a powerful yet straightforward statistical model that predicts binary outcomes by modeling the probability of class membership. It is particularly well-suited for high-dimensional text data and benefits from being easily interpretable. Regularization techniques can further enhance its performance by preventing overfitting.

Business Applications:

- **Document Classification:** Categorizes documents into predefined classes (e.g., news categorization, product reviews).
- **Customer Sentiment Analysis:** Provides probabilistic insights into customer opinions, supporting strategic decision-making.

Illustrative Code Example (Using scikit-learn):

```
from sklearn.linear_model import LogisticRegression

# Build a pipeline for Logistic Regression with
CountVectorizer
```

```
lr_pipeline = make_pipeline(CountVectorizer(), LogisticRegression(max_iter=1000))

# Train the Logistic Regression classifier

lr_pipeline.fit(X_train, y_train)

# Predict sentiment on the test set

y_pred_lr = lr_pipeline.predict(X_test)

print("Logistic Regression Accuracy:", accuracy_score(y_test, y_pred_lr))

print("Classification Report:\n", classification_report(y_test, y_pred_lr))
```

3. Support Vector Machines (SVM)

Overview:
Support Vector Machines are powerful classifiers that operate by finding the optimal hyperplane that separates classes in a high-dimensional feature space. SVMs are particularly effective in scenarios where the decision boundary is complex. With the appropriate kernel functions, they can handle non-linear relationships, making them versatile for various text classification tasks.

Business Applications:

- **Fine-Grained Sentiment Analysis:** Captures subtle differences in sentiment by defining clear decision boundaries.
- **Topic Classification:** Efficiently separates documents into different topics or categories based on textual features.

Illustrative Code Example (Using scikit-learn):

```
from sklearn.svm import LinearSVC
```

```
# Build a pipeline for SVM with CountVectorizer

svm_pipeline = make_pipeline(CountVectorizer(),
LinearSVC())

# Train the SVM classifier

svm_pipeline.fit(X_train, y_train)

# Predict sentiment on the test set

y_pred_svm = svm_pipeline.predict(X_test)

print("SVM Accuracy:", accuracy_score(y_test, y_pred_svm))

print("Classification Report:\n", classification_report(y_test,
y_pred_svm))
```

Strategic Business Impact

- **Cost-Efficiency and Speed:**
  Classical NLP algorithms, due to their relatively lower computational requirements, enable rapid prototyping and deployment, which is crucial for time-sensitive business decisions.
- **Interpretability:**
  These models offer clear insights into which features drive classification, making it easier to explain decisions to stakeholders and ensuring alignment with compliance and governance standards.
- **Scalability:**
  When integrated with robust feature extraction techniques (like BoW, TF-IDF, and n-gram models), these algorithms scale effectively across large corpora, supporting enterprise-level analytics and decision-making.

- **Adaptability:**
  Classical approaches serve as reliable baselines that can be enhanced with ensemble methods or integrated with modern deep learning models, ensuring a future-proof investment in NLP infrastructure.

In summary, classical statistical and machine learning approaches, including Naive Bayes, Logistic Regression, and SVM, continue to play a pivotal role in enterprise NLP applications. Their balance of efficiency, interpretability, and effectiveness makes them indispensable for tasks like document classification and sentiment analysis. By leveraging these methods, businesses can rapidly deploy robust NLP solutions that drive strategic insights and support data-driven decision-making in a dynamic corporate landscape.

Hidden Markov Models and CRFs

Sequence Modeling for Named Entity Recognition and Part-of-Speech Tagging

Sequence modeling is a critical component of many NLP tasks such as Named Entity Recognition (NER) and Part-of-Speech (POS) tagging. Two classical approaches that have been widely adopted for these tasks are Hidden Markov Models (HMMs) and Conditional Random Fields (CRFs). Both methods model sequences but differ in how they treat dependencies between observations and labels.

Hidden Markov Models (HMMs)

Overview:
HMMs are generative probabilistic models that assume an underlying sequence of hidden states (e.g., POS tags or entity labels) which generate observable outputs (words). They model the joint probability of the observed sequence and the hidden state sequence, leveraging two main components:

- **Transition Probabilities:**
  The likelihood of moving from one hidden state to another.
- **Emission Probabilities:**
  The likelihood of observing a word given a specific hidden state.

Applications in NLP:

- **Part-of-Speech Tagging:**
  HMMs assign POS tags to each word by modeling the probabilities of tag sequences.
- **Basic Named Entity Recognition:**
  Early NER systems used HMMs to capture entity patterns, though they often struggled with overlapping and contextual features.

Challenges:

- HMMs assume conditional independence between observations given the hidden state, which may oversimplify real-world language dependencies.
- They are generative models and do not directly model the conditional probability of labels given the observations.

Conditional Random Fields (CRFs)

Overview:
CRFs are discriminative models that directly estimate the conditional probability of a label sequence given an observation sequence. This allows them to incorporate overlapping, non-independent features without making strong independence assumptions. CRFs excel in sequence labeling tasks by:

- **Modeling Context:**
  Capturing the dependencies between neighboring labels.

- **Feature Flexibility:**
  Incorporating various features (e.g., word shapes, prefixes, suffixes) that are crucial for tasks like NER and POS tagging.

Applications in NLP:

- **Named Entity Recognition:**
  CRFs effectively capture context and entity boundaries, making them a popular choice for NER.
- **Part-of-Speech Tagging:**
  They improve tagging accuracy by considering the entire sequence context and a wide range of features.

Benefits Over HMMs:

- CRFs can integrate rich feature sets without violating the model assumptions.
- They optimize the conditional probability directly, often leading to improved performance in practical applications.

Illustrative Example: CRF for Named Entity Recognition

Below is a simplified example using the sklearn-crfsuite library to build a CRF model for a basic NER task. This example demonstrates how to prepare features, train the model, and evaluate its performance.

```
# Install the package if necessary:

# !pip install sklearn-crfsuite

import sklearn_crfsuite

from sklearn_crfsuite import metrics

# Sample dataset: each sentence is a list of tuples (word, label)
```

```
# Labels: 'O' = Outside, 'B-PER' = Beginning of a Person Entity, 'I-PER' = Inside a Person Entity
train_sentences = [
    [("John", "B-PER"), ("lives", "O"), ("in", "O"), ("New", "B-LOC"), ("York", "I-LOC")],
    [("Mary", "B-PER"), ("visited", "O"), ("Paris", "B-LOC")],
]
test_sentences = [
    [("Alice", "B-PER"), ("is", "O"), ("from", "O"), ("London", "B-LOC")],
]
# Feature extraction for each token in a sentence
def word2features(sent, i):
    word = sent[i][0]
    features = {
        'bias': 1.0,
        'word.lower()': word.lower(),
        'word.isupper()': word.isupper(),
        'word.istitle()': word.istitle(),
        'word.isdigit()': word.isdigit(),
    }
    # Add features from previous word
    if i > 0:
```

```
        word1 = sent[i-1][0]
        features.update({
            '-1:word.lower()': word1.lower(),
            '-1:word.istitle()': word1.istitle(),
            '-1:word.isupper()': word1.isupper(),
        })
    else:
        features['BOS'] = True  # Beginning of sentence

    # Add features from next word
    if i < len(sent) - 1:
        word1 = sent[i+1][0]
        features.update({
            '+1:word.lower()': word1.lower(),
            '+1:word.istitle()': word1.istitle(),
            '+1:word.isupper()': word1.isupper(),
        })
    else:
        features['EOS'] = True  # End of sentence
    return features
def sent2features(sent):
    return [word2features(sent, i) for i in range(len(sent))]
```

```
def sent2labels(sent):
    return [label for token, label in sent]
def sent2tokens(sent):
    return [token for token, label in sent]
# Prepare training and test data
X_train = [sent2features(s) for s in train_sentences]
y_train = [sent2labels(s) for s in train_sentences]
X_test = [sent2features(s) for s in test_sentences]
y_test = [sent2labels(s) for s in test_sentences]
# Initialize and train the CRF model
crf = sklearn_crfsuite.CRF(
    algorithm='lbfgs',
    c1=0.1,  # Coefficient for L1 penalty
    c2=0.1,  # Coefficient for L2 penalty
    max_iterations=100,
    all_possible_transitions=True
)
crf.fit(X_train, y_train)
# Predict on the test set
y_pred = crf.predict(X_test)
# Evaluate the model
print("CRF Model Performance on Test Set:")
```

```
print(metrics.flat_classification_report(y_test, y_pred,
labels=["B-PER", "I-PER", "B-LOC", "I-LOC", "O"]))
```

Explanation:

- **Feature Engineering:**
  The word2features function generates a rich set of features for each word, including lowercase conversion, capitalization flags, and neighboring word features.
- **Data Preparation:**
  The training and test datasets are transformed into feature representations suitable for CRF training.
- **Model Training:**
  The CRF model is trained using the lbfgs algorithm with regularization parameters c1 and c2 to prevent overfitting.
- **Evaluation:**
  The model's performance is evaluated using a flat classification report that breaks down precision, recall, and F1-score for each label.

In summary, Hidden Markov Models and Conditional Random Fields represent two pivotal approaches in classical sequence modeling for NLP. While HMMs laid the groundwork for understanding sequential dependencies in language, CRFs have become the preferred choice for tasks such as NER and POS tagging due to their flexibility and superior performance in handling overlapping and interdependent features. By leveraging these models, enterprises can build sophisticated NLP pipelines that effectively extract structured insights from unstructured text, thereby driving enhanced decision-making and operational efficiency.

Evaluation Metrics

Precision, Recall, F1 Score, and Other KPIs for Measuring Effectiveness and Business Impact

Evaluation metrics are essential to understanding the performance and business impact of NLP systems. In the context of classical statistical and machine learning approaches for tasks such as document classification, sentiment analysis, and named entity recognition, metrics like precision, recall, and F1 score provide clear, interpretable measures of model effectiveness. These KPIs not only inform technical improvements but also drive strategic decisions by linking model performance to real-world outcomes.

Key Evaluation Metrics

1. **Precision**

- **Definition:** The ratio of true positive predictions to the total predicted positives.
- **Business Impact:** High precision means that when the model predicts a positive outcome (e.g., a document classified as relevant or a sentiment as positive), it is likely to be correct. This is crucial for applications where false positives can lead to wasted resources or misdirected efforts, such as targeted marketing or fraud detection.

2. **Recall (Sensitivity)**

- **Definition:** The ratio of true positive predictions to the total actual positives.
- **Business Impact:** High recall indicates that the model is effectively capturing the majority of relevant instances. This is important in scenarios like spam detection or medical text analysis, where missing a positive case can have significant negative consequences.

3. **F1 Score**

- **Definition:** The harmonic mean of precision and recall, providing a single metric that balances both concerns.

- **Business Impact:** The F1 score is particularly useful when there is an uneven class distribution or when both false positives and false negatives carry significant business risk. It allows decision-makers to evaluate overall model effectiveness comprehensively.

4. **Additional KPIs:**

- **Accuracy:** Measures the proportion of correctly classified instances across all predictions.
- **Confusion Matrix:** Provides detailed insight into true positives, false positives, true negatives, and false negatives.
- **ROC-AUC:** Evaluates the model's ability to distinguish between classes across different threshold settings.
- **Business-Specific Metrics:** In some cases, custom KPIs (e.g., cost savings, conversion rates) may be derived to directly measure the business impact of model performance.

Illustrative Example: Evaluating a Sentiment Analysis Model

Below is an example in Python using scikit-learn to compute precision, recall, F1 score, and other metrics for a sentiment analysis classifier. This example assumes that we have a test set with true labels and predictions from a model.

```
from sklearn.metrics import accuracy_score, precision_score, recall_score, f1_score, confusion_matrix, classification_report

import numpy as np

# Sample true labels and predicted labels from a sentiment analysis model

# 1 represents positive sentiment, 0 represents negative sentiment

y_true = np.array([1, 0, 1, 1, 0, 0, 1, 0, 1, 0])
```

```
y_pred = np.array([1, 0, 1, 0, 0, 0, 1, 1, 1, 0])
# Calculate evaluation metrics
accuracy = accuracy_score(y_true, y_pred)
precision = precision_score(y_true, y_pred)
recall = recall_score(y_true, y_pred)
f1 = f1_score(y_true, y_pred)
conf_matrix = confusion_matrix(y_true, y_pred)
# Display the results
print("Accuracy:", accuracy)
print("Precision:", precision)
print("Recall:", recall)
print("F1 Score:", f1)
print("Confusion Matrix:\n", conf_matrix)
# Detailed classification report
print("\nClassification Report:\n",
classification_report(y_true, y_pred))
```

Explanation:

- **Accuracy:**
  The overall proportion of correct predictions.
- **Precision:**
  Indicates the correctness of positive predictions.
- **Rccall:**
  Measures the model's ability to capture all actual positive cases.

- **F1 Score:**
  Balances precision and recall to provide a single, robust performance metric.
- **Confusion Matrix:**
  Offers a granular view of model errors, showing counts of true positives, false positives, true negatives, and false negatives.
- **Classification Report:**
  Provides an aggregated view of all key metrics, enabling a quick assessment of model performance across classes.

Strategic Business Impact

- **Operational Efficiency:**
  Optimized models with high precision and recall reduce manual review and correction, saving time and resources.
- **Risk Mitigation:**
  In applications like fraud detection or medical diagnostics, minimizing false negatives (via high recall) is critical to reducing risk.
- **Enhanced Customer Experience:**
  Accurate sentiment analysis and document classification lead to better-targeted customer interactions, boosting satisfaction and loyalty.
- **Data-Driven Decision Making:**
  Clear, interpretable metrics enable stakeholders to make informed decisions about model updates, resource allocation, and strategic planning.

Conclusion

Measuring the effectiveness of NLP models through precision, recall, F1 score, and additional KPIs is vital for both technical evaluation and business strategy. By understanding and monitoring these metrics, enterprises can ensure that their NLP systems not only perform well in controlled evaluations but also deliver tangible benefits in real-world applications. This robust evaluation framework supports continuous improvement, operational excellence, and strategic alignment with overall business objectives.

Chapter 6: Word Embeddings and Vector Representations

Introduction to Vector Space Models

The transformation of words into vector representations has revolutionized natural language processing by enabling models to capture semantic and syntactic relationships in a continuous space. At the heart of this approach lies the concept of the **vector space model**, which represents words as dense vectors in a high-dimensional space.

Theoretical Background: Distributed Representations

Vector Space Model Overview:

- **Traditional Representation vs. Distributed Representation:** Traditional representations, such as one-hot encoding, suffer from sparsity and fail to capture inter-word relationships. In contrast, distributed representations map each word to a dense vector, where semantic similarity is reflected by spatial proximity in the vector space.
- **Semantic Similarity and Context:**
  Word embeddings are generated such that words appearing in similar contexts have similar vector representations. This concept, often summarized by the phrase "You shall know a word by the company it keeps," is formalized in the **distributional hypothesis**.

Key Models for Learning Embeddings:

- **Word2Vec:**
  Developed by Mikolov et al., Word2Vec introduced two architectures - Continuous Bag-of-Words (CBOW) and Skip-Gram - which learn embeddings by predicting a target word from its context or vice versa.

- **GloVe (Global Vectors):**
  GloVe leverages global co-occurrence statistics to generate word vectors, integrating both local context and overall corpus statistics.

- **FastText:**
  An extension of Word2Vec, FastText considers subword information (e.g., character n-grams) to generate embeddings, which enhances performance for rare words and morphologically rich languages.

Benefits for NLP Applications:

- **Semantic Reasoning:**
  Vector representations enable arithmetic operations (e.g., *king* − *man* + *woman* ≈ *queen*), highlighting their ability to capture analogical relationships.

- **Reduced Dimensionality:**
  Dense vectors reduce the dimensionality compared to one-hot representations, making downstream tasks more computationally efficient.

- **Generalization:**
  Models built on embeddings can generalize better to unseen data due to the continuous nature of the representation space.

Illustrative Example: Learning Word Embeddings with Gensim's Word2Vec

The following Python code demonstrates how to train a Word2Vec model using the Gensim library. This example shows how to convert raw text into distributed word representations.

```
import gensim

from gensim.models import Word2Vec

import nltk
```

```
from nltk.tokenize import word_tokenize

# Sample corpus: list of sentences (each sentence is a string)

corpus = [

    "The company reported a significant increase in revenue this quarter.",

    "Customer satisfaction is a key metric for business success.",

    "Innovative product design and efficient operations drive growth.",

    "The market trends indicate a shift towards sustainable practices.",

    "Effective communication and collaboration are vital for success."

]

# Tokenize the corpus (convert each sentence to a list of words)

tokenized_corpus = [word_tokenize(sentence.lower()) for sentence in corpus]

# Train a Word2Vec model using the Skip-Gram architecture

model = Word2Vec(sentences=tokenized_corpus, vector_size=100, window=5, min_count=1, sg=1, workers=2, epochs=100)

# Example: Get the vector representation for the word "success"

word_vector = model.wv["success"]

print("Vector representation for 'success':\n", word_vector)
```

```
# Finding similar words to "growth"
similar_words = model.wv.most_similar("growth", topn=5)
print("\nWords similar to 'growth':")
for word, similarity in similar_words:
    print(f"{word}: {similarity:.2f}")
```

Explanation:

- **Preprocessing:**
  The code tokenizes a small corpus into words, ensuring the text is in lowercase to standardize the input.
- **Training the Model:**
  We train a Word2Vec model using the Skip-Gram architecture (sg=1), which predicts context words given a target word. The model learns dense vector representations (embeddings) for each word in the vocabulary.
- **Extracting and Using Embeddings:**
  The vector for the word "success" is printed, and similar words to "growth" are identified based on cosine similarity. This demonstrates how embeddings can capture semantic relationships.

Strategic Business Impact

- **Enhanced Semantic Understanding:**
  By representing words as vectors, NLP systems can capture nuanced relationships, leading to better performance in tasks such as sentiment analysis, document classification, and machine translation.
- **Scalability and Efficiency:**
  Dense vector representations allow for more efficient

computation and storage, facilitating real-time applications such as chatbots and recommendation systems.

- **Data-Driven Insights:**
  The ability to perform vector arithmetic and similarity searches enables businesses to uncover hidden insights from textual data, driving more informed strategic decisions.

In summary, the vector space model and distributed representations of words form the foundation of modern NLP. By transforming raw text into continuous, dense vectors, these models capture intricate semantic relationships and contextual nuances that are essential for a wide range of applications. Enterprises that harness the power of word embeddings can achieve significant improvements in model performance, operational efficiency, and strategic insight, making them a critical component of contemporary NLP pipelines.

Word2Vec, GloVe, and FastText

Key Embedding Techniques and Practical Guidelines for Enterprise-Scale Implementation

Word embeddings have become a cornerstone of modern NLP, enabling machines to capture semantic and syntactic nuances through dense, continuous vector representations. Among the leading techniques, **Word2Vec**, **GloVe**, and **FastText** have established themselves as robust methods for generating high-quality embeddings.

1. Word2Vec

Overview:
Word2Vec, developed by Mikolov et al., employs neural networks to learn word embeddings from large corpora. It offers two primary architectures:

- **Continuous Bag-of-Words (CBOW):** Predicts a target word from its surrounding context.

- **Skip-Gram:** Predicts surrounding context words given a target word.

These models effectively capture semantic relationships, allowing for vector arithmetic (e.g., *king* − *man* + *woman* ≈ *queen*).

Practical Guidelines for Enterprise Implementation:

- **Data Preparation:** Ensure extensive, diverse corpora to capture the vocabulary nuances of your domain.
- **Parameter Tuning:** Optimize hyperparameters such as vector size, window size, and training epochs based on domain-specific needs.
- **Infrastructure:** Utilize distributed computing frameworks to process large-scale datasets efficiently.
- **Integration:** Seamlessly integrate trained embeddings into downstream NLP pipelines such as sentiment analysis, document classification, or recommendation systems.

Illustrative Code Example (Using Gensim):

```
import gensim

from gensim.models import Word2Vec

import nltk

from nltk.tokenize import word_tokenize

# Sample corpus: list of sentences

corpus = [

    "The company reported significant revenue growth last quarter.",

    "Customer satisfaction is a key metric for business success.",
```

```
    "Innovative product design drives competitive advantage.",
    "Operational efficiency is critical for sustainable growth.",
    "Strategic investments in technology boost market performance."
]
# Preprocess: Tokenize and convert to lowercase
tokenized_corpus = [word_tokenize(sentence.lower()) for sentence in corpus]
# Train Word2Vec model using the Skip-Gram architecture (sg=1)
word2vec_model = Word2Vec(sentences=tokenized_corpus, vector_size=100, window=5, min_count=1, sg=1, workers=4, epochs=100)
# Retrieve and display the embedding for a sample word
print("Word2Vec embedding for 'growth':")
print(word2vec_model.wv["growth"])
# Find words similar to "growth"
similar_words = word2vec_model.wv.most_similar("growth", topn=5)
print("\nWords similar to 'growth':")
for word, similarity in similar_words:
    print(f"{word}: {similarity:.2f}")
```

2. GloVe (Global Vectors for Word Representation)

Overview:

GloVe, introduced by Pennington et al., combines the strengths of global matrix factorization and local context window methods. It constructs embeddings by aggregating global word-word co-occurrence statistics, offering robust representations that excel in capturing the overall structure of the corpus.

Practical Guidelines for Enterprise Implementation:

- **Precomputed Models:** Consider using pre-trained GloVe embeddings (available in various dimensions) as a baseline, especially when domain-specific corpora are limited.
- **Customization:** Fine-tune pre-trained embeddings on your proprietary data to capture industry-specific language.
- **Scalability:** Leverage high-performance computing resources to handle the computational intensity of co-occurrence matrix factorization.
- **Evaluation:** Rigorously validate embeddings on downstream tasks to ensure they meet business performance criteria.

Loading Pre-Trained GloVe Embeddings Example:

```
import numpy as np

def load_glove_embeddings(file_path):

    embeddings = {}

    with open(file_path, 'r', encoding='utf8') as f:

        for line in f:

            values = line.split()
```

```
        word = values[0]
        vector = np.asarray(values[1:], dtype='float32')
        embeddings[word] = vector
    return embeddings

# Example usage: Load a small GloVe embedding file (e.g., glove.6B.100d.txt)
# glove_embeddings = load_glove_embeddings("path/to/glove.6B.100d.txt")
# print("GloVe embedding for 'growth':", glove_embeddings.get("growth"))
```

Note: The GloVe embedding file must be downloaded separately from GloVe's website.

3. FastText

Overview:
FastText, developed by Facebook AI Research, extends Word2Vec by incorporating subword information. Instead of learning embeddings for whole words only, FastText represents each word as a bag of character n-grams. This approach enhances the model's ability to handle rare words, misspellings, and morphologically rich languages.

Practical Guidelines for Enterprise Implementation:

- **Handling Out-of-Vocabulary (OOV) Words:** Use FastText to generate embeddings for unseen words by leveraging their subword structure.
- **Domain Adaptation:** FastText is particularly effective in industries with highly specialized terminology, as it can generate robust embeddings even for low-frequency words.

- **Model Fine-Tuning:** Fine-tune FastText models on domain-specific corpora to improve relevance and accuracy.
- **Deployment:** Ensure the model supports incremental updates, allowing continuous learning as new data becomes available.

Illustrative Code Example (Using Gensim's FastText):

```
from gensim.models import FastText

# Train a FastText model on the same tokenized corpus

fasttext_model = FastText(sentences=tokenized_corpus, vector_size=100, window=5, min_count=1, workers=4, sg=1, epochs=100)

# Retrieve and display the embedding for a sample word

print("FastText embedding for 'efficiency':")

print(fasttext_model.wv["efficiency"])

# Find words similar to "efficiency"

similar_words_ft = fasttext_model.wv.most_similar("efficiency", topn=5)

print("\nWords similar to 'efficiency':")

for word, similarity in similar_words_ft:

    print(f"{word}: {similarity:.2f}")
```

Enterprise-Scale Implementation Best Practices

1. **Infrastructure Considerations:**

   - **Scalability:** Deploy models on distributed architectures (e.g., cloud platforms, GPU clusters) to manage large-scale training.

- **Storage:** Utilize scalable storage solutions (e.g., data lakes) to handle vast corpora and embedding matrices.
- **Integration:** Ensure seamless integration with existing data pipelines and downstream analytics systems.

2. **Model Maintenance:**

- **Version Control:** Implement model versioning to track changes and facilitate reproducibility.
- **Continuous Learning:** Regularly update embeddings with new data to maintain relevance.
- **Monitoring:** Establish performance metrics and monitoring systems to track model efficacy in real-world applications.

3. **Data Privacy and Compliance:**

- **Anonymization:** Ensure sensitive data is anonymized before training.
- **Governance:** Adhere to corporate and regulatory guidelines for data handling and model deployment.

4. **Evaluation and Fine-Tuning:**

- **Benchmarking:** Evaluate embeddings on standard NLP tasks (e.g., similarity, analogy tests) as well as domain-specific applications.
- **Custom Tuning:** Fine-tune hyperparameters based on business use cases to optimize performance.

In summary, Word2Vec, GloVe, and FastText each offer distinct advantages in generating word embeddings, forming the backbone of modern NLP applications. By understanding the theoretical underpinnings and practical considerations for each technique, enterprises can deploy robust, scalable embedding models that drive enhanced semantic understanding, operational efficiency, and strategic insights. With thoughtful infrastructure planning, continuous maintenance, and rigorous evaluation, these embedding techniques become powerful tools for leveraging the vast potential of textual data in a business context.

Evaluation and Practical Considerations

Best Practices for Embedding Selection, Dimensionality, and Interpretability

Choosing the right word embeddings and configuring them appropriately is critical for building high-performing NLP systems. In enterprise applications, where model performance directly influences business outcomes, evaluating and selecting the best embeddings require a balanced approach. This involves not only measuring quantitative performance but also ensuring that the embeddings are interpretable and scalable. Below are key best practices and practical considerations:

1. Embedding Selection

Key Considerations:

- **Domain Relevance:**
  Choose embeddings that align with your domain. Pre-trained embeddings like Word2Vec, GloVe, or FastText offer general-purpose representations, but fine-tuning or training on domain-specific corpora can lead to significant improvements in tasks such as sentiment analysis, document classification, and recommendation systems.
- **Performance Benchmarks:**
  Evaluate embeddings using standard NLP benchmarks such as analogy tests, similarity tasks, or downstream task performance. This provides an objective measure of how well the embeddings capture semantic relationships.

- **Out-of-Vocabulary (OOV) Handling:**
  For applications with a high frequency of rare or evolving terminology, FastText's subword modeling can be advantageous as it generates representations for words not seen during training.

2. Dimensionality

Balancing Trade-offs:

- **Expressiveness vs. Efficiency:**
  Higher-dimensional embeddings can capture more subtle semantic nuances but may increase computational requirements and risk overfitting, especially when training data is limited.

- **Optimal Dimension Selection:**
  Empirical experimentation is often required. Typical dimensions range from 100 to 300 for many applications, but tasks with complex semantics or large vocabularies might benefit from 400 dimensions or more.

- **Scalability:**
  Consider the impact on downstream systems. Lower-dimensional embeddings can speed up training and inference, particularly in real-time applications, while higher-dimensional embeddings might be more suitable for batch processing scenarios.

3. Interpretability

Ensuring Transparency and Insight:

- **Visualization:**
  Use dimensionality reduction techniques (e.g., t-SNE or PCA) to visualize the embedding space. This can help identify clusters of semantically similar words and validate that the model captures expected linguistic patterns.

- **Semantic Coherence:**
  Check for logical analogies and relationships, such as vector

arithmetic (e.g., *king* − *man* + *woman* ≈ *queen*). Such tests provide intuitive validation of the embeddings' quality.

- **Feature Importance:**
  In applications where interpretability is key (e.g., legal or compliance domains), ensure that embedding-driven features can be traced back to meaningful word characteristics or contextual cues.

Illustrative Example: Evaluating and Visualizing Embeddings with t-SNE

The following Python code demonstrates how to evaluate and visualize word embeddings using t-SNE, a popular technique for reducing dimensionality and interpreting high-dimensional data.

```
import matplotlib.pyplot as plt

from sklearn.manifold import TSNE

import numpy as np

# Example: Using a pre-trained Word2Vec model (assumed to be loaded as 'word2vec_model')

# For illustration, we select a subset of words from the vocabulary.

words = ["company", "revenue", "growth", "customer", "satisfaction", "market", "performance", "innovation", "strategy", "efficiency"]

word_vectors = np.array([word2vec_model.wv[word] for word in words])

# Use t-SNE to reduce the embeddings to 2 dimensions for visualization

tsne = TSNE(n_components=2, random_state=42, perplexity=5, n_iter=300)
```

```
reduced_vectors = tsne.fit_transform(word_vectors)
# Plot the results
plt.figure(figsize=(10, 6))
for i, word in enumerate(words):
    plt.scatter(reduced_vectors[i, 0], reduced_vectors[i, 1], marker='o', color='blue')
    plt.text(reduced_vectors[i, 0] + 0.01, reduced_vectors[i, 1] + 0.01, word, fontsize=12)
plt.title("t-SNE Visualization of Selected Word Embeddings")
plt.xlabel("Dimension 1")
plt.ylabel("Dimension 2")
plt.grid(True)
plt.show()
```

Explanation:

- **Subset Selection:**
  A small subset of words is chosen to illustrate semantic relationships relevant to enterprise contexts.
- **Dimensionality Reduction:**
  t-SNE reduces high-dimensional embeddings into two dimensions, enabling visualization of clusters and semantic proximities.
- **Interpretability:**
  Visual inspection of the plot can help confirm that semantically related words (e.g., *growth*, *revenue*, *performance*) are close together, offering insights into the model's effectiveness.

Conclusion

Embedding selection, dimensionality, and interpretability are fundamental pillars for the successful deployment of NLP systems at scale. Enterprises should:

- Choose embeddings that are both domain-relevant and performance-validated.
- Balance the trade-offs between expressive power and computational efficiency when selecting dimensionality.
- Employ visualization and semantic tests to ensure the embeddings provide meaningful, interpretable insights.

By following these best practices, organizations can deploy word embeddings that not only improve the performance of NLP applications but also enhance strategic decision-making and operational efficiency in a business context.

Part III: Deep Learning and Advanced Architectures
Chapter 7: Neural Network Foundations for NLP

Feedforward Networks and MLPs

Deep learning has transformed NLP by enabling models to learn complex patterns directly from data. At the heart of many advanced architectures lie feedforward networks and multi-layer perceptrons (MLPs), which form the building blocks for more sophisticated models.

Understanding Feedforward Networks and MLPs

Feedforward Networks:

- **Structure:**
  A feedforward network is a type of neural network where information moves in one direction—from input to output—without cycles or loops.
- **Layers:**
  It consists of an input layer, one or more hidden layers, and an output layer. Each layer is made up of neurons (or nodes) that perform linear transformations followed by a non-linear activation function.

Multi-Layer Perceptrons (MLPs):

- **Definition:**
  MLPs are a class of feedforward networks that have one or more hidden layers, allowing them to learn non-linear representations.
- **Key Components:**
  - **Weights and Biases:** Parameters learned during training that define how input data is transformed.

- **Activation Functions:** Non-linear functions (e.g., ReLU, sigmoid, tanh) applied to the output of each layer to capture complex patterns.
- **Backpropagation:** The algorithm used to update network parameters by propagating the error gradient backward through the network.

Basic Deep Learning Concepts in an NLP Context

1. **Input Representation:**
   In NLP, input data is typically represented as vectors. This could be via one-hot encodings, TF-IDF features, or word embeddings. These vectors are fed into the MLP as input features.
2. **Activation Functions:**
   Activation functions introduce non-linearity into the network, enabling it to learn more complex relationships:

- **ReLU (Rectified Linear Unit):**
  $\mathrm{ReLU}(x)=\max(0,x)$
  Commonly used for hidden layers due to its computational efficiency and reduced likelihood of vanishing gradients.
- **Sigmoid:**
  $\sigma(x)=\frac{1}{1+e^{-x}}$
  Often used in output layers for binary classification tasks.
- **Tanh:**
  $\tanh(x)=\frac{e^{x}-e^{-x}}{e^{x}+e^{-x}}$
  Outputs values between -1 and 1, used in some NLP applications to capture both positive and negative activations.

3. **Backpropagation:**
   The backpropagation algorithm computes gradients of the loss function with respect to network parameters. It then uses these

gradients to update the weights and biases using an optimization algorithm (e.g., stochastic gradient descent).

4. **Loss Function:**
   For classification tasks, a common loss function is the cross-entropy loss, which measures the difference between the predicted probabilities and the actual labels.

Illustrative Example: Building an MLP for Text Classification

Below is an example using PyTorch to construct a simple MLP for an NLP classification task. The model takes pre-processed text features (e.g., word embeddings or TF-IDF vectors) as input and predicts a class label.

```
import torch

import torch.nn as nn

import torch.optim as optim

import torch.nn.functional as F

# Define a simple MLP for classification

class SimpleMLP(nn.Module):

    def __init__(self, input_size, hidden_size, num_classes):

        super(SimpleMLP, self).__init__()

        # Define layers

        self.fc1 = nn.Linear(input_size, hidden_size)  # First
hidden layer

        self.fc2 = nn.Linear(hidden_size, num_classes)   # Output
layer
```

```
    def forward(self, x):
        # Forward pass through the network
        # Linear transformation followed by ReLU activation
        out = F.relu(self.fc1(x))
        # Final linear transformation to obtain class scores
        out = self.fc2(out)
        return out
# Parameters
input_size = 300     # Example input dimension (e.g., size of word embeddings or TF-IDF features)
hidden_size = 128    # Size of the hidden layer
num_classes = 2      # Binary classification (e.g., positive/negative sentiment)
learning_rate = 0.001
# Instantiate the model, loss function, and optimizer
model = SimpleMLP(input_size, hidden_size, num_classes)
criterion = nn.CrossEntropyLoss()
optimizer = optim.Adam(model.parameters(), lr=learning_rate)
# Example training loop (dummy data)
# Assume we have some pre-processed feature vectors (X) and labels (y)
# Here, we generate random data for demonstration purposes
batch_size = 16
```

```
num_epochs = 5
X = torch.randn(batch_size, input_size)     # Random feature matrix
y = torch.randint(0, num_classes, (batch_size,)) # Random labels (0 or 1)
for epoch in range(num_epochs):
    # Forward pass
    outputs = model(X)
    loss = criterion(outputs, y)
        # Backward pass and optimization
    optimizer.zero_grad()  # Zero the gradients from the previous step
    loss.backward()       # Compute gradients via backpropagation
    optimizer.step()      # Update model parameters
    print(f"Epoch [{epoch+1}/{num_epochs}], Loss: {loss.item():.4f}")
# Model evaluation (for demonstration, using the same dummy data)
with torch.no_grad():
    predicted = torch.argmax(model(X), dim=1)
    accuracy = (predicted == y).float().mean()
    print(f"Training Accuracy: {accuracy.item() * 100:.2f}%")
```

Explanation:

- **Model Definition:**
  The SimpleMLP class defines an MLP with one hidden layer. The input layer takes a feature vector of size 300, the hidden layer has 128 neurons with ReLU activation, and the output layer produces class scores for binary classification.
- **Loss and Optimizer:**
  Cross-entropy loss is used for classification, and the Adam optimizer updates the weights based on the gradients computed during backpropagation.
- **Training Loop:**
  A simple training loop demonstrates how the model processes input data, computes the loss, performs backpropagation, and updates its parameters.
- **Evaluation:**
  The training accuracy is computed by comparing the predicted labels with the true labels, showcasing how model performance is tracked.

In summary, feedforward networks and MLPs serve as fundamental building blocks in NLP, enabling models to learn non-linear relationships from text data. By understanding key deep learning concepts - such as activation functions, backpropagation, and loss optimization - NLP practitioners can design efficient and scalable models. Whether used in simple text classification tasks or as components in more complex architectures, these neural network foundations play a critical role in driving the performance and business impact of modern NLP systems.

Convolutional Neural Networks (CNNs) for NLP

Architecture Design and Use Cases for Text Classification and Sentiment Analysis

Convolutional Neural Networks (CNNs) have emerged as a powerful architecture in the NLP domain, particularly for tasks such as text classification and sentiment analysis. Originally designed for computer vision, CNNs have been successfully adapted for text processing by treating sequences of word embeddings as "images" where convolutional filters capture local patterns - such as n-grams - and hierarchical features in text.

Architecture Design

Key Components:

1. **Embedding Layer:**

- **Purpose:** Converts words into dense vector representations (e.g., via pre-trained embeddings or learned during training).
- **NLP Impact:** Captures semantic relationships between words and provides a robust input representation for the CNN.

2. **Convolutional Layers:**

- **Filters:** Multiple filters with varying kernel sizes (e.g., 2, 3, 4, or 5) capture different n-gram features.
- **Activation Functions:** ReLU is commonly used to introduce non-linearity.
- **Sliding Window:** Filters slide over the text to extract local features.

3. **Pooling Layers:**

- **Max-Pooling:** Selects the most significant feature from each filter's output, reducing dimensionality and emphasizing the most relevant features.
- **Global Pooling:** Often used to aggregate information over the entire sequence, making the model invariant to the position of features.

4. **Fully Connected (Dense) Layers:**

- **Purpose:** Integrate features from the pooling layers to perform final classification.
- **Dropout:** Regularization technique to reduce overfitting.

5. **Output Layer:**

- **Softmax or Sigmoid:** Depending on whether the task is multi-class classification or binary classification (e.g., sentiment analysis).

Use Cases in NLP

- **Text Classification:**
  CNNs excel at categorizing documents, news articles, and customer reviews by automatically learning hierarchical features that discriminate between classes.
- **Sentiment Analysis:**
  By capturing local n-gram features that indicate sentiment (e.g., "not good", "extremely satisfied"), CNNs can robustly classify text into positive, negative, or neutral sentiments.
- **Other Applications:**
  CNNs are also applied to tasks like question classification, spam detection, and even more complex applications when integrated with other architectures.

Illustrative Example: CNN for Text Classification Using PyTorch

The following example demonstrates a simple CNN for text classification. This network leverages an embedding layer, convolutional layers with multiple filter sizes, max pooling, and fully connected layers to classify text into two categories (e.g., positive or negative sentiment).

```
import torch
import torch.nn as nn
import torch.optim as optim
import torch.nn.functional as F
class TextCNN(nn.Module):
  def __init__(self, vocab_size, embed_dim, num_classes,
filter_sizes, num_filters, dropout=0.5):
      super(TextCNN, self).__init__()
      # Embedding layer: transforms token indices into
embeddings.
      self.embedding = nn.Embedding(vocab_size,
embed_dim)
      # Convolution layers for each filter size
      self.convs = nn.ModuleList([
        nn.Conv2d(1, num_filters, (fs, embed_dim)) for fs in
filter_sizes
      ])
      # Dropout layer for regularization
      self.dropout = nn.Dropout(dropout)
      # Fully connected layer: combines features from different
filters.
      self.fc = nn.Linear(len(filter_sizes) * num_filters,
num_classes)
```

```
    def forward(self, x):
        # x: [batch_size, sequence_length]
        x = self.embedding(x)  # Shape: [batch_size, sequence_length, embed_dim]
        x = x.unsqueeze(1)     # Shape: [batch_size, 1, sequence_length, embed_dim]
        # Apply convolution and ReLU activation on each filter
        conv_results = [F.relu(conv(x)).squeeze(3) for conv in self.convs]
        # Each conv_result: [batch_size, num_filters, sequence_length - filter_size + 1]
        # Apply max pooling over time for each filter
        pooled = [F.max_pool1d(feature_map, feature_map.size(2)).squeeze(2) for feature_map in conv_results]
        # Each pooled: [batch_size, num_filters]
        # Concatenate pooled features
        cat = torch.cat(pooled, dim=1)  # Shape: [batch_size, num_filters * len(filter_sizes)]
        # Apply dropout
        cat = self.dropout(cat)
        # Final fully connected layer for classification
        out = self.fc(cat)
        return out
# Hyperparameters and Model Initialization
```

```
vocab_size = 5000        # Size of the vocabulary

embed_dim = 100          # Dimension of word embeddings

num_classes = 2          # Binary classification (e.g.,
positive/negative sentiment)

filter_sizes = [3, 4, 5] # Different filter sizes to capture tri-
grams, 4-grams, and 5-grams

num_filters = 100        # Number of filters per filter size

dropout = 0.5

# Instantiate the model

model = TextCNN(vocab_size, embed_dim, num_classes,
filter_sizes, num_filters, dropout)

print(model)

# Define loss function and optimizer

criterion = nn.CrossEntropyLoss()

optimizer = optim.Adam(model.parameters(), lr=0.001)

# Dummy data for demonstration: batch_size=16,
sequence_length=50

batch_size = 16

sequence_length = 50

dummy_inputs = torch.randint(0, vocab_size, (batch_size,
sequence_length))  # Random token indices

dummy_labels = torch.randint(0, num_classes, (batch_size,))
# Random labels

# Training step demonstration
```

```
model.train()
optimizer.zero_grad()
outputs = model(dummy_inputs)  # Forward pass
loss = criterion(outputs, dummy_labels)  # Compute loss
loss.backward()  # Backpropagation
optimizer.step()  # Update weights
print(f"Loss: {loss.item():.4f}")
```

Explanation:

- **Embedding Layer:**
  Converts token indices into dense embeddings, serving as the input representation for the CNN.
- **Convolutional Layers:**
  Multiple convolutional filters with different kernel sizes slide over the embedding matrix, capturing local n-gram features.
- **Max Pooling:**
  Each convolutional feature map undergoes max pooling to extract the most salient feature from each filter.
- **Concatenation and Dropout:**
  The pooled features are concatenated into a single vector and regularized using dropout.
- **Fully Connected Layer:**
  The concatenated feature vector is passed through a dense layer that outputs class scores, enabling text classification.
- **Training Loop:**
  A simple training step is demonstrated using a dummy batch of

data to illustrate the forward pass, loss computation, and weight updates via backpropagation.

In summary, CNNs for NLP provide a robust framework for capturing local and hierarchical patterns in text, making them highly effective for tasks like text classification and sentiment analysis. By designing architectures that incorporate embedding layers, convolutional filters of various sizes, and pooling mechanisms, enterprises can develop models that extract meaningful features from unstructured text data. The flexibility and performance of CNN-based approaches empower organizations to deploy scalable NLP solutions that drive actionable insights and support strategic decision-making in dynamic business environments.

Recurrent Neural Networks

Handling Sequence Data in NLP

Recurrent Neural Networks (RNNs) and their gated variants—Long Short-Term Memory (LSTM) and Gated Recurrent Unit (GRU)—are foundational architectures designed to process sequential data. In NLP, these models excel at tasks that involve language modeling, sequence prediction, and complex generative tasks, such as text generation, translation, and dialogue systems.

Recurrent Neural Networks (RNNs)

Overview:

- **Sequential Data Handling:**
  RNNs are specifically designed to process sequences by maintaining a hidden state that carries information from previous time steps. This capability allows RNNs to capture dependencies and patterns in language data.

- **Architecture:**
  At each time step t, an RNN takes an input xt and updates its hidden state ht using the previous state ht−1 and current input:

$$ht=\sigma(Whh\cdot ht-1+Wxh\cdot xt+bh)$$

where σ is an activation function (commonly tanh), and Whh and Wxh are weight matrices.

- **Challenges:**
  Standard RNNs often struggle with long-term dependencies due to issues like vanishing or exploding gradients, making it difficult to capture context over long sequences.

Long Short-Term Memory (LSTM)

Overview:

- **Addressing Long-Term Dependencies:**
  LSTMs introduce gated mechanisms to control the flow of information, effectively addressing the vanishing gradient problem inherent in standard RNNs. They maintain a cell state that can preserve information over long sequences.

- **Key Components:**

  - **Input Gate:** Controls how much new information is added to the cell state.

  - **Forget Gate:** Determines how much of the previous cell state should be retained.

  - **Output Gate:** Controls how much information from the cell state is exposed to the next layer.

- **Formulation:**

The core equations for an LSTM cell are:

$$f_t = \sigma(W_f \cdot [h_{t-1}, x_t] + b_f) \quad \text{(Forget Gate)}$$

$$i_t = \sigma(W_i \cdot [h_{t-1}, x_t] + b_i) \quad \text{(Input Gate)}$$

$$\tilde{C}_t = \tanh(W_C \cdot [h_{t-1}, x_t] + b_C) \quad \text{(Candidate Cell State)}$$

$$C_t = f_t * C_{t-1} + i_t * \tilde{C}_t \quad \text{(Cell State Update)}$$

$$o_t = \sigma(W_o \cdot [h_{t-1}, x_t] + b_o) \quad \text{(Output Gate)}$$

$$h_t = o_t * \tanh(C_t) \quad \text{(Hidden State)}$$

Use Cases:

- **Language Modeling:**
  LSTMs are widely used for predicting the next word in a sequence, forming the backbone of language models.
- **Text Generation:**
  They power generative tasks like creative writing and dialogue generation by learning complex dependencies in language.

Gated Recurrent Unit (GRU)

Overview:

- **Simplified Alternative:**
  GRUs simplify the LSTM architecture by combining the forget and input gates into a single update gate and eliminating the explicit cell state. Despite this simplification, GRUs often achieve comparable performance with fewer parameters.
- **Key Components:**
  - **Update Gate:** Balances between retaining the previous hidden state and incorporating the new candidate.
  - **Reset Gate:** Determines how much past information to forget.
- **Formulation:**

The GRU cell is defined as:

$$z_t = \sigma(W_z \cdot [h_{t-1}, x_t] + b_z) \quad \text{(Update Gate)}$$
$$r_t = \sigma(W_r \cdot [h_{t-1}, x_t] + b_r) \quad \text{(Reset Gate)}$$
$$\tilde{h}_t = \tanh(W \cdot [r_t * h_{t-1}, x_t] + b) \quad \text{(Candidate Activation)}$$
$$h_t = (1 - z_t) * h_{t-1} + z_t * \tilde{h}_t \quad \text{(Hidden State Update)}$$

Use Cases:

- **Efficient Sequence Modeling:**
  GRUs are especially useful when computational efficiency is a priority, as they require fewer parameters and computations compared to LSTMs.
- **Real-Time Applications:**
  Their streamlined architecture makes GRUs a good fit for real-time NLP tasks such as speech recognition and live sentiment analysis.

Illustrative Example: Building an LSTM for Text Classification in PyTorch

Below is an example demonstrating how to construct an LSTM-based model for text classification. This model takes a sequence of word embeddings as input and outputs a class label.

```
import torch

import torch.nn as nn

import torch.optim as optim

class LSTMClassifier(nn.Module):

    def __init__(self, vocab_size, embed_dim, hidden_dim,
output_dim, n_layers, dropout):

        super(LSTMClassifier, self).__init__()
```

```
        # Embedding layer
        self.embedding = nn.Embedding(vocab_size,
embed_dim)
        # LSTM layer(s)
        self.lstm = nn.LSTM(embed_dim, hidden_dim,
num_layers=n_layers,
                            batch_first=True, dropout=dropout,
bidirectional=False)
        # Fully connected layer for classification
        self.fc = nn.Linear(hidden_dim, output_dim)
        # Dropout layer for regularization
        self.dropout = nn.Dropout(dropout)
        def forward(self, x):
        # x: [batch_size, sequence_length]
        embedded = self.embedding(x)  # [batch_size,
sequence_length, embed_dim]
        lstm_out, (hidden, cell) = self.lstm(embedded)
        # Using the last hidden state for classification
        hidden = self.dropout(hidden[-1])  # [batch_size,
hidden_dim]
        out = self.fc(hidden)  # [batch_size, output_dim]
        return out
# Hyperparameters
vocab_size = 5000     # Size of the vocabulary
```

```
embed_dim = 100      # Dimension of word embeddings

hidden_dim = 128     # Hidden state dimension for LSTM

output_dim = 2       # Number of classes (e.g.,
positive/negative sentiment)

n_layers = 2         # Number of LSTM layers

dropout = 0.5        # Dropout rate

# Initialize the model, loss function, and optimizer

model = LSTMClassifier(vocab_size, embed_dim, hidden_dim,
output_dim, n_layers, dropout)

criterion = nn.CrossEntropyLoss()

optimizer = optim.Adam(model.parameters(), lr=0.001)

# Dummy data for demonstration: batch_size=16,
sequence_length=50

batch_size = 16

sequence_length = 50

dummy_inputs = torch.randint(0, vocab_size, (batch_size,
sequence_length))

dummy_labels = torch.randint(0, output_dim, (batch_size,))

# Training step demonstration

model.train()

optimizer.zero_grad()

outputs = model(dummy_inputs)

loss = criterion(outputs, dummy_labels)

loss.backward()
```

```
optimizer.step()
print(f"LSTM Training Loss: {loss.item():.4f}")
```

Explanation:

- **Embedding Layer:**
  Converts token indices into dense vectors, serving as input for the LSTM.
- **LSTM Layers:**
  The LSTM processes the sequence of embeddings and produces hidden states. The last hidden state is used for classification.
- **Fully Connected Layer:**
  Maps the hidden state to the output class scores.
- **Training Loop:**
  A simple training step demonstrates forward propagation, loss calculation, backpropagation, and parameter updates.

Conclusion

Recurrent Neural Networks and their gated variants, LSTMs and GRUs, provide robust solutions for modeling sequential data in NLP. By handling long-term dependencies and capturing contextual nuances, these architectures enable applications ranging from language modeling and text generation to sentiment analysis and machine translation. Understanding their internal mechanisms and practical implementation considerations is key to leveraging their full potential in enterprise-scale NLP systems. Whether choosing LSTMs for their robust memory mechanisms or GRUs for computational efficiency, these recurrent models form the backbone of modern sequence processing tasks in NLP.

Chapter 8: Transformers and Attention Mechanisms

The Attention Revolution

The introduction of attention mechanisms has fundamentally transformed natural language processing. Often referred to as the "Attention Revolution," this paradigm shift moves away from the sequential processing of recurrent architectures to a model that can capture relationships between all parts of a sequence simultaneously. This comprehensive approach provides a robust theoretical framework and practical benefits that are critical for modern enterprise applications.

Theoretical Aspects of Attention

- **Global Context Modeling:**
  Unlike Recurrent Neural Networks (RNNs) that process inputs sequentially, attention mechanisms allow the model to consider all words in the input sequence concurrently. This global context modeling ensures that each token can directly attend to every other token, capturing long-range dependencies without the bottleneck of sequential processing.
- **Dynamic Weighting:**
  Attention assigns dynamic weights to different parts of the input based on their relevance to the task at hand. This means that the model can focus on the most informative elements of the sequence, enhancing the representation of key features while minimizing the influence of less important tokens.
- **Scalability and Parallelism:**
  By eliminating the inherent sequential nature of RNNs, transformers enable massive parallelization during training. This leads to significant improvements in training speed and efficiency, especially when processing large datasets—a critical requirement for enterprise-scale implementations.

- **Self-Attention Mechanism:**
  Self-attention is the core component of transformer architectures. It computes a weighted representation of each token by considering its similarity with every other token in the sequence. Mathematically, self-attention is computed as:

$$\text{Attention}(Q, K, V) = \text{softmax}\left(\frac{QK^T}{\sqrt{d_k}}\right)V$$

where Q (queries), K (keys), and V (values) are derived from the input representations, and dk is the dimensionality of the keys.

Practical Aspects and Differences from Recurrent Structures

- **Parallel Processing:**
  Transformers enable simultaneous processing of all tokens, whereas RNNs process tokens sequentially. This significantly reduces training time and allows for scaling on modern hardware (e.g., GPUs, TPUs).

- **Handling Long-Term Dependencies:**
  While RNNs and LSTMs can struggle with long-term dependencies due to vanishing gradients, attention mechanisms directly model relationships between distant tokens. This direct path for gradient flow results in more effective learning over long sequences.

- **Simpler Architecture for Sequence Modeling:**
  The transformer architecture discards recurrence entirely, relying solely on attention and positional encodings to maintain order information. This not only simplifies the model design but also improves the interpretability of learned relationships within the data.

- **Enhanced Flexibility:**
  Attention mechanisms are highly adaptable and can be stacked to form deep architectures. They provide fine-grained control over which parts of the input the model attends to, making them

suitable for diverse tasks such as language translation, summarization, and question answering.

Illustrative Example: Self-Attention Implementation in PyTorch

Below is a simplified implementation of a self-attention mechanism using PyTorch. This example demonstrates how queries, keys, and values are computed and how attention weights are derived.

```
import torch

import torch.nn as nn

import torch.nn.functional as F

class SelfAttention(nn.Module):

    def __init__(self, embed_dim, heads):

        super(SelfAttention, self).__init__()

        self.embed_dim = embed_dim

        self.heads = heads

        self.head_dim = embed_dim // heads

        assert (

            self.head_dim * heads == embed_dim

        ), "Embedding dimension must be divisible by number of
heads"

        # Define linear layers for queries, keys, and values

        self.query = nn.Linear(embed_dim, embed_dim)

        self.key = nn.Linear(embed_dim, embed_dim)
```

```
        self.value = nn.Linear(embed_dim, embed_dim)
        # Final linear layer
        self.fc_out = nn.Linear(embed_dim, embed_dim)
    def forward(self, x):
        # x shape: [batch_size, seq_length, embed_dim]
        batch_size, seq_length, embed_dim = x.shape
        # Compute queries, keys, and values
        Q = self.query(x)  # [batch_size, seq_length, embed_dim]
        K = self.key(x)
        V = self.value(x)
        # Reshape for multi-head attention
        Q = Q.view(batch_size, seq_length, self.heads,
self.head_dim).transpose(1,2)
        K = K.view(batch_size, seq_length, self.heads,
self.head_dim).transpose(1,2)
        V = V.view(batch_size, seq_length, self.heads,
self.head_dim).transpose(1,2)
        # Compute energy scores: [batch_size, heads, seq_length,
seq_length]
        energy = torch.matmul(Q, K.transpose(-2, -1)) /
(self.head_dim ** 0.5)
        # Apply softmax to get attention weights
        attention = torch.softmax(energy, dim=-1)
        # Multiply attention weights with values
```

```
        out = torch.matmul(attention, V)  # [batch_size, heads,
seq_length, head_dim]

        # Concatenate heads

        out = out.transpose(1,2).contiguous().view(batch_size,
seq_length, embed_dim)

        # Pass through final linear layer

        out = self.fc_out(out)

        return out

# Example usage

embed_dim = 128

heads = 8

batch_size = 4

seq_length = 10

# Random input tensor representing embedded words in a
sequence

x = torch.rand(batch_size, seq_length, embed_dim)

# Initialize self-attention layer and forward pass

self_attention = SelfAttention(embed_dim, heads)

output = self_attention(x)

print("Output shape from self-attention:", output.shape)
```

Explanation:

- **Input Preparation:**
  The input xxx represents a batch of sequences with word embeddings.
- **Multi-Head Attention:**
  The queries, keys, and values are computed and split into multiple heads. This allows the model to capture diverse types of relationships simultaneously.
- **Energy Calculation and Softmax:**
  The energy scores between queries and keys are computed and normalized with softmax to produce attention weights.
- **Aggregation and Output:**
  The attention weights are used to aggregate the values, and the results from all heads are concatenated and passed through a final linear layer.

In summary, the attention mechanism has revolutionized the way we model language by enabling direct, parallelized access to contextual information across entire sequences. Unlike recurrent structures, attention-based models - exemplified by transformers - offer enhanced scalability, efficiency, and the ability to capture long-range dependencies with ease. These advantages have driven their widespread adoption in enterprise applications, making them indispensable for tasks ranging from translation and summarization to sentiment analysis and beyond. Through both theoretical insights and practical implementations, the attention revolution continues to propel NLP into a new era of innovation and efficiency.

Transformer Model Architecture

Understanding the Encoder-Decoder Framework, Positional Embeddings, and Self-Attention

The transformer architecture has reshaped NLP by introducing a highly parallelizable, attention-based framework that efficiently captures long-range dependencies in text. Unlike traditional recurrent models, transformers rely on an encoder-decoder framework and self-attention mechanisms to process entire sequences in parallel.

1. Encoder-Decoder Framework

Overview:
The transformer model is divided into two main parts:

- **Encoder:**
  Processes the input sequence and converts it into a continuous representation. It consists of multiple identical layers, each containing:
  - **Self-Attention Sub-Layer:** Allows each token in the input to attend to every other token.
  - **Feedforward Neural Network:** Applies non-linear transformations to the output of the self-attention mechanism.
  - **Residual Connections and Layer Normalization:** Help in stabilizing training and allow for deeper networks.
- **Decoder:**
  Generates the output sequence one token at a time by:
  - **Masked Self-Attention:** Ensures that predictions for a given token depend only on previous tokens (maintaining autoregressive behavior).

- **Encoder-Decoder Attention:** Allows the decoder to attend to the encoder's output, effectively integrating the context from the input sequence.
- **Feedforward Network:** Further processes the integrated information.
- **Residual Connections and Layer Normalization:** Similar to the encoder, these ensure robust gradient flow and stable training.

Key Benefits:

- **Parallelization:** Both the encoder and decoder can process tokens simultaneously (except for the autoregressive constraint in the decoder), leading to significant speed improvements.
- **Scalability:** The architecture scales well with increasing data and computational resources.

2. Positional Embeddings

Need for Positional Information:
Since transformers process input sequences in parallel, they lack inherent sequential order. Positional embeddings are added to the input embeddings to inject information about the relative or absolute position of tokens in the sequence.

Mechanism:

- **Sinusoidal Positional Encodings:**
  A popular method introduced in the original transformer paper uses sine and cosine functions of different frequencies to encode position. These encodings have the property that the relative positions can be inferred from the encodings.

Mathematical Formulation:

$$PE_{(pos,2i)} = \sin\left(\frac{pos}{10000^{\frac{2i}{d_{model}}}}\right)$$
$$PE_{(pos,2i+1)} = \cos\left(\frac{pos}{10000^{\frac{2i}{d_{model}}}}\right)$$

where *pos* is the position and *i* is the dimension index.

3. Self-Attention Mechanism

Core Concept:

Self-attention allows the model to weigh the importance of each token relative to every other token in the sequence. This mechanism enables the capture of global dependencies without regard to the distance between tokens.

Computation Steps:

1. **Projection:**
   The input embeddings are projected into three vectors: Queries (Q), Keys (K), and Values (V) using learned linear transformations.

2. **Attention Scores:**
   Compute the dot-product between the queries and keys, scale by $\sqrt{d_k}$, and apply the softmax function to obtain attention weights.

$$\text{Attention}(Q, K, V) = \text{softmax}\left(\frac{QK^T}{\sqrt{d_k}}\right) V$$

3. **Multi-Head Attention:**
   The mechanism is performed in parallel multiple times (heads), allowing the model to attend to information from different representation subspaces. The outputs from each head are concatenated and linearly transformed.

Illustrative Code Example: Simplified Transformer Block

Below is a simplified PyTorch implementation of a transformer encoder block that includes positional embeddings, self-attention, and a feedforward layer.

```
import torch

import torch.nn as nn

import math

class PositionalEncoding(nn.Module):

    def __init__(self, d_model, max_len=5000):

        super(PositionalEncoding, self).__init__()

        pe = torch.zeros(max_len, d_model)

        position = torch.arange(0, max_len,
dtype=torch.float).unsqueeze(1)

        div_term = torch.exp(torch.arange(0, d_model, 2).float() *
(-math.log(10000.0) / d_model))

        pe[:, 0::2] = torch.sin(position * div_term)

        pe[:, 1::2] = torch.cos(position * div_term)

        pe = pe.unsqueeze(0)  # Shape: [1, max_len, d_model]

        self.register_buffer('pe', pe)

    def forward(self, x):

        # x: [batch_size, seq_length, d_model]

        x = x + self.pe[:, :x.size(1)]

        return x

class TransformerEncoderBlock(nn.Module):
```

```
    def __init__(self, d_model, n_heads, d_ff, dropout=0.1):
        super(TransformerEncoderBlock, self).__init__()
        self.self_attn =
nn.MultiheadAttention(embed_dim=d_model,
num_heads=n_heads, dropout=dropout)
        self.linear1 = nn.Linear(d_model, d_ff)
        self.dropout = nn.Dropout(dropout)
        self.linear2 = nn.Linear(d_ff, d_model)
        self.norm1 = nn.LayerNorm(d_model)
        self.norm2 = nn.LayerNorm(d_model)
        self.activation = nn.ReLU()  # or use GELU
    def forward(self, src, src_mask=None):
        # src: [seq_length, batch_size, d_model] (note:
nn.MultiheadAttention expects seq_length first)
        src2, _ = self.self_attn(src, src, src, attn_mask=src_mask)
        src = self.norm1(src + self.dropout(src2))
        src2 =
self.linear2(self.dropout(self.activation(self.linear1(src))))
        src = self.norm2(src + self.dropout(src2))
        return src
# Hyperparameters
d_model = 128
n_heads = 8
d_ff = 512
```

```
seq_length = 20

batch_size = 4

# Example input: random embeddings for a batch of sequences

input_embeddings = torch.rand(batch_size, seq_length,
d_model)  # [batch_size, seq_length, d_model]

# Positional Encoding

pos_encoder = PositionalEncoding(d_model)

embedded_input = pos_encoder(input_embeddings)

# Transpose for MultiheadAttention: [seq_length, batch_size,
d_model]

embedded_input = embedded_input.transpose(0, 1)

# Transformer Encoder Block

encoder_block = TransformerEncoderBlock(d_model,
n_heads, d_ff)

output = encoder_block(embedded_input)

print("Output shape from Transformer Encoder Block:",
output.shape)
```

Explanation:

- **Positional Encoding:**
  The PositionalEncoding class generates sinusoidal positional embeddings and adds them to the input embeddings, ensuring that token order is incorporated.
- **Self-Attention:**
  The TransformerEncoderBlock utilizes PyTorch's built-in

MultiheadAttention layer to implement self-attention. The residual connection and layer normalization ensure stable training.

- **Feedforward Network:**
  A two-layer feedforward network with ReLU activation further processes the output from the self-attention layer.
- **Input and Output Shapes:**
  The input embeddings (after positional encoding) are transposed to match the expected shape for multi-head attention. The final output retains the same shape as the input, providing a transformed representation that can be fed into subsequent layers or the decoder.

In summary, the transformer architecture represents a paradigm shift in NLP by leveraging an encoder-decoder framework combined with positional embeddings and self-attention mechanisms. This design enables the model to capture global dependencies and process sequences in parallel, offering significant advantages over traditional recurrent models. With the ability to scale and efficiently learn complex patterns, transformers have become the backbone of modern NLP applications, powering tasks from translation and summarization to sentiment analysis and beyond. The provided code exemplifies a simplified transformer encoder block, illustrating how these core components work together to create rich, contextualized representations of text.

Mainstream Transformer Variants

BERT, GPT, RoBERTa, and Beyond

In recent years, transformer-based models have redefined the landscape of NLP, setting new benchmarks across a wide range of tasks. Major variants - such as BERT, GPT, and RoBERTa - have not only advanced state-of-the-art performance but have also reshaped industry paradigms by enabling applications that require deep contextual understanding and generative capabilities.

BERT (Bidirectional Encoder Representations from Transformers)

Overview:

- **Architecture:**
  BERT utilizes a deep, bidirectional transformer encoder to capture context from both left and right simultaneously. This bidirectionality allows the model to develop a nuanced understanding of language, making it particularly effective for tasks like question answering, named entity recognition, and sentiment analysis.
- **Key Innovations:**
  - **Masked Language Modeling (MLM):**
    During pre-training, BERT masks a percentage of the input tokens and learns to predict them, enabling the model to learn rich, contextual representations.
  - **Next Sentence Prediction (NSP):**
    BERT is also trained on a task that determines if two sentences logically follow each other, which improves its understanding of sentence relationships.

Enterprise Impact:
BERT's deep contextual understanding makes it a versatile choice for fine-tuning on specific tasks, enhancing performance in areas such as customer support automation, document analysis, and compliance monitoring.

Illustrative Code Example (Using Hugging Face Transformers):

```
from transformers import BertTokenizer, BertModel
import torch
# Load pre-trained BERT model and tokenizer
tokenizer = BertTokenizer.from_pretrained('bert-base-
uncased')
model = BertModel.from_pretrained('bert-base-uncased')
# Sample input text
text = "Enterprise AI solutions require robust language
understanding."
inputs = tokenizer(text, return_tensors="pt")
# Obtain BERT embeddings
with torch.no_grad():
    outputs = model(**inputs)
# Extract the last hidden state for each token
last_hidden_states = outputs.last_hidden_state
print("BERT last hidden state shape:",
last_hidden_states.shape)
```

GPT (Generative Pre-trained Transformer)

Overview:

- **Architecture:**
  GPT is built upon the transformer decoder architecture and is designed for generative tasks. It processes text sequentially in an autoregressive manner, generating coherent and contextually appropriate text.

- **Key Innovations:**
  - **Autoregressive Language Modeling:**
    GPT predicts the next token in a sequence, enabling it to generate human-like text. Its architecture emphasizes fluency and creativity, making it ideal for tasks like text completion, summarization, and conversational agents.
- **Generational Advancements:**
  With iterations like GPT-2 and GPT-3, the models have grown in scale, demonstrating impressive capabilities in few-shot learning and zero-shot tasks.

Enterprise Impact:
GPT models empower applications that require high-quality text generation, such as chatbots, automated content creation, and interactive virtual assistants.

Illustrative Code Example (Using Hugging Face Transformers):

```
from transformers import GPT2Tokenizer,
GPT2LMHeadModel

import torch

# Load pre-trained GPT-2 model and tokenizer

tokenizer = GPT2Tokenizer.from_pretrained('gpt2')

model = GPT2LMHeadModel.from_pretrained('gpt2')

# Sample prompt text

prompt = "The future of enterprise AI is"

inputs = tokenizer(prompt, return_tensors="pt")
```

```
# Generate text continuation
output_sequences = model.generate(
    input_ids=inputs['input_ids'],
    max_length=50,
    temperature=0.7,
    top_p=0.9,
    do_sample=True,
    num_return_sequences=1
)
# Decode the generated text
generated_text = tokenizer.decode(output_sequences[0],
skip_special_tokens=True)
print("Generated Text:\n", generated_text)
```

RoBERTa (Robustly Optimized BERT Pretraining Approach)

Overview:

- **Architecture:**
  RoBERTa builds on BERT's architecture but improves its performance by training on larger datasets, longer sequences, and removing the next sentence prediction objective. It uses dynamic masking during training, which further enhances its contextual representations.

- **Key Innovations:**
  - **Optimized Pre-training:**
    RoBERTa leverages more robust training strategies and a larger corpus to refine BERT's underlying principles.
  - **Dynamic Masking:**
    This approach re-masks input sequences dynamically during training, allowing for a more comprehensive learning of language patterns.

Enterprise Impact:
RoBERTa's improved performance and robustness make it an attractive option for high-stakes NLP tasks, such as legal document analysis, financial sentiment prediction, and complex information extraction systems.

Illustrative Code Example (Using Hugging Face Transformers):

```
from transformers import RobertaTokenizer, RobertaModel

import torch

# Load pre-trained RoBERTa model and tokenizer

tokenizer = RobertaTokenizer.from_pretrained('roberta-base')

model = RobertaModel.from_pretrained('roberta-base')

# Sample input text

text = "Advanced AI models are transforming enterprise workflows."

inputs = tokenizer(text, return_tensors="pt")

# Obtain RoBERTa embeddings
```

```
with torch.no_grad():
    outputs = model(**inputs)
# Extract the last hidden state for each token
last_hidden_states = outputs.last_hidden_state
print("RoBERTa last hidden state shape:",
last_hidden_states.shape)
```

Other Notable Transformer Models

- **T5 (Text-To-Text Transfer Transformer):**
  T5 reframes every NLP problem as a text-to-text task, unifying a diverse range of tasks under a single framework. Its flexibility allows for a streamlined approach to tasks like translation, summarization, and question answering.
- **XLNet:**
  XLNet combines ideas from autoregressive and autoencoding models, addressing limitations of BERT by modeling bidirectional contexts in a permutation-based framework. It often outperforms BERT on several benchmarks by capturing a richer context.
- **DistilBERT:**
  DistilBERT is a smaller, faster, and lighter version of BERT that retains 95% of its performance. It is ideal for enterprise applications where computational efficiency and latency are critical.

Conclusion

The advent of transformer models has catalyzed a significant paradigm shift in NLP. BERT, GPT, and RoBERTa, among others, exemplify how transformer architectures can be tailored to different tasks - ranging from contextual understanding and language generation to robust classification and sentiment analysis. Their ability to leverage vast amounts of data, parallelize computations, and capture intricate language nuances has not only pushed the boundaries of state-of-the-art performance but also redefined the way enterprises implement AI-driven solutions. By adopting these models, organizations can unlock unprecedented levels of insight and efficiency, driving innovation across various business domains.

Chapter 9: Pretrained Language Models

Model Selection Criteria

Selecting the appropriate pretrained language model is a critical decision that directly influences the overall return on investment (ROI), operational efficiency, and the strategic impact of NLP solutions. In this phase of deployment, enterprises must weigh multiple factors - domain specificity, hardware constraints, and project ROI - to ensure that the selected model not only meets performance expectations but also aligns with broader corporate objectives.

1. Domain Specificity

Overview:
Models pre-trained on generic corpora (e.g., Wikipedia, news articles) may not capture the nuances of industry-specific language. For enterprise applications in specialized domains such as legal, financial, or medical sectors, fine-tuning on domain-specific data is essential. This process allows models to learn the particular jargon, terminologies, and contextual patterns unique to the business, leading to more accurate predictions and actionable insights.

Key Considerations:

- **Corpus Relevance:**
  Assess whether the pretrained model's original training data aligns with the target domain. If there is a significant domain gap, consider additional pre-training or fine-tuning on in-domain datasets.

- **Customization:**
  Look for models that offer flexible fine-tuning capabilities, enabling iterative improvements and rapid adaptation to evolving domain requirements.

2. Hardware Constraints

Overview:
The computational footprint of pretrained models can vary dramatically, with models such as GPT-3 requiring extensive GPU resources, while lighter variants like DistilBERT offer a more resource-efficient alternative. Enterprises must balance the model's performance with the available hardware infrastructure to ensure cost-effective and timely deployment.

Key Considerations:

- **Model Size and Complexity:**
  Evaluate the trade-off between model size (number of parameters) and performance. Larger models often deliver higher accuracy but come with increased computational demands.
- **Latency and Throughput:**
  For real-time applications, it is imperative to select models that can deliver low latency and high throughput without compromising on quality.
- **Scalability:**
  Ensure that the chosen model can be deployed on existing hardware or cloud infrastructure with the ability to scale as the volume of data and request frequency grows.

3. Project ROI

Overview:
The ultimate goal of any enterprise initiative is to achieve a measurable return on investment. When selecting a pretrained model, it is crucial to consider not only the technical merits but also the broader business implications. This includes evaluating the cost of training, deployment, and maintenance against the expected benefits in efficiency, customer satisfaction, and revenue growth.

Key Considerations:

- **Cost-Benefit Analysis:**
  Assess the total cost of ownership, including licensing fees, computational resources, and engineering effort, versus the potential improvements in business outcomes.
- **Time-to-Market:**
  Models that require minimal fine-tuning and quick integration can accelerate deployment, enabling faster realization of benefits.
- **Performance Metrics:**
  Establish key performance indicators (KPIs) aligned with business objectives, such as improved sentiment analysis accuracy, enhanced document classification precision, or reduced manual review time.

Illustrative Example: Selecting and Fine-Tuning a Pretrained Model Using Hugging Face Transformers

The following Python code snippet demonstrates how to select a model—based on its balance of performance and efficiency—and fine-tune it for a specific text classification task. This example uses a BERT variant, which can be adapted based on domain-specific requirements and hardware constraints.

```
from transformers import BertTokenizer, BertForSequenceClassification, Trainer, TrainingArguments

import torch

from datasets import load_dataset

# Load a pretrained BERT model and tokenizer

model_name = "bert-base-uncased"  # Consider variants like "distilbert-base-uncased" for lower hardware demands
```

```
tokenizer = BertTokenizer.from_pretrained(model_name)

model =
BertForSequenceClassification.from_pretrained(model_name,
num_labels=2)

# Load a sample dataset (e.g., sentiment analysis dataset)

dataset = load_dataset("imdb")

# For demonstration, we use a subset of the training data

train_data =
dataset["train"].shuffle(seed=42).select(range(2000))

test_data = dataset["test"].shuffle(seed=42).select(range(500))

# Tokenization function

def tokenize_function(example):

   return tokenizer(example["text"], padding="max_length",
truncation=True)

# Tokenize datasets

train_data = train_data.map(tokenize_function, batched=True)

test_data = test_data.map(tokenize_function, batched=True)

# Set format for PyTorch

train_data.set_format("torch", columns=["input_ids",
"attention_mask", "label"])

test_data.set_format("torch", columns=["input_ids",
"attention_mask", "label"])

# Define training arguments with attention to hardware
constraints and ROI (time-to-market)

training_args = TrainingArguments(
```

```
    output_dir="./results",
    num_train_epochs=3,
    per_device_train_batch_size=16,  # Adjust batch size based
on hardware capabilities
    per_device_eval_batch_size=16,
    warmup_steps=500,
    weight_decay=0.01,
    logging_dir="./logs",
    evaluation_strategy="epoch",
    logging_steps=100,
    save_total_limit=2,
)
# Initialize Trainer
trainer = Trainer(
    model=model,
    args=training_args,
    train_dataset=train_data,
    eval_dataset=test_data,
)
# Fine-tune the model
trainer.train()
# Evaluate the fine-tuned model
eval_results = trainer.evaluate()
```

```
print("Evaluation Results:", eval_results)
```

Explanation:

- **Model Selection:**
  We selected the bert-base-uncased model for its robust performance. Depending on hardware constraints, lighter alternatives such as distilbert-base-uncased might be chosen.
- **Dataset and Tokenization:**
  The model is fine-tuned on a subset of the IMDb dataset. Tokenization is performed to ensure the text is transformed into an appropriate format for the model.
- **Training Configuration:**
  Training parameters are configured to balance computational efficiency (e.g., batch sizes) with effective learning (e.g., warmup steps, weight decay).
- **Evaluation:**
  The evaluation step provides quantitative metrics that can be compared against business KPIs, ensuring that the model meets project ROI expectations.

In summary, choosing the right pretrained language model for enterprise applications involves a multidimensional evaluation process. By carefully considering domain specificity, hardware constraints, and project ROI, organizations can deploy models that not only meet technical benchmarks but also drive strategic business outcomes. The example provided demonstrates how to leverage the Hugging Face Transformers library for model fine-tuning, encapsulating best practices that ensure robust, scalable, and cost-effective NLP solutions.

Fine-Tuning Strategies

Transfer Learning, Domain Adaptation, and Hyperparameter Optimization for Corporate Deployments

Fine-tuning pretrained language models is a powerful strategy that leverages transfer learning to adapt robust, general-purpose NLP systems to specific business contexts. By fine-tuning, organizations can tailor these models to industry-specific language, optimize performance on targeted tasks, and achieve measurable improvements in key business metrics. The process encompasses several strategic elements:

1. Transfer Learning

Overview:

- **Leveraging Pretrained Models:**
  Pretrained language models (e.g., BERT, GPT, RoBERTa) capture a wide range of linguistic patterns and contextual knowledge from vast, diverse datasets. Transfer learning enables organizations to harness this pre-existing expertise and adapt it to new, domain-specific tasks with significantly reduced training time and data requirements.

- **Benefits for Enterprises:**

  - **Faster Deployment:** Reduces the need for extensive training from scratch, speeding up time-to-market.

  - **Improved Performance:** Enhances model accuracy on specialized tasks by building on a strong general foundation.

  - **Cost Efficiency:** Minimizes computational and data resource demands, critical in budget-sensitive corporate environments.

2. Domain Adaptation

Overview:

- **Customization to Specific Domains:**
  Domain adaptation involves further pre-training or fine-tuning on data that is representative of the target domain (e.g., legal, medical, financial). This process helps the model learn domain-specific terminologies, expressions, and contextual nuances that general-purpose models might overlook.

- **Approach:**

  - **Collect Domain-Specific Data:** Gather representative corpora from internal documents, industry publications, or specialized datasets.

  - **Incremental Fine-Tuning:** First, fine-tune the pretrained model on a large domain-specific dataset, then fine-tune on task-specific data for optimal results.

  - **Continuous Learning:** Update the model periodically as new domain data becomes available to keep it current with industry trends.

3. Hyperparameter Optimization

Overview:

- **Tailoring Training Dynamics:**
  Hyperparameter optimization is the process of tuning model parameters (e.g., learning rate, batch size, number of epochs, dropout rate) to achieve the best performance on a validation set. These parameters have a significant impact on model convergence and overall performance.

- **Best Practices:**
  - **Grid Search / Random Search:** Experiment with various combinations of hyperparameters to find the optimal set.
  - **Automated Optimization Tools:** Leverage tools such as Ray Tune, Optuna, or Hyperopt to efficiently explore the hyperparameter space.
  - **Early Stopping:** Monitor performance on a validation set and stop training when improvements plateau to avoid overfitting.

Illustrative Example: Fine-Tuning a Pretrained Model with Domain Adaptation and Hyperparameter Tuning

Below is an example using the Hugging Face Transformers library to fine-tune a pretrained BERT model on a domain-specific text classification task. This example incorporates basic transfer learning and outlines a framework for hyperparameter optimization.

```
from transformers import BertTokenizer, BertForSequenceClassification, Trainer, TrainingArguments

from datasets import load_dataset

import numpy as np

# Load a pretrained BERT model and tokenizer

model_name = "bert-base-uncased"  # For cost efficiency, consider 'distilbert-base-uncased' if needed

tokenizer = BertTokenizer.from_pretrained(model_name)

model = BertForSequenceClassification.from_pretrained(model_name, num_labels=2)
```

```
# Domain Adaptation: Load a domain-specific dataset (for demonstration, we use the IMDB dataset as a proxy)

dataset = load_dataset("imdb")

train_data = dataset["train"].shuffle(seed=42).select(range(2000))

test_data = dataset["test"].shuffle(seed=42).select(range(500))

# Tokenization function for domain-specific text

def tokenize_function(example):

    return tokenizer(example["text"], padding="max_length", truncation=True)

# Tokenize datasets

train_data = train_data.map(tokenize_function, batched=True)

test_data = test_data.map(tokenize_function, batched=True)

# Set format for PyTorch

train_data.set_format("torch", columns=["input_ids", "attention_mask", "label"])

test_data.set_format("torch", columns=["input_ids", "attention_mask", "label"])

# Define training arguments with hyperparameter considerations

training_args = TrainingArguments(

    output_dir="./results",

    num_train_epochs=3,              # Adjust epochs based on convergence
```

```
    per_device_train_batch_size=16,    # Adjust batch size
according to hardware

    per_device_eval_batch_size=16,

    warmup_steps=500,              # Learning rate warmup for
stable convergence

    weight_decay=0.01,             # Regularization to prevent
overfitting

    evaluation_strategy="epoch",

    logging_dir="./logs",

    logging_steps=100,

    save_total_limit=2,

)

# Initialize Trainer with our model, training arguments, and
datasets

trainer = Trainer(

    model=model,

    args=training_args,

    train_dataset=train_data,

    eval_dataset=test_data,

)

# Fine-tune the model (this process integrates both transfer
learning and domain adaptation)

trainer.train()

# Evaluate the fine-tuned model
```

```
eval_results = trainer.evaluate()
print("Evaluation Results:", eval_results)
```

Explanation:

- **Model Selection and Transfer Learning:**
  The pretrained bert-base-uncased model is selected for its proven performance and is further adapted to the domain by fine-tuning on a dataset representative of the target domain.
- **Domain Adaptation:**
  Although IMDB is used here as a demonstration, in a real-world scenario, this dataset should be replaced with domain-specific data (e.g., legal or medical texts).
- **Hyperparameter Optimization:**
  Training arguments such as learning rate warmup, weight decay, and batch size are carefully selected. In production, these can be tuned further using automated optimization frameworks.
- **Evaluation:**
  The model's performance is assessed on a held-out test set, ensuring that the fine-tuning has translated into tangible improvements for the specific application.

In summary, Fine-tuning pretrained language models is a strategic enabler for deploying advanced NLP solutions in corporate environments. By leveraging transfer learning, domain adaptation, and systematic hyperparameter optimization, organizations can customize state-of-the-art models to meet specific business needs while balancing computational costs and performance gains. This tailored approach not only maximizes ROI but also ensures that the deployed models deliver actionable insights, drive operational efficiency, and maintain a competitive edge in dynamic market conditions.

Performance Evaluation and Maintenance

Strategies for Model Lifecycle Management, Versioning, and Continuous Improvement

The deployment of pretrained language models into production environments is not the end of the development cycle; rather, it marks the beginning of a dynamic process of performance evaluation and maintenance. For enterprise NLP applications, managing the lifecycle of models - from initial deployment through versioning and continuous improvement - is critical to ensuring sustained accuracy, reliability, and business impact. Below, we outline best practices and strategies for robust lifecycle management of NLP models.

1. Performance Evaluation

Ongoing Assessment:

- **Monitoring Key Metrics:**
  Regularly track performance metrics such as accuracy, precision, recall, and F1 score, as well as latency and throughput for real-time applications. Monitoring these metrics in production helps detect degradation in performance, which may indicate concept drift or data distribution changes.
- **Validation and Testing:**
  Utilize hold-out validation sets and periodic A/B testing to compare model versions. This ensures that any updates lead to measurable improvements and do not inadvertently harm model performance.
- **User Feedback:**
  Incorporate feedback loops from end users and stakeholders to assess the qualitative aspects of the model's outputs. This real-world feedback is invaluable for understanding practical impact.

Example: Evaluating with Hugging Face Trainer

```
from transformers import Trainer, TrainingArguments
# Assume `model`, `train_dataset`, and `eval_dataset` are already defined
training_args = TrainingArguments(
    output_dir="./model_checkpoints",
    evaluation_strategy="epoch",
    logging_steps=50,
    save_strategy="epoch",
    load_best_model_at_end=True,
    metric_for_best_model="accuracy",
)
trainer = Trainer(
    model=model,
    args=training_args,
    train_dataset=train_dataset,
    eval_dataset=eval_dataset,
)
# Evaluate the model
eval_results = trainer.evaluate()
print("Evaluation Results:", eval_results)
```

2. Model Versioning

Why Versioning Matters:

- **Traceability and Reproducibility:**
  Versioning enables teams to track changes, reproduce results, and rollback to previous versions if necessary. This is especially important in regulated industries or high-stakes applications.
- **Experimentation:**
  Maintain multiple versions of models to compare different fine-tuning strategies or hyperparameter settings. Tools like MLflow or DVC (Data Version Control) can be integrated to manage model versions and associated metadata.

Best Practices:

- **Naming Conventions:**
  Adopt clear naming conventions for model versions, including dates, hyperparameter configurations, and dataset versions.
- **Automated Logging:**
  Integrate automated logging to capture configuration, training metrics, and evaluation outcomes. This creates a comprehensive audit trail.

Example: Model Versioning with MLflow

```
import mlflow

import mlflow.pytorch

# Start an MLflow run to log model parameters and metrics

with mlflow.start_run(run_name="BERT_FineTune_v1"):

    mlflow.log_param("learning_rate", 0.001)
```

```
mlflow.log_param("batch_size", 16)

    # Train the model (trainer.train() is assumed to be run previously)

trainer.train()

    # Evaluate the model

eval_results = trainer.evaluate()

mlflow.log_metrics(eval_results)

    # Log the model

mlflow.pytorch.log_model(model, "model")

    print("Model version logged in MLflow with metrics:", eval_results)
```

3. Continuous Improvement and Maintenance

Strategies for Ongoing Model Health:

- **Regular Retraining:**
  Schedule periodic retraining sessions to incorporate new data and adjust for changes in language usage, market trends, or regulatory requirements. Automated pipelines can trigger retraining based on performance thresholds.
- **Monitoring and Alerts:**
  Implement monitoring systems that continuously track key performance indicators (KPIs) and send alerts when performance dips below predetermined thresholds. This can involve integrating with cloud monitoring services or custom dashboards.
- **Feedback Loops:**
  Use user interactions and feedback to fine-tune and improve the

model over time. This can include supervised learning updates or unsupervised drift detection techniques.

- **Model Distillation and Compression:**
  As models evolve, consider distilling larger models into smaller, more efficient versions to reduce inference latency and resource consumption while maintaining performance.

Example: Setting Up a Monitoring Alert with Python (Pseudo-code)

```
import time

import requests

def monitor_model_performance(api_endpoint, threshold=0.80):

    while True:

        # Simulated call to a performance API endpoint

        response = requests.get(api_endpoint)

        performance = response.json().get("accuracy", 0)

        if performance < threshold:

            print(f"Alert: Model accuracy dropped below {threshold * 100}%. Current accuracy: {performance * 100}%")

            # Trigger alert mechanism (e.g., send email, notify Slack, etc.)

        else:

            print(f"Model performing well: {performance * 100}% accuracy.")
```

```
    time.sleep(3600)  # Check every hour
# Example API endpoint for monitoring
monitor_model_performance("http://your-monitoring-endpoint/api/performance")
```

Conclusion

The performance evaluation and maintenance of pretrained language models are ongoing, critical processes for ensuring that NLP solutions continue to deliver high value in enterprise applications. By implementing rigorous monitoring, versioning, and continuous improvement strategies, organizations can manage the full lifecycle of their models effectively. This proactive approach not only safeguards model performance against concept drift and changing data distributions but also drives innovation, operational efficiency, and competitive advantage in a rapidly evolving business landscape.

Part IV: Special Topics and Emerging Trends
Chapter 10: Multilingual NLP

Challenges in Multilingual Contexts

Data Scarcity, Linguistic Nuances, and the Necessity of Domain-Specific Corpora

As organizations increasingly operate on a global scale, the demand for multilingual NLP has grown exponentially. However, building robust multilingual models comes with significant challenges that can impede performance and generalizability. These challenges include data scarcity, the complexity of linguistic nuances across different languages, and the critical need for domain-specific corpora tailored to various regional and cultural contexts.

1. Data Scarcity

Issue Overview:

- **Limited Resources:**
  While large corpora are available for high-resource languages (e.g., English, Spanish), many languages lack sufficient annotated data to train robust NLP models. This scarcity is particularly pronounced for low-resource or endangered languages.
- **Implications:**
  - **Poor Model Generalization:** Limited data can lead to models that overfit to available examples and fail to generalize well to new inputs.
  - **Increased Annotation Costs:** Collecting and annotating data for low-resource languages is time-consuming and expensive.

Strategies to Mitigate Data Scarcity:

- **Transfer Learning and Multilingual Models:**
  Leverage pretrained multilingual models (e.g., mBERT, XLM-R) that learn language-agnostic features across multiple languages.
- **Data Augmentation:**
  Utilize data augmentation techniques such as back-translation or synthetic data generation to expand the available dataset.
- **Crowdsourcing and Community Engagement:**
  Engage native speakers and linguistic communities to create and annotate corpora, ensuring cultural and contextual accuracy.

2. Linguistic Nuances

Issue Overview:

- **Complex Language Structures:**
  Languages vary widely in their syntactic, semantic, and morphological properties. For example, agglutinative languages (e.g., Turkish, Finnish) exhibit complex word formations, while tonal languages (e.g., Mandarin) encode meaning through pitch variations.
- **Idioms and Cultural Context:**
  Idiomatic expressions and culturally specific references often do not translate directly across languages, complicating tasks like sentiment analysis and machine translation.

Implications:

- **Model Performance:**
  Failing to account for these nuances can lead to inaccuracies in tasks such as translation, named entity recognition, and sentiment analysis.

- **Interpretability:**
  Linguistic subtleties may be lost, reducing the model's ability to capture the true meaning of text in different languages.

Strategies to Address Linguistic Nuances:

- **Incorporate Linguistic Features:**
  Enhance models by integrating part-of-speech tags, syntactic dependencies, and morphological features.
- **Language-Specific Preprocessing:**
  Implement tailored tokenization, normalization, and segmentation techniques that respect the structural peculiarities of each language.
- **Cross-Lingual Transfer Learning:**
  Employ models that learn shared representations across languages to better capture the inherent linguistic diversity.

3. Necessity of Domain-Specific Corpora

Issue Overview:

- **Domain Relevance:**
  Generic multilingual datasets may not capture the specialized terminology and context needed for industry-specific applications (e.g., legal, medical, technical domains).
- **Cultural and Regional Variations:**
  Domain-specific corpora must consider regional dialects, cultural idioms, and industry jargon to be truly effective.

Implications:

- **Task Performance:**
  Models trained on generic corpora might underperform in specialized domains due to a lack of relevant vocabulary and contextual understanding.

- **Business Impact:**
  Inaccurate language processing can lead to misinterpretations, compliance issues, or poor customer experiences in enterprise applications.

Strategies for Building Domain-Specific Corpora:

- **Targeted Data Collection:**
  Focus on gathering texts from industry-specific sources such as legal documents, medical journals, or financial reports.
- **Collaboration with Experts:**
  Work with domain experts to annotate and curate corpora that reflect the nuanced language of the field.
- **Adaptive Fine-Tuning:**
  Fine-tune multilingual models on these domain-specific datasets to enhance performance in targeted applications.

Illustrative Example: Data Augmentation for a Low-Resource Language

To illustrate a strategy for addressing data scarcity in multilingual contexts, consider the use of back-translation for augmenting a low-resource dataset. The following Python code demonstrates how to perform back-translation using the Hugging Face Transformers library.

```
from transformers import MarianMTModel, MarianTokenizer

# Load a pretrained MarianMT model for translation (e.g., English <-> Romanian)

src_lang = "en"

tgt_lang = "ro"
```

```
model_name = f'Helsinki-NLP/opus-mt-{src_lang}-
{tgt_lang}'

tokenizer = MarianTokenizer.from_pretrained(model_name)

model = MarianMTModel.from_pretrained(model_name)

def back_translate(text):

    # Translate text from English to Romanian

    translated =
model.generate(**tokenizer.prepare_seq2seq_batch([text],
return_tensors="pt"))

    tgt_text = tokenizer.decode(translated[0],
skip_special_tokens=True)

    # Translate back from Romanian to English using the
reverse model

    reverse_model_name = f'Helsinki-NLP/opus-mt-{tgt_lang}-
{src_lang}'

    reverse_tokenizer =
MarianTokenizer.from_pretrained(reverse_model_name)

    reverse_model =
MarianMTModel.from_pretrained(reverse_model_name)

    back_translated =
reverse_model.generate(**reverse_tokenizer.prepare_seq2seq_
batch([tgt_text], return_tensors="pt"))

    return reverse_tokenizer.decode(back_translated[0],
skip_special_tokens=True)

# Example usage
```

```
original_text = "The company's annual report highlighted significant growth."

augmented_text = back_translate(original_text)

print("Original Text:", original_text)

print("Back-Translated Text:", augmented_text)
```

Explanation:

- **Back-Translation:**
  The code translates an English text to Romanian and then back to English. This technique can generate paraphrased versions of the original text, thereby augmenting the dataset.
- **Utility for Low-Resource Languages:**
  Such techniques help expand the available training data, improving model generalization when annotated data is scarce.

In summary, addressing the challenges in multilingual NLP requires a multi-faceted approach that tackles data scarcity, respects linguistic nuances, and leverages domain-specific corpora. By integrating strategies such as transfer learning, linguistic-aware preprocessing, and data augmentation techniques like back-translation, enterprises can build robust multilingual systems. These systems are essential for delivering accurate, culturally relevant, and industry-specific NLP solutions that drive global business success.

Cross-Lingual Embeddings

Bridging Language Barriers in Globalized Business Environments

In a globalized business landscape, the ability to seamlessly process and analyze text across multiple languages is a critical enabler for international operations, customer support, market analysis, and regulatory compliance. Cross-lingual embeddings provide a powerful solution to bridge language barriers by mapping words from different languages into a shared semantic space. This unified representation facilitates cross-lingual information retrieval, machine translation, sentiment analysis, and more, ensuring that insights are not confined to a single language.

Theoretical Foundations and Approaches

1. Unified Semantic Space:

Cross-lingual embeddings aim to represent words from different languages in the same vector space. Words with similar meanings, regardless of language, are positioned closely together. This alignment allows models to transfer knowledge from high-resource languages to low-resource ones.

2. Approaches to Learning Cross-Lingual Embeddings:

- **Joint Training:**
  Multilingual models like mBERT (multilingual BERT) and XLM-R (XLM-RoBERTa) are trained on data from multiple languages simultaneously. They learn language-agnostic representations that work well across languages.

- **Mapping-Based Methods:**
  Methods like MUSE (Multilingual Unsupervised or Supervised Embeddings) align independently trained monolingual embeddings into a shared space using a bilingual dictionary or unsupervised techniques.

- **Adversarial Learning:**
  Some approaches employ adversarial training to minimize the discrepancy between embeddings from different languages, encouraging the model to produce similar representations for semantically equivalent words.

3. Business Applications:

- **Cross-Lingual Information Retrieval:**
  Users can query in one language and retrieve documents in another, enhancing search capabilities in multinational environments.
- **Multilingual Sentiment Analysis:**
  Companies can analyze customer feedback across different regions and languages without training separate models for each language.
- **Knowledge Transfer:**
  Insights learned from high-resource languages can be transferred to improve NLP applications in low-resource languages, reducing data requirements and development time.

Illustrative Example: Using mBERT for Cross-Lingual Embedding Extraction

The following example demonstrates how to extract cross-lingual embeddings using a multilingual pretrained model (mBERT) from the Hugging Face Transformers library. We will show how similar words in different languages align in the shared embedding space.

```
from transformers import BertTokenizer, BertModel

import torch

import numpy as np

from sklearn.metrics.pairwise import cosine_similarity

# Load the multilingual BERT (mBERT) model and tokenizer

model_name = "bert-base-multilingual-cased"

tokenizer = BertTokenizer.from_pretrained(model_name)
```

```
model = BertModel.from_pretrained(model_name)

def get_embedding(text):

    """Obtain the embedding of the [CLS] token for a given
text."""

    inputs = tokenizer(text, return_tensors="pt",
truncation=True, padding=True)

    with torch.no_grad():

        outputs = model(**inputs)

    # The [CLS] token embedding is the first token in the
last_hidden_state

    cls_embedding = outputs.last_hidden_state[0][0]

    return cls_embedding.numpy()

# Sample words or phrases in different languages

word_en = "economy"

word_fr = "économie"

word_es = "economía"

word_de = "Wirtschaft"  # 'Economy' in German, though not
a direct translation of 'economy'

# Get embeddings for each word

emb_en = get_embedding(word_en)

emb_fr = get_embedding(word_fr)

emb_es = get_embedding(word_es)

emb_de = get_embedding(word_de)

# Compute cosine similarities between embeddings
```

```
embeddings = np.stack([emb_en, emb_fr, emb_es, emb_de])
similarity_matrix = cosine_similarity(embeddings)
print("Cosine Similarity Matrix:")
print(similarity_matrix)
```

Explanation:

- **Model Loading:**
  We use bert-base-multilingual-cased (mBERT), which has been pretrained on multiple languages and can produce language-agnostic embeddings.
- **Embedding Extraction:**
  The embedding for each input text is obtained from the [CLS] token in the model's output. This token is generally used to capture the overall meaning of the sequence.
- **Cosine Similarity:**
  We compute cosine similarity between embeddings to measure semantic similarity. A high similarity between "economy," "économie," and "economía" indicates that the model successfully aligns their meanings in a shared vector space, even though they are in different languages.

Practical Considerations for Enterprise Deployment

Data Quality and Domain Adaptation:

- Ensure that your cross-lingual model is fine-tuned or further pre-trained on domain-specific multilingual corpora if necessary. This adaptation improves the model's performance on specialized vocabulary and context relevant to your business.

Scalability and Inference Efficiency:

- Leverage optimized libraries and hardware acceleration (e.g., GPUs, TPUs) to handle the increased computational demands of multilingual models in production environments.

Integration with Downstream Systems:

- Cross-lingual embeddings can be integrated into existing NLP pipelines, powering applications such as multilingual search engines, automated translation systems, and customer sentiment analysis across different markets.

In summary, Cross-lingual embeddings offer a transformative solution for bridging language barriers in globalized business environments. By mapping words from diverse languages into a unified semantic space, these techniques facilitate robust multilingual applications, enhancing information retrieval, sentiment analysis, and knowledge transfer across linguistic boundaries. With practical approaches such as joint training in models like mBERT, mapping-based methods, and adversarial techniques, enterprises can deploy cross-lingual NLP systems that drive global insights and competitive advantage in an increasingly interconnected world.

Machine Translation Platforms

State-of-the-Art Tools and Workflows for Real-Time, Enterprise Translation Solutions

As global businesses expand their reach, effective and efficient communication across languages becomes paramount. Machine translation platforms have evolved from simple rule-based systems to sophisticated, neural network-based solutions that deliver high-quality, real-time translations. This transformation has been driven by advances in deep learning, particularly the development of transformer-based architectures. In enterprise environments, the integration of state-of-the-art machine translation tools enables seamless cross-lingual communication, enhances customer engagement, and supports international operations.

Key Components of Modern Machine Translation Platforms

1. **Neural Machine Translation (NMT) Models:**

- **Transformer-Based Models:**
  Models such as MarianMT, mBART, and M2M-100 leverage transformer architectures to capture long-range dependencies and produce fluent, contextually accurate translations.

- **Sequence-to-Sequence (Seq2Seq) Architectures:**
  These architectures use encoder-decoder frameworks with attention mechanisms to translate text from a source language to a target language.

2. **Real-Time Translation Workflows:**

- **API Integration:**
  Modern translation platforms provide RESTful APIs or SDKs, enabling integration with web, mobile, and enterprise applications for real-time translation services.

- **Scalable Deployment:**
  Leveraging cloud-based infrastructure and container orchestration (e.g., Docker and Kubernetes) allows organizations to scale translation services to meet demand, ensuring low latency and high throughput.

- **Continuous Improvement:**
  Platforms often include tools for monitoring translation quality, user feedback loops, and continuous fine-tuning, ensuring that the system evolves alongside changing language usage and domain-specific terminology.

3. **Quality Assurance and Post-Editing:**

- **Automated Quality Metrics:**
Evaluation metrics such as BLEU, METEOR, and TER are used to gauge translation quality.

- **Human-in-the-Loop:**
For critical applications, machine translations are supplemented with human post-editing to ensure accuracy and cultural appropriateness.

State-of-the-Art Tools for Machine Translation

Hugging Face Transformers and MarianMT:

- Hugging Face provides robust implementations of MarianMT models, which are highly effective for many language pairs and can be fine-tuned on domain-specific data.
- These models are optimized for both accuracy and speed, making them suitable for real-time translation tasks.

Other Notable Platforms:

- **Google Cloud Translation API:**
A widely used commercial service that supports a vast number of languages with high accuracy and seamless integration.
- **Microsoft Translator:**
Provides comprehensive translation services integrated with other Microsoft Azure tools.
- **Amazon Translate:**
A cloud-based translation service designed for scalability and real-time applications.

Illustrative Example: Real-Time Translation with MarianMT Using Hugging Face Transformers

The following code snippet demonstrates how to set up a real-time translation workflow using the MarianMT model from Hugging Face. This example translates an input text from English to French.

```
from transformers import MarianMTModel, MarianTokenizer

# Define source and target languages

src_lang = "en"

tgt_lang = "fr"

model_name = f'Helsinki-NLP/opus-mt-{src_lang}-{tgt_lang}'

# Load MarianMT model and tokenizer

tokenizer = MarianTokenizer.from_pretrained(model_name)

model = MarianMTModel.from_pretrained(model_name)

def translate_text(text):

    """

    Translate the input text from English to French using MarianMT.

    """

    # Prepare the input text for translation

    inputs = tokenizer(text, return_tensors="pt", truncation=True, padding="longest")
```

```
    # Generate translation using the model
    translated_tokens = model.generate(**inputs)
      # Decode the generated tokens to get the translated text
    translated_text = tokenizer.decode(translated_tokens[0],
skip_special_tokens=True)
    return translated_text
# Example usage
input_text = "Global enterprises need robust translation
solutions to communicate effectively."
translated_output = translate_text(input_text)
print("Original Text:", input_text)
print("Translated Text (English to French):",
translated_output)
```

Explanation:

- **Model Loading:**
  We load the MarianMT model and its tokenizer tailored for English-to-French translation.
- **Translation Function:**
  The function translate_text tokenizes the input, generates translated tokens with the model, and decodes them into human-readable text.
- **Real-Time Application:**
  This code can be integrated into a real-time API endpoint to serve translation requests across various applications, ensuring minimal latency and high-quality output.

Practical Considerations for Enterprise Deployment

1. **Integration and Scalability:**

- **APIs and Microservices:**
  Deploy translation models as microservices within a cloud infrastructure to allow easy scaling and integration with existing enterprise systems.

- **Load Balancing and Caching:**
  Implement caching mechanisms for frequently translated phrases and load balancing to distribute translation requests evenly, ensuring consistent performance.

2. **Quality Monitoring and Continuous Improvement:**

- **Automated Feedback:**
  Use automated evaluation metrics to monitor translation quality continuously.

- **Human Feedback:**
  Incorporate user feedback and periodic human review to fine-tune models, especially for domain-specific applications.

- **Regular Updates:**
  Stay updated with the latest advancements in NMT and periodically update models to maintain competitive edge and accuracy.

3. **Data Privacy and Compliance:**

- **Security Measures:**
  Ensure data privacy through encryption and compliance with relevant regulations (e.g., GDPR) when handling sensitive or personal information.

- **Custom Models:**
  In scenarios with strict compliance requirements, consider training custom models on in-house data to mitigate privacy risks.

Conclusion

Machine translation platforms have reached a level of sophistication that enables real-time, enterprise-grade translation solutions. By leveraging state-of-the-art tools like MarianMT, along with robust workflows that emphasize scalability, quality assurance, and continuous improvement, organizations can effectively bridge language barriers in a globalized business environment. The combination of advanced neural architectures, seamless API integration, and rigorous quality monitoring ensures that translation services not only meet but exceed the demands of modern enterprises, fostering better communication, enhanced customer engagement, and improved operational efficiency.

Chapter 11: Dialogue Systems and Conversational AI

Chatbots and Virtual Assistants

Architecture Patterns from Rule-Based Systems to Advanced Generative Models

The evolution of dialogue systems and conversational AI has been marked by a transition from simple, rule-based architectures to complex, generative models capable of producing context-aware, human-like responses. This progression reflects the growing demands of enterprise applications for robust, scalable, and intelligent virtual assistants that can effectively manage customer interactions, support internal processes, and drive business outcomes.

1. Rule-Based Systems

Overview:

- **Deterministic Responses:**
  Early chatbots were built on rule-based systems, relying on predefined patterns, keywords, and scripted responses. These systems use decision trees or state machines to navigate user inputs and produce fixed replies.
- **Advantages:**
  - **Predictability:** Responses are consistent and controlled.
  - **Simplicity:** Easy to design and implement for narrow tasks.
  - **Low Computational Cost:** Minimal resource requirements.
- **Limitations:**
  - **Limited Flexibility:** Inability to handle unexpected or complex user inputs.

- **Scalability Issues:** Expanding the rule set for diverse conversations becomes increasingly complex.

Example:

A simple rule-based chatbot might use pattern matching with regular expressions:

```
import re

def rule_based_response(user_input):

    if re.search(r'\b(hi|hello|hey)\b', user_input, re.IGNORECASE):

        return "Hello! How can I assist you today?"

    elif re.search(r'\b(problem|issue|trouble)\b', user_input, re.IGNORECASE):

        return "I'm sorry to hear that you're facing issues. Could you please provide more details?"

    else:

        return "I'm not sure I understand. Can you please rephrase?"

# Example interaction

user_input = "Hi, I have a problem with my order."

print("Chatbot:", rule_based_response(user_input))
```

2. Retrieval-Based and Template-Based Models

Overview:

- **Pattern Matching with Context:**
  Retrieval-based systems leverage a database of pre-written responses and use similarity metrics to select the most appropriate reply based on the current input and conversation history.

- **Template-Based Systems:**
  These systems use templates with fill-in-the-blank slots, which are dynamically populated with context-specific information. They offer more flexibility than pure rule-based methods while retaining a level of predictability.

- **Advantages:**

  - **Improved Response Relevance:** More context-aware compared to static rule-based systems.
  - **Efficiency:** Faster response times due to pre-stored replies.

- **Limitations:**

  - **Static Nature:** Cannot generate novel responses.
  - **Scalability:** Requires a large repository of templates or responses to cover various scenarios.

3. Generative Models

Overview:

- **End-to-End Neural Dialogue Systems:**
  Modern conversational AI systems leverage deep learning architectures to generate responses dynamically. Models such as sequence-to-sequence (Seq2Seq) networks with attention mechanisms, and more recently, transformer-based models, have pushed the boundaries of conversational AI.

- **Transformer-Based Models:**
  Architectures like GPT (Generative Pre-trained Transformer) and BERT-based dialogue systems generate coherent and contextually rich responses. They process entire conversation histories to produce replies that can adapt to evolving contexts.
- **Advantages:**
  - **Flexibility and Adaptability:** Can generate a wide range of responses, handle ambiguous inputs, and adapt to new topics.
  - **Contextual Understanding:** Leverage large-scale pretraining to understand nuances in conversation.
  - **Personalization:** Capable of incorporating user-specific data for tailored interactions.
- **Challenges:**
  - **Computational Intensity:** Require significant resources for training and inference.
  - **Quality Control:** May generate unpredictable or inappropriate responses if not properly fine-tuned and monitored.
  - **Data Requirements:** Demand large, high-quality datasets to learn effective conversational patterns.

Illustrative Example:

Below is an example of generating responses using a pretrained generative model (GPT-2) from the Hugging Face Transformers library:

```
from transformers import GPT2LMHeadModel,
GPT2Tokenizer

import torch
```

```
# Load the GPT-2 model and tokenizer

model_name = "gpt2"  # For more robust conversational capabilities, consider GPT-2 variants fine-tuned for dialogue

tokenizer = GPT2Tokenizer.from_pretrained(model_name)

model = GPT2LMHeadModel.from_pretrained(model_name)

def generate_response(prompt, max_length=100, temperature=0.7):

    # Encode the prompt

    inputs = tokenizer.encode(prompt, return_tensors="pt")

        # Generate a response using the model

    outputs = model.generate(

        inputs,

        max_length=max_length,

        temperature=temperature,

        pad_token_id=tokenizer.eos_token_id,

        do_sample=True,

        top_p=0.9,

        num_return_sequences=1

    )

    # Decode and return the response

    response = tokenizer.decode(outputs[0], skip_special_tokens=True)

    return response
```

```
# Example interaction
prompt = "User: Hi, I'm having trouble with my account login.\nChatbot:"
response = generate_response(prompt)
print("Chatbot Response:\n", response)
```

Explanation:

- **Model Loading and Tokenization:**
  The GPT-2 model is loaded along with its tokenizer. The input prompt is encoded to create a tensor suitable for the model.
- **Response Generation:**
  The model generates a response based on the input prompt using parameters such as temperature (which controls randomness) and top_p (which controls nucleus sampling for diversity).
- **Dynamic Interaction:**
  The generated response is decoded and returned, simulating a dynamic, context-aware conversational exchange.

Enterprise Applications and Considerations

- **Hybrid Approaches:**
  In many real-world deployments, hybrid systems combine retrieval-based components with generative models. The retrieval system handles common or straightforward queries, while the generative model tackles more complex or open-ended conversations.
- **Integration with Business Systems:**
  Chatbots and virtual assistants must integrate seamlessly with enterprise systems (e.g., CRM, databases, support ticketing systems) to provide contextually rich and actionable responses.

- **Continuous Learning and Monitoring:**
  Implement mechanisms for continuous model improvement, including user feedback loops, regular retraining, and performance monitoring to ensure that the dialogue system remains effective over time.

- **Ethical Considerations:**
  Ensure that conversational AI adheres to ethical standards and regulatory requirements, particularly in handling sensitive data and avoiding biased or inappropriate responses.

In summary, from rule-based systems to advanced generative models, the architecture patterns of chatbots and virtual assistants have evolved to meet the diverse needs of modern enterprises. While rule-based and retrieval-based approaches offer predictability and efficiency, generative models bring flexibility, context-awareness, and natural language fluency that are critical for sophisticated conversational AI applications. By integrating these architectures with robust monitoring, continuous improvement strategies, and seamless enterprise system integration, organizations can deploy virtual assistants that not only enhance customer engagement but also drive significant operational efficiencies and business growth.

Context Management

Handling Context Carryover, Personalization, and User Experience Optimization

Modern dialogue systems must excel not only at understanding isolated user inputs but also at managing ongoing, multi-turn conversations. Effective context management is crucial for creating conversational AI that feels natural, personalized, and responsive. This involves carrying context from one turn to the next, adapting to user preferences, and optimizing the overall user experience.

1. Handling Context Carryover

Overview:
Multi-turn conversations require the system to maintain a memory of previous interactions. This "context carryover" allows the model to:

- **Understand Continuity:** Recognize follow-up questions and references to earlier parts of the conversation.
- **Resolve Ambiguities:** Use prior context to disambiguate pronouns or vague references (e.g., "it," "that product").
- **Provide Consistency:** Ensure responses are coherent over multiple turns.

Techniques:

- **Dialogue State Tracking:**
  Maintain an explicit representation of the conversation state (e.g., slots and intents) to inform response generation.
- **Memory Networks:**
  Utilize neural architectures designed to store and retrieve context over long conversations.
- **Concatenated Histories:**
  Include previous utterances as part of the input to generative models (e.g., transformers), though this approach must balance context length with computational efficiency.

2. Personalization

Overview:
Personalization tailors interactions based on user preferences, history, and behavioral data. By incorporating personalization, a dialogue system can:

- **Enhance Engagement:** Offer recommendations and responses that resonate with the user.

- **Improve Satisfaction:** Address specific user needs and adapt to communication styles.
- **Build Trust:** Create a more human-like and empathetic interaction experience.

Techniques:

- **User Profiles:**
  Integrate user-specific data (e.g., previous interactions, preferences, purchase history) into the dialogue context.
- **Adaptive Learning:**
  Continuously update the user model based on ongoing interactions.
- **Contextual Memory:**
  Store long-term user context across sessions to inform future conversations.

3. User Experience Optimization

Overview:
Optimizing user experience in dialogue systems involves ensuring that responses are not only contextually appropriate and personalized but also timely, clear, and engaging. This requires balancing technical performance with interaction design.

Techniques:

- **Real-Time Response Generation:**
  Implement efficient architectures that reduce latency.
- **Error Handling and Clarification:**
  Proactively detect and manage ambiguities or misunderstandings, prompting users for clarification when necessary.

- **Multi-Modal Interactions:**
  Incorporate visual or interactive elements where applicable to enhance the dialogue experience.

Illustrative Example: Managing Multi-Turn Conversations with Context

Below is a simplified Python example that demonstrates how to manage context and personalization in a multi-turn conversation. This example uses a class-based approach to maintain conversation state across multiple user interactions.

```
class Chatbot:

    def __init__(self):

        # Initialize conversation history and user profile

        self.history = []

        self.user_profile = {}


    def update_history(self, user_input, bot_response):

        # Append the latest exchange to the conversation history

        self.history.append({"user": user_input, "bot":
bot_response})


    def update_user_profile(self, key, value):

        # Update user profile with personalized information

        self.user_profile[key] = value
```

```
    def generate_response(self, user_input):
        # Simple heuristic to demonstrate context awareness
        if "name" in user_input.lower():
            response = "I didn't catch your name. What should I
call you?"
        elif "my name is" in user_input.lower():
            # Extract user name from the input
            name = user_input.split("my name is")[-
1].strip().split()[0]
            self.update_user_profile("name", name)
            response = f"Nice to meet you, {name}! How can I help
you today?"
        elif "how are you" in user_input.lower():
            # Example of using conversation history
            response = "I'm just a chatbot, but I'm here to help!
What can I do for you today?"
        elif "recommend" in user_input.lower() and "name" in
self.user_profile:
            response = f"{self.user_profile['name']}, based on your
interests, I recommend checking out our latest offerings."
        else:
            response = "Can you please provide more details so I
can better assist you?"
        self.update_history(user_input, response)
        return response
```

```
# Simulate a multi-turn conversation
chatbot = Chatbot()
# Turn 1: User introduces themselves
user_input = "Hi, my name is Alice."
response = chatbot.generate_response(user_input)
print("Bot:", response)
# Turn 2: Follow-up query
user_input = "How are you?"
response = chatbot.generate_response(user_input)
print("Bot:", response)
# Turn 3: User asks for a recommendation
user_input = "Can you recommend something for me?"
response = chatbot.generate_response(user_input)
print("Bot:", response)
# Review conversation history
print("\nConversation History:")
for turn in chatbot.history:
    print(turn)
```

Explanation:

- **Context Tracking:**
  The chatbot maintains a history list to record each turn of the

conversation, which can later be used for advanced context management and to inform responses.

- **User Profile and Personalization:**
  The user_profile dictionary stores user-specific information (e.g., name), allowing the system to personalize subsequent responses.
- **Response Generation:**
  The generate_response method uses simple heuristics to demonstrate context-aware and personalized responses based on user input and conversation history.

In summary, effective context management and handling of multi-turn conversations are essential for creating dialogue systems that feel natural and engaging. By maintaining context carryover, integrating user personalization, and optimizing the overall user experience, enterprises can build conversational AI solutions that not only respond accurately but also adapt to the evolving needs of users. As illustrated, even a simplified approach to tracking conversation history and user profiles can significantly enhance the quality and relevance of interactions, laying the groundwork for more sophisticated implementations in real-world applications.

Voice-Activated Systems

Integrating ASR and TTS for Cohesive Conversational Solutions

As enterprises strive to create natural, accessible interactions with technology, voice-activated systems have emerged as a critical component of modern dialogue systems and conversational AI. These systems seamlessly combine Automatic Speech Recognition (ASR) and Text-to-Speech (TTS) to create a cohesive end-to-end solution. By integrating these technologies, organizations can develop applications that allow users to interact with digital systems through natural speech - whether in customer service, virtual assistance, or hands-free operation environments.

1. Automatic Speech Recognition (ASR)

Overview:
ASR converts spoken language into written text. Modern ASR systems leverage deep learning models trained on extensive audio datasets to achieve high accuracy in diverse acoustic environments. Key features include:

- **Noise Robustness:**
  The ability to accurately transcribe speech even in noisy environments.
- **Speaker Adaptation:**
  Customization to recognize individual voices or accents.
- **Real-Time Processing:**
  Ensuring low latency for interactive applications.

Applications:

- Voice search and command interfaces.
- Real-time transcription services.
- Integration in virtual assistants for dynamic conversational interactions.

2. Text-to-Speech (TTS)

Overview:
TTS systems convert text into natural-sounding speech. Recent advances using neural network-based models such as Tacotron 2 and WaveNet have significantly improved the naturalness and expressiveness of synthesized speech. Key features include:

- **Expressiveness:**
  The ability to modulate tone, pace, and emotion to better mimic human speech.

- **Customization:**
  Support for different voices, languages, and dialects to suit specific applications.

- **Low Latency:**
  Fast processing to ensure seamless interaction in real-time systems.

Applications:

- Reading out notifications, messages, or search results.
- Interactive voice response (IVR) systems.
- Accessibility tools for visually impaired users.

3. Integrating ASR and TTS for Cohesive Solutions

Workflow:
A complete voice-activated system typically follows these steps:

1. **User Speech Input:**
   The user speaks into a microphone, and the ASR module captures and transcribes the speech into text.

2. **Natural Language Processing (NLP):**
   The transcribed text is processed by a dialogue system or conversational AI engine to generate an appropriate response.

3. **Response Generation:**
   The system formulates a text response, which is then fed into the TTS module.

4. **Voice Output:**
   The TTS module converts the text response into synthesized speech, which is played back to the user.

Benefits:

- **Enhanced User Experience:**
  Users interact with the system naturally using their voice.
- **Accessibility:**
  Provides an alternative interface for users with disabilities.
- **Operational Efficiency:**
  Enables hands-free operation in environments where manual input is impractical.

Illustrative Example: Integrating ASR and TTS in Python

The following Python example demonstrates a simple voice-activated system that captures user speech, transcribes it using an ASR system, and responds with synthesized speech using a TTS engine.

```
import speech_recognition as sr
from gtts import gTTS
import os
import tempfile
def recognize_speech():
    # Initialize the recognizer
    r = sr.Recognizer()
    with sr.Microphone() as source:
        print("Please speak now...")
        audio = r.listen(source)
    try:
```

```
        # Recognize speech using Google's speech recognition
service
        text = r.recognize_google(audio)
        print("You said: " + text)
        return text
    except sr.UnknownValueError:
        print("Sorry, I could not understand the audio.")
        return ""
    except sr.RequestError as e:
        print("Could not request results; {0}".format(e))
        return ""
def text_to_speech(text):
    # Convert text to speech using gTTS
    tts = gTTS(text=text, lang='en')
    # Use a temporary file to save the audio
    with tempfile.NamedTemporaryFile(delete=True,
suffix='.mp3') as fp:
        tts.save(fp.name)
        # Play the audio file using a system call (platform-specific)
        os.system(f"start {fp.name}" if os.name == "nt" else
f"mpg321 {fp.name}")
def voice_activated_system():
    user_text = recognize_speech()
```

```
    if user_text:
        response_text = f"You said: {user_text}. How can I assist you further?"
        print("Bot:", response_text)
        text_to_speech(response_text)

# Run the voice-activated system
if __name__ == "__main__":
    voice_activated_system()
```

Explanation:

- **ASR Implementation:**
  The recognize_speech() function uses the speech_recognition library to capture audio from the microphone and transcribe it using Google's speech recognition service.
- **TTS Implementation:**
  The text_to_speech() function converts text into speech using the Google Text-to-Speech (gTTS) library and plays the generated audio.
- **System Workflow:**
  The voice_activated_system() function ties together ASR and TTS to simulate a simple conversational interaction where the system repeats back what the user said and asks how it can further assist.

Conclusion

Integrating ASR and TTS into voice-activated systems creates a powerful, cohesive solution that enables natural, real-time communication across languages and devices. By leveraging state-of-the-art ASR and TTS technologies, enterprises can build conversational AI applications that offer enhanced user experiences, improved accessibility, and operational efficiency. The example provided demonstrates the basic building blocks of such systems, forming the foundation for more advanced, scalable implementations in a global business context.

Chapter 12: Explainability, Ethics, and Compliance in NLP

Model Interpretability

Explaining Outputs and Mitigating the "Black Box" Perception to Align with Corporate Governance

As organizations increasingly rely on advanced NLP models to drive strategic decisions, ensuring model transparency and interpretability becomes crucial. The "black box" nature of many deep learning models can hinder stakeholder trust, regulatory compliance, and effective governance. To address these concerns, enterprises are adopting techniques that explain model predictions, enabling decision-makers to understand, audit, and validate the outputs. This not only builds trust but also aligns with corporate governance standards and ethical guidelines.

Key Objectives for Model Interpretability

- **Transparency:**
  Providing clear insights into how a model arrives at its predictions helps demystify the decision-making process.
- **Accountability:**
  Interpretability facilitates error analysis and bias detection, ensuring models adhere to ethical standards and regulatory requirements.
- **User Trust:**
  Explaining model outputs in understandable terms fosters confidence among users and stakeholders, crucial for applications in sensitive domains like finance, healthcare, and legal.
- **Auditability:**
  Well-documented and interpretable models simplify the auditing process, allowing organizations to trace and justify decisions based on model outputs.

Techniques for Enhancing Model Interpretability

- **Feature Importance Analysis:**
  Tools such as SHAP (SHapley Additive exPlanations) and LIME (Local Interpretable Model-Agnostic Explanations) help quantify the contribution of each feature to the model's predictions.

- **Attention Visualization:**
  In transformer-based models, visualizing attention weights can reveal which parts of the input the model focused on during prediction, offering intuitive insights into its behavior.

- **Layer-wise Relevance Propagation:**
  This technique backpropagates prediction scores to input features, highlighting the areas that most strongly influenced the outcome.

Illustrative Example: Explaining a Text Classification Model with SHAP

The following Python example demonstrates how to use SHAP to interpret the predictions of a logistic regression classifier trained on TF-IDF features. This approach helps reveal which words in a text contribute most significantly to its predicted sentiment.

```
import shap

import numpy as np

import pandas as pd

from sklearn.feature_extraction.text import TfidfVectorizer

from sklearn.linear_model import LogisticRegression

# Sample dataset: Texts with sentiment labels (1: Positive, 0:
Negative)
```

```
texts = [
    "I love this product!",
    "This product is terrible.",
    "I am very satisfied with this service.",
    "The service was not good at all."
]
labels = [1, 0, 1, 0]
# Vectorize the text data using TF-IDF
vectorizer = TfidfVectorizer()
X = vectorizer.fit_transform(texts)
# Train a Logistic Regression classifier
model = LogisticRegression()
model.fit(X, labels)
# Define a function to predict probabilities for SHAP
def predict_proba(x):
    return model.predict_proba(x)
# Convert sparse matrix to dense format for SHAP
X_dense = X.toarray()
# Use SHAP's KernelExplainer for model-agnostic explanation
explainer = shap.KernelExplainer(predict_proba,
shap.kmeans(X_dense, 2))
# Explain a single prediction: a new text sample
test_text = "I am extremely happy with the excellent service."
```

```
test_vector = vectorizer.transform([test_text]).toarray()
shap_values = explainer.shap_values(test_vector)
# Visualize the explanation for the positive class (index 1)
shap.initjs()
shap.force_plot(explainer.expected_value[1], shap_values[1],
vectorizer.get_feature_names_out(), matplotlib=True)
```

Explanation:

- **Data Preparation and Model Training:**
  A TF-IDF vectorizer transforms textual data into numerical features, which are then used to train a logistic regression classifier for sentiment analysis.
- **SHAP Integration:**
  The KernelExplainer from SHAP is used to approximate the contribution of each word (feature) in the input text to the predicted probability of positive sentiment.
- **Visualization:**
  The force plot generated by SHAP provides an intuitive visualization of how individual words contribute to the final prediction. Positive contributions (pushing the prediction towards positive sentiment) and negative contributions are clearly highlighted, making the model's decision process transparent.

In summary, by incorporating interpretability techniques such as SHAP, organizations can effectively explain the outputs of their NLP models, addressing the "black box" challenge. This transparency not only satisfies corporate governance and regulatory requirements but also fosters trust among users and stakeholders. Ultimately, explainable models are better positioned to support informed decision-making and continuous improvement, ensuring that advanced NLP systems deliver reliable, ethical, and impactful insights in a corporate setting.

Bias, Fairness, and Responsible AI

Identifying and Addressing Ethical Risks in Training Data and Model Outputs

As NLP models become integral to enterprise decision-making, addressing ethical risks and ensuring fairness is paramount. Bias in training data and model outputs can lead to discriminatory practices, misrepresentation, and unintended harm. Responsible AI initiatives focus on mitigating these risks by identifying sources of bias, applying fairness metrics, and implementing strategies to ensure that models operate equitably across all user groups.

Key Challenges in Bias and Fairness

1. **Data Bias:**

- **Representation Bias:**
  When training data disproportionately represents certain demographics, leading to skewed model performance.
- **Historical Bias:**
  Inherited biases from historical data can perpetuate stereotypes and unfair outcomes.
- **Sampling Bias:**
  When the data collection process systematically excludes certain groups, resulting in models that do not generalize well.

2. **Model Bias:**

- **Algorithmic Bias:**
  Even with balanced data, the choice of model architecture and learning algorithms can introduce bias.

- **Outcome Bias:**
  Biases manifest in predictions, where the model may favor or penalize certain groups, leading to unfair treatment in applications like sentiment analysis, hiring, or loan approvals.

3. **Ethical and Legal Implications:**

- **Regulatory Compliance:**
  Organizations must adhere to ethical guidelines and regulatory standards such as GDPR, ensuring that AI systems do not reinforce discrimination.

- **Trust and Transparency:**
  Fair and interpretable models are crucial for maintaining stakeholder trust and ensuring accountability in AI-driven decisions.

Strategies for Mitigating Bias and Ensuring Fairness

1. **Bias Auditing and Monitoring:**

- **Pre-training Audits:**
  Analyze training data for representativeness and balance. Use statistical tests and visualization techniques to detect biases.

- **Post-deployment Monitoring:**
  Continuously monitor model outputs using fairness metrics and real-world feedback to detect and address any emerging bias.

2. **Fairness-Aware Training:**

- **Data Augmentation and Rebalancing:**
  Augment underrepresented groups in the training data or apply re-sampling techniques to ensure a more balanced dataset.

- **Adversarial Debiasing:**
  Incorporate adversarial techniques to learn representations that are invariant to sensitive attributes (e.g., gender, ethnicity).

3. **Transparency and Interpretability:**

- **Explainable AI Tools:**
  Use model interpretability tools (e.g., SHAP, LIME) to understand and communicate how decisions are made, ensuring that biases can be identified and rectified.

- **Documentation and Accountability:**
  Maintain detailed documentation of data sources, modeling choices, and fairness evaluation procedures to facilitate audits and stakeholder communication.

4. **Ethical Guidelines and Governance:**

- **Ethics Review Boards:**
  Establish internal committees to review AI projects and ensure adherence to ethical standards.

- **User-Centric Design:**
  Engage diverse user groups during model development to capture a wide range of perspectives and minimize unintended harm.

Illustrative Example: Using SHAP to Identify Bias in a Sentiment Analysis Model

The following Python code demonstrates how to use SHAP to interpret the predictions of a sentiment analysis model. By visualizing feature contributions, we can identify whether specific words or phrases disproportionately affect outcomes, potentially highlighting biases.

```
import shap

import numpy as np
```

```
import pandas as pd

from sklearn.feature_extraction.text import TfidfVectorizer

from sklearn.linear_model import LogisticRegression

# Sample dataset: Texts with sentiment labels (1: Positive, 0:
Negative)

texts = [

    "I love this product!",          # Likely positive

    "This product is terrible.",     # Likely negative

    "I am very satisfied with this service.",

    "The service was not good at all."

]

labels = [1, 0, 1, 0]

# Vectorize the text data using TF-IDF

vectorizer = TfidfVectorizer()

X = vectorizer.fit_transform(texts)

# Train a Logistic Regression classifier

model = LogisticRegression()

model.fit(X, labels)

# Define a prediction function for SHAP

def predict_proba(x):

    return model.predict_proba(x)

# Convert sparse matrix to dense format for SHAP

X_dense = X.toarray()
```

```
# Use SHAP's KernelExplainer for model-agnostic explanation

explainer = shap.KernelExplainer(predict_proba,
shap.kmeans(X_dense, 2))

# Explain a single prediction: A new text sample that might
show bias

test_text = "The product is amazing, but the service is
terrible."

test_vector = vectorizer.transform([test_text]).toarray()

shap_values = explainer.shap_values(test_vector)

# Visualize the explanation for the positive class (index 1)

shap.initjs()

shap.force_plot(explainer.expected_value[1], shap_values[1],
vectorizer.get_feature_names_out(), matplotlib=True)
```

Explanation:

- **Data Preparation and Model Training:**
  A TF-IDF vectorizer converts the text into numerical features, and a logistic regression classifier is trained on this dataset.
- **SHAP Integration:**
  The KernelExplainer is used to compute SHAP values, quantifying the impact of each feature (word) on the model's prediction.
- **Bias Detection:**
  By visualizing the force plot, stakeholders can inspect if certain words (e.g., adjectives associated with gender or ethnicity) are

unduly influencing the model's sentiment predictions. Identifying such patterns is the first step toward mitigating bias through rebalancing or retraining.

In summary, ensuring fairness and responsible AI in NLP involves rigorous processes for identifying and mitigating bias throughout the model lifecycle. By employing robust auditing methods, fairness-aware training techniques, and transparency tools like SHAP, organizations can demystify the decision-making process of complex models. This not only aligns with corporate governance and ethical standards but also builds trust among users and stakeholders, paving the way for equitable and accountable AI solutions in a diverse, global marketplace.

Regulatory and Compliance Considerations

Navigating Data Privacy Laws, Security Protocols, and Ethical Review Boards

In today's data-driven world, enterprises leveraging NLP must prioritize compliance with stringent data privacy laws and ethical standards. Regulations such as GDPR (General Data Protection Regulation) and CCPA (California Consumer Privacy Act) impose strict guidelines on data collection, storage, and processing, ensuring that user privacy and data security are maintained. Additionally, security protocols and oversight by ethical review boards play a critical role in maintaining transparency and accountability.

Key Regulatory Frameworks

1. **GDPR (General Data Protection Regulation):**

- **Scope:** Applies to any organization processing personal data of individuals in the European Union.
- **Key Provisions:**

- **Data Minimization:** Collect only the data necessary for the specified purpose.
- **Consent:** Ensure explicit consent is obtained from users for data processing.
- **Right to Erasure:** Allow users to request deletion of their data ("right to be forgotten").
- **Data Protection Impact Assessments (DPIAs):** Conduct assessments to identify and mitigate privacy risks.

2. **CCPA (California Consumer Privacy Act):**

- **Scope:** Focuses on the rights of California residents regarding their personal information.
- **Key Provisions:**
    - **Consumer Rights:** Grants users rights to know, delete, and opt-out of data sales.
    - **Transparency:** Requires companies to disclose data collection and sharing practices.
    - **Security Requirements:** Mandates implementation of reasonable security measures to protect user data.

Security Protocols

- **Data Encryption:**
  Encrypt data both in transit and at rest to prevent unauthorized access. Utilize industry-standard protocols (e.g., TLS, AES) to secure communications and storage.
- **Access Control:**
  Implement robust authentication and authorization mechanisms to restrict data access to authorized personnel only.

- **Audit Trails:**
  Maintain detailed logs of data access and processing activities to facilitate auditing and regulatory compliance.
- **Anonymization and Pseudonymization:**
  Remove or mask personally identifiable information (PII) to minimize privacy risks while retaining analytical value.

Ethical Review and Oversight

- **Ethical Review Boards:**
  Establish internal or external review boards to assess the ethical implications of NLP projects. These boards ensure that data collection, model training, and deployment practices align with ethical standards and societal values.
- **Transparent Documentation:**
  Maintain thorough documentation of data sources, processing methodologies, and model decision-making processes. This transparency supports both internal audits and external regulatory reviews.
- **User Consent and Communication:**
  Clearly communicate to users how their data will be used, stored, and protected. Provide mechanisms for users to give, withdraw, or modify their consent.

Illustrative Example: Data Anonymization in Python

Below is a Python example demonstrating how to anonymize a dataset by removing or masking PII. In this scenario, we use a simple approach to anonymize names and email addresses using regular expressions. This technique is an important part of complying with GDPR and CCPA requirements.

```
import re
import pandas as pd
# Sample dataset with personal data
data = {
    "Name": ["Alice Johnson", "Bob Smith", "Charlie Davis"],
    "Email": ["alice.johnson@example.com",
"bob.smith@example.com", "charlie.davis@example.com"],
    "Feedback": [
        "I really enjoyed the product. Thank you, Alice!",
        "The service could be improved, says Bob.",
        "Charlie thinks the new feature is great."
    ]
}
df = pd.DataFrame(data)


# Function to anonymize personal information
def anonymize_text(text):
    # Mask email addresses
    text = re.sub(r'\b[\w\.-]+@[\w\.-]+\.\w+\b', '[EMAIL]',
text)
    # Mask names (assuming first name followed by last name)
    text = re.sub(r'\b[A-Z][a-z]+\s[A-Z][a-z]+\b', '[NAME]',
text)
```

```
    return text

# Apply anonymization to the dataset

df['Anonymized_Feedback'] =
df['Feedback'].apply(anonymize_text)

df['Anonymized_Name'] = '[NAME]'

df['Anonymized_Email'] = '[EMAIL]'

print("Original Data:")

print(df[['Name', 'Email', 'Feedback']])

print("\nAnonymized Data:")

print(df[['Anonymized_Name', 'Anonymized_Email',
'Anonymized_Feedback']])
```

Explanation:

- **Regular Expressions for PII:**
  The anonymize_text function uses regular expressions to identify and mask email addresses and names.
- **Data Transformation:**
  The script applies the anonymization function to a dataset, replacing sensitive information with placeholders (e.g., [NAME], [EMAIL]).
- **Compliance:**
  Such anonymization is a critical step in ensuring that the data processing pipeline complies with data protection laws like GDPR and CCPA.

Conclusion

Navigating regulatory and compliance considerations in NLP involves a multi-layered approach that spans technical, organizational, and ethical dimensions. By implementing robust security protocols, ensuring transparency through ethical review boards, and adopting data anonymization techniques, organizations can build NLP solutions that not only deliver business value but also uphold the highest standards of data privacy and ethical responsibility. This proactive approach is essential for maintaining stakeholder trust and meeting the rigorous demands of global regulatory frameworks.

Chapter 13: Industry-Specific Implementations

Financial Services

Automating Sentiment Analysis for Market Insights, Compliance Checks, and Fraud Detection

In the financial services industry, timely and accurate analysis of textual data is essential for maintaining a competitive edge, ensuring regulatory compliance, and detecting fraudulent activities. Advanced NLP techniques—especially automated sentiment analysis—play a pivotal role in extracting actionable insights from a wide array of unstructured data sources such as news articles, social media posts, earnings call transcripts, and internal communications.

1. Market Insights through Sentiment Analysis

Overview:
Financial institutions leverage sentiment analysis to gauge market sentiment by analyzing news headlines, financial reports, and social media chatter. By understanding whether public sentiment is positive, neutral, or negative regarding a particular stock, sector, or the market as a whole, traders and analysts can make more informed investment decisions.

Key Benefits:

- **Real-Time Monitoring:** Enables tracking of market sentiment as events unfold, providing an edge in volatile markets.
- **Investment Strategy:** Helps refine trading strategies by correlating sentiment trends with market performance.
- **Risk Management:** Assists in early identification of potential downturns or overreactions.

Illustrative Code Example: Using FinBERT for Market Sentiment Analysis

FinBERT is a transformer-based model fine-tuned for financial sentiment analysis. The following example demonstrates how to use FinBERT to analyze the sentiment of a financial news headline.

```
from transformers import AutoTokenizer,
AutoModelForSequenceClassification

import torch

import numpy as np

# Load the FinBERT model and tokenizer

model_name = "yiyanghkust/finbert-tone"

tokenizer = AutoTokenizer.from_pretrained(model_name)

model =
AutoModelForSequenceClassification.from_pretrained(model_
name)

# Sample financial news headline

headline = "Company XYZ's quarterly earnings surpass analyst
expectations, driving up stock prices."

# Tokenize and process the input text

inputs = tokenizer(headline, return_tensors="pt",
truncation=True, padding=True)

outputs = model(**inputs)

# Obtain raw sentiment scores and apply softmax for
probabilities
```

```
scores = outputs.logits.detach().numpy()[0]

probabilities = np.exp(scores) / np.sum(np.exp(scores))

# Interpret sentiment: 0 -> negative, 1 -> neutral, 2 -> positive
(based on model's training)

sentiment_labels = ['negative', 'neutral', 'positive']

predicted_sentiment =
sentiment_labels[np.argmax(probabilities)]

print("Headline:", headline)

print("Sentiment Probabilities:", probabilities)

print("Predicted Sentiment:", predicted_sentiment)
```

2. Compliance Checks with NLP

Overview:
Financial institutions must adhere to stringent compliance regulations that govern communication, data handling, and reporting practices. NLP can automate compliance checks by scanning emails, reports, and chat logs for prohibited language, insider trading hints, or any irregular communication patterns that may trigger regulatory scrutiny.

Key Benefits:

- **Risk Mitigation:** Early detection of non-compliant language helps prevent regulatory breaches.
- **Automated Monitoring:** Continuous, real-time monitoring of communications reduces manual oversight burdens.
- **Audit Trail:** Provides detailed logs and explanations for compliance audits.

Example Approach:
A compliance system might flag communications containing terms related to insider trading or unauthorized disclosures. Advanced NLP techniques can use keyword extraction combined with sentiment and contextual analysis to assess the risk level of communications.

```
import re

def compliance_check(text):

    # Define a set of sensitive keywords related to insider trading or non-compliant behavior

    sensitive_keywords = ["insider", "confidential", "leak", "non-public", "unauthorized"]

    # Check if any sensitive keyword is present in the text

    flagged = any(re.search(r'\b' + keyword + r'\b', text, re.IGNORECASE) for keyword in sensitive_keywords)

    if flagged:

        return "Potential Compliance Issue Detected"

    else:

        return "No Issues Detected"

# Example usage

communication = "Please ensure that all confidential information remains within our team."

print("Compliance Check:", compliance_check(communication))
```

3. Fraud Detection through Text Analysis

Overview:
Fraud detection in financial services can be significantly enhanced by analyzing text communications for anomalies or indicators of fraudulent behavior. NLP can analyze emails, transaction notes, and internal communications to identify suspicious patterns that might indicate collusion, money laundering, or other fraudulent activities.

Key Benefits:

- **Anomaly Detection:** Identify unusual language patterns that deviate from normal operational communications.
- **Early Warning Systems:** Flag potential fraud risks in real-time, enabling proactive investigation.
- **Cost Savings:** Reduce the reliance on manual monitoring and investigations through automated analysis.

Example Approach:
A fraud detection system might use clustering or anomaly detection techniques on extracted text features to identify communications that warrant further investigation.

```
from sklearn.feature_extraction.text import TfidfVectorizer

from sklearn.cluster import DBSCAN

import numpy as np

# Sample communications from internal channels

communications = [

    "The monthly financial report is ready for review.",

    "Ensure that all transactions are recorded accurately.",
```

```
    "We have a tip about unusual transactions involving offshore accounts.",
    "Please schedule a meeting to discuss the latest market trends.",
    "Suspicious activity detected in the recent transaction logs."
]
# Vectorize communications using TF-IDF
vectorizer = TfidfVectorizer(stop_words='english')
X = vectorizer.fit_transform(communications)
# Use DBSCAN to detect anomalies; communication clusters with very few members may indicate outliers
clustering = DBSCAN(eps=0.5, min_samples=2, metric='cosine').fit(X.toarray())
labels = clustering.labels_
# Identify potential fraud-related communications (outliers are labeled as -1)
fraud_indicators = [comm for comm, label in zip(communications, labels) if label == -1]
print("Communications:", communications)
print("Cluster Labels:", labels)
print("Potential Fraud Indicators (Outliers):", fraud_indicators)
```

Explanation:

- **TF-IDF Vectorization:**
  Transforms communications into a numerical format that captures the importance of each word.
- **Clustering with DBSCAN:**
  DBSCAN identifies outliers (labeled as -1), which could indicate communications that deviate from normal patterns and potentially signal fraudulent behavior.
- **Actionable Insights:**
  Communications flagged as outliers are reviewed by compliance teams for further investigation.

In summary, in the financial services industry, automating sentiment analysis, compliance checks, and fraud detection through advanced NLP techniques drives significant business value. By leveraging models like FinBERT for market sentiment, implementing rule-based and machine learning approaches for compliance, and applying clustering techniques for anomaly detection, enterprises can enhance decision-making, ensure regulatory compliance, and mitigate fraud risk. These automated solutions not only improve operational efficiency but also provide timely insights in a rapidly changing financial landscape, ultimately supporting more informed, data-driven strategies in the sector.

Healthcare and Life Sciences

Patient Data Processing, Clinical Documentation, and Medical Text Analysis for Improved Outcomes

In the healthcare and life sciences sector, the integration of NLP into clinical workflows is revolutionizing patient care, streamlining administrative processes, and enhancing research outcomes. Advanced NLP techniques facilitate the automated extraction and analysis of patient data, clinical documentation, and unstructured medical text, enabling healthcare providers to derive actionable insights, improve diagnostic accuracy, and optimize treatment plans. This transformation not only boosts operational efficiency but also contributes to enhanced patient outcomes while ensuring adherence to strict regulatory and privacy standards.

Key Applications in Healthcare and Life Sciences

1. **Patient Data Processing:**

- **Electronic Health Records (EHRs):**
  Automate the extraction of structured data from EHRs by processing clinical narratives, lab reports, and radiology notes. This assists in creating comprehensive patient profiles for better care coordination.

- **Clinical Data Integration:**
  Combine data from multiple sources (e.g., wearable devices, patient portals, and genomic data) to form a holistic view of patient health, enabling personalized medicine.

2. **Clinical Documentation:**

- **Automated Summarization:**
  Generate concise summaries of lengthy clinical notes to support faster decision-making by clinicians.

- **Named Entity Recognition (NER):**
  Identify critical medical entities such as medications, diagnoses, procedures, and lab results to support accurate record-keeping and compliance reporting.

- **Clinical Coding:**
  Assist in mapping clinical narratives to standardized codes (e.g., ICD-10, SNOMED) to improve billing accuracy and streamline administrative workflows.

3. **Medical Text Analysis:**

- **Diagnostic Decision Support:**
  Analyze medical literature and patient histories to aid in differential diagnosis and treatment recommendations.

- **Outcome Prediction:**
  Leverage predictive models to analyze historical clinical data and forecast patient outcomes, readmission risks, or adverse events.

- **Research and Drug Discovery:**
  Extract insights from published research, clinical trial data, and patents to identify emerging trends and support the development of new therapeutics.

Challenges and Considerations

- **Data Privacy and Security:**
  Handling sensitive patient data requires strict adherence to HIPAA, GDPR, and other healthcare-specific regulations. Robust data anonymization, encryption, and secure data handling protocols are essential.

- **Domain-Specific Language:**
  Medical texts are characterized by complex terminologies, abbreviations, and jargon. Models need to be fine-tuned on domain-specific corpora (e.g., ClinicalBERT, BioBERT) to achieve high accuracy.

- **Interoperability:**
  Integrating NLP solutions into existing healthcare IT systems (such as EHRs and hospital management systems) requires adherence to interoperability standards like HL7 and FHIR.

Illustrative Example: Using ClinicalBERT for Medical Text Analysis

Below is a practical example demonstrating how to leverage a domain-specific pretrained language model, such as ClinicalBERT, for classifying clinical text. This example uses the Hugging Face Transformers library to process a sample clinical note and output a prediction that could be used to flag critical information or assist in clinical decision-making.

```
from transformers import AutoTokenizer, AutoModelForSequenceClassification

import torch

import numpy as np

# Load a pretrained ClinicalBERT model and its tokenizer

model_name = "emilyalsentzer/Bio_ClinicalBERT"

tokenizer = AutoTokenizer.from_pretrained(model_name)

model = AutoModelForSequenceClassification.from_pretrained(model_name, num_labels=2)  # Assuming binary classification for demonstration

# Sample clinical note for analysis

clinical_note = (

    "The patient, a 65-year-old male with a history of hypertension and diabetes, presented with chest pain and shortness of breath. "

    "ECG showed signs of myocardial infarction. Immediate intervention with angioplasty was recommended."
```

```
)
# Tokenize the clinical note
inputs = tokenizer(clinical_note, return_tensors="pt",
truncation=True, padding=True)
# Obtain model predictions
with torch.no_grad():
    outputs = model(**inputs)
# Extract logits and convert to probabilities using softmax
logits = outputs.logits.numpy()[0]
probabilities = np.exp(logits) / np.sum(np.exp(logits))
predicted_label = np.argmax(probabilities)
label_names = {0: "Non-critical", 1: "Critical"}  # Example
mapping
print("Clinical Note:", clinical_note)
print("Prediction Probabilities:", probabilities)
print("Predicted Label:", label_names[predicted_label])
```

Explanation:

- **Model and Tokenizer Loading:**
  The code loads a ClinicalBERT model fine-tuned for clinical text analysis. Such models are specifically designed to understand medical jargon and contextual nuances within clinical narratives.
- **Tokenization and Input Preparation:**
  The clinical note is tokenized and formatted as input to the

model, ensuring proper handling of long texts through truncation and padding.

- **Prediction and Interpretation:**
  The model outputs logits which are converted to probabilities using a softmax function. The predicted label indicates whether the note is classified as "Critical" (indicating potential high risk or need for immediate intervention) or "Non-critical."

In summary, implementing advanced NLP solutions in healthcare and life sciences enables organizations to transform vast amounts of unstructured clinical data into actionable insights. By automating patient data processing, clinical documentation, and medical text analysis, these technologies empower healthcare providers to make faster, more informed decisions, ultimately improving patient outcomes. With careful attention to data privacy, domain-specific language, and interoperability, enterprise-scale NLP solutions can be seamlessly integrated into healthcare systems, driving operational efficiency and enhancing the quality of care delivered.

Manufacturing and Supply Chain

Demand Forecasting, Supplier Communications, and Operational Efficiency Drivers

In the highly competitive manufacturing and supply chain sector, leveraging advanced NLP and AI techniques is critical for driving operational efficiency and informed decision-making. By automating the analysis of textual data - from supplier communications and market reports to social media and internal documents - companies can extract actionable insights that directly impact demand forecasting, supplier relations, and overall operational performance.

1. Demand Forecasting

Overview:
Demand forecasting is essential for optimizing production schedules,

managing inventory levels, and aligning supply chain operations. While traditional methods rely on historical sales and economic data, modern approaches integrate NLP to analyze external textual data such as:

- Market sentiment from news articles and social media.
- Industry reports and expert commentary.
- Customer reviews and feedback.

Benefits:

- **Enhanced Accuracy:** Combining numerical time-series data with insights derived from unstructured text can lead to more robust forecasting models.
- **Proactive Planning:** Early detection of shifts in consumer sentiment or market trends allows companies to adjust production and inventory strategies in real-time.
- **Risk Mitigation:** Identifying potential supply chain disruptions or shifts in demand can help mitigate risks and reduce costs.

2. Supplier Communications

Overview:
Supplier communications are a vital source of information for monitoring supplier performance, identifying potential delays, and ensuring quality control. NLP techniques can automatically extract and categorize key information from emails, contracts, and reports to:

- Detect issues in supply chain communications.
- Monitor supplier sentiment and performance indicators.
- Automate response workflows and escalate concerns as needed.

Benefits:

- **Efficiency Gains:** Automating the review process reduces manual effort and minimizes human error.
- **Improved Supplier Relationships:** Timely insights into supplier performance enable proactive management and negotiation.
- **Enhanced Transparency:** Clear, structured data from communications aids in compliance and auditing processes.

3. Operational Efficiency Drivers

Overview:
Operational efficiency in manufacturing and supply chain management is driven by the ability to streamline processes, reduce waste, and optimize resource allocation. NLP contributes by:

- Automating documentation and report generation.
- Analyzing production logs and maintenance reports to predict equipment failures.
- Integrating qualitative insights with quantitative data to enhance decision-making processes.

Benefits:

- **Cost Reduction:** Enhanced process automation leads to significant reductions in operational costs.
- **Time Savings:** Rapid extraction and analysis of text data free up human resources for strategic tasks.
- **Data-Driven Insights:** Combining multiple data sources allows for holistic insights that drive continuous improvement and innovation.

Illustrative Example: Integrating NLP for Demand Forecasting

Below is a Python example demonstrating how to integrate sentiment analysis from supplier communications into a demand forecasting model. In this simplified scenario, we use the VADER sentiment analyzer from NLTK to extract sentiment scores from supplier messages and then combine these scores with historical demand data to forecast future demand using linear regression.

Step 1: Sentiment Analysis on Supplier Communications

```
import pandas as pd
from nltk.sentiment.vader import SentimentIntensityAnalyzer
import nltk
# Download VADER lexicon
nltk.download('vader_lexicon')
# Sample supplier communications data
data = {
    "date": ["2023-01-01", "2023-01-02", "2023-01-03", "2023-01-04"],
    "communication": [
        "The shipment will be on time.",
        "There might be slight delays due to weather conditions.",
        "We are facing significant issues with quality control.",
        "Everything is proceeding as planned."
    ]
```

```
}
supplier_df = pd.DataFrame(data)
supplier_df['date'] = pd.to_datetime(supplier_df['date'])
# Initialize VADER sentiment analyzer
sia = SentimentIntensityAnalyzer()
# Calculate sentiment score for each communication
supplier_df['sentiment'] =
supplier_df['communication'].apply(lambda x:
sia.polarity_scores(x)['compound'])
print("Supplier Communications with Sentiment Scores:")
print(supplier_df)
```

Step 2: Demand Forecasting with Sentiment as a Feature

```
import numpy as np
from sklearn.linear_model import LinearRegression
from sklearn.model_selection import train_test_split
# Sample historical demand data (e.g., units sold per day)
demand_data = {
   "date": ["2023-01-01", "2023-01-02", "2023-01-03", "2023-01-
04"],
   "demand": [150, 160, 140, 155]
}
```

```
demand_df = pd.DataFrame(demand_data)

demand_df['date'] = pd.to_datetime(demand_df['date'])

# Merge supplier sentiment with demand data on the date

merged_df = pd.merge(demand_df, supplier_df[['date',
'sentiment']], on="date")

print("\nMerged Data:")

print(merged_df)

# Prepare features and target for forecasting

X = merged_df[['sentiment']].values  # Feature: sentiment
score

y = merged_df['demand'].values       # Target: demand

# Split the data for training and testing

X_train, X_test, y_train, y_test = train_test_split(X, y,
test_size=0.25, random_state=42)

# Train a linear regression model

model = LinearRegression()

model.fit(X_train, y_train)

# Predict demand using the model

y_pred = model.predict(X_test)

print("\nPredicted Demand:", y_pred)

print("Actual Demand:", y_test)
```

Explanation:

- **Sentiment Analysis:**
  Supplier communications are analyzed using VADER to derive a compound sentiment score for each message.
- **Data Integration:**
  Sentiment scores are merged with historical demand data, providing an additional feature that may correlate with demand fluctuations.
- **Demand Forecasting:**
  A simple linear regression model is trained using the sentiment score as a predictor, illustrating how qualitative insights from supplier communications can enhance demand forecasting models.

Conclusion

In the manufacturing and supply chain sector, integrating NLP into operational workflows unlocks new levels of efficiency and strategic insight. By automating sentiment analysis of supplier communications and combining these insights with traditional demand forecasting methods, organizations can better predict market needs, optimize production schedules, and streamline supplier interactions. These advancements not only drive cost reductions and time savings but also enable a more agile and responsive supply chain capable of thriving in a dynamic global marketplace.

Part V: Enterprise Solutions and Deployment Roadmaps
Chapter 14: Infrastructure and Cloud Strategy

On-Premises vs. Cloud vs. Hybrid

Cost-Benefit Analysis, Scalability Considerations, and Vendor Selection

As enterprises expand their digital footprint and integrate advanced NLP and AI solutions, the underlying infrastructure strategy becomes a pivotal decision point. Organizations must choose between on-premises, cloud, or hybrid deployments - each with distinct advantages, challenges, and cost implications. A careful cost-benefit analysis, evaluation of scalability requirements, and judicious vendor selection are critical to align IT investments with business objectives and ensure sustainable growth.

1. On-Premises, Cloud, and Hybrid: An Overview

- **On-Premises:**
  - **Definition:**
    Deploying and managing hardware and software within the organization's own data centers.
  - **Advantages:**
    - Full control over security, data governance, and customization.
    - Often preferred by industries with strict regulatory requirements.
  - **Challenges:**
    - High upfront capital expenditure and ongoing maintenance costs.

- Limited scalability; scaling up often requires additional capital investment.

- **Cloud-Based:**
  - **Definition:**
    Leveraging third-party cloud service providers (e.g., AWS, Azure, Google Cloud) to host and manage applications and data.
  - **Advantages:**
    - Elastic scalability and cost-efficiency through pay-as-you-go models.
    - Rapid deployment and integration with other cloud-native services.
  - **Challenges:**
    - Ongoing operational expenses can add up over time.
    - Potential concerns over data privacy and control, depending on the industry.
- **Hybrid:**
  - **Definition:**
    A blend of on-premises and cloud solutions, combining the control of local infrastructure with the scalability and flexibility of cloud services.
  - **Advantages:**
    - Optimizes cost and performance by storing sensitive data on-premises while leveraging cloud resources for peak loads.
    - Flexibility to adapt to changing business needs.

- **Challenges:**
  - Complexity in integration and managing data across multiple environments.
  - Requires careful orchestration and robust security measures to maintain consistency and compliance.

2. Cost-Benefit Analysis

When evaluating infrastructure strategies, key factors include:

- **Capital Expenditure (CapEx) vs. Operational Expenditure (OpEx):**
  - *On-Premises:*
    Typically involves high CapEx for hardware, licensing, and setup costs; lower OpEx over time if utilization is high.
  - *Cloud:*
    Shifts costs to OpEx with a pay-as-you-go model, offering flexibility but potentially higher costs for sustained high utilization.
  - *Hybrid:*
    Balances CapEx and OpEx by keeping critical operations on-premises while leveraging cloud services for burst capacity.
- **Total Cost of Ownership (TCO):**
  Consider not only direct costs (hardware, software, licensing) but also indirect costs (maintenance, staffing, energy consumption, downtime).
- **Scalability and Performance:**
  - *Cloud and Hybrid models* offer rapid scalability to handle varying workloads, while on-premises solutions may require substantial lead time and capital to scale.

- **Compliance and Security Requirements:**
  Industries with stringent regulatory requirements may prefer on-premises or hybrid solutions for greater control over sensitive data, even if it means higher initial costs.

3. Scalability Considerations

- **Cloud:**
  - Offers virtually unlimited scalability, leveraging auto-scaling groups and distributed computing resources.
  - Supports global deployment, reducing latency through regional data centers.
- **On-Premises:**
  - Scalability is limited by physical capacity and requires significant capital investment.
  - Upgrading infrastructure often involves downtime and complex migration processes.
- **Hybrid:**
  - Provides flexibility by combining the reliability of on-premises infrastructure with the dynamic scalability of the cloud.
  - Requires robust orchestration tools to seamlessly manage workloads between environments.

4. Vendor Selection

Key Criteria for Vendor Selection:

- **Service Level Agreements (SLAs) and Reliability:**
  Evaluate vendor SLAs for uptime, performance, and support. Ensure they align with your business requirements.

- **Cost Structure:**
  Compare pricing models (e.g., on-demand, reserved instances, volume discounts) and assess long-term cost implications.
- **Security and Compliance:**
  Ensure the vendor adheres to relevant regulatory standards (e.g., GDPR, HIPAA) and provides robust security features such as encryption, identity management, and auditing.
- **Integration and Ecosystem:**
  Assess the vendor's compatibility with your existing systems and the availability of complementary services (e.g., data analytics, machine learning platforms).
- **Global Reach:**
  For enterprises operating internationally, vendor support in multiple regions and languages is critical.

Illustrative Code Example: Estimating Cloud Infrastructure Costs

Below is a simplified Python script that estimates cloud infrastructure costs based on usage parameters. This example demonstrates how you might programmatically compare costs for compute resources.

```
def estimate_cloud_costs(instance_hours,
instance_type="standard", region="us-east-1"):
    # Example pricing (USD per hour) for illustration purposes
    pricing = {
        "standard": 0.10,     # Standard instance price per hour
        "high_memory": 0.20,  # High-memory instance price per
hour
        "gpu": 0.90           # GPU-enabled instance price per hour
```

```
    }
    # Retrieve cost per hour for the instance type
    cost_per_hour = pricing.get(instance_type, 0.10)
      # Total estimated cost
    total_cost = instance_hours * cost_per_hour
    return total_cost
# Example usage:
instance_hours = 720  # e.g., one month of continuous usage
cost_standard = estimate_cloud_costs(instance_hours,
instance_type="standard")
cost_high_memory = estimate_cloud_costs(instance_hours,
instance_type="high_memory")
cost_gpu = estimate_cloud_costs(instance_hours,
instance_type="gpu")
print("Estimated Monthly Costs:")
print(f"Standard Instance: ${cost_standard:.2f}")
print(f"High-Memory Instance: ${cost_high_memory:.2f}")
print(f"GPU-Enabled Instance: ${cost_gpu:.2f}")
```

Explanation:

- **Instance Hours:**
  The script calculates cost estimates based on instance usage measured in hours.

- **Instance Types:**
  Different instance types (e.g., standard, high_memory, gpu) have varied pricing. This simple function retrieves a cost per hour based on the instance type and multiplies by the number of hours.
- **Cost Comparison:**
  The output provides a basic comparison to help decision-makers understand the cost implications of different infrastructure choices.

In summary. choosing between on-premises, cloud, and hybrid infrastructure strategies requires a detailed analysis of cost, scalability, and vendor capabilities. Enterprises must evaluate both CapEx and OpEx, balance performance requirements with regulatory and security considerations, and carefully select vendors that meet their operational needs. By leveraging cost estimation tools and robust vendor evaluations, organizations can develop an infrastructure strategy that supports advanced NLP applications and other enterprise solutions while optimizing for efficiency, flexibility, and long-term growth.

Containerization and Microservices

Best Practices for Model Deployment Using Docker, Kubernetes, and Serverless Architectures

In today's rapidly evolving digital landscape, deploying machine learning models at scale requires a flexible, efficient, and resilient infrastructure. Containerization and microservices have emerged as essential strategies for achieving these objectives, enabling organizations to package, deploy, and manage applications consistently across diverse environments. By leveraging Docker for containerization, Kubernetes for orchestration, and serverless architectures for on-demand scalability, enterprises can optimize deployment workflows, reduce time-to-market, and enhance operational efficiency.

1. Containerization with Docker

Overview:
Docker provides a standardized platform to package applications and their dependencies into isolated containers. This ensures consistency across development, testing, and production environments, and simplifies collaboration between teams.

Best Practices:

- **Lightweight Images:**
  Use minimal base images (e.g., Alpine Linux) to reduce the container size and improve startup times.
- **Layer Caching:**
  Organize Dockerfiles to maximize the use of cached layers, reducing build times during iterative development.
- **Security:**
  Regularly update container images, limit container privileges, and scan images for vulnerabilities.
- **Environment Variables:**
  Use environment variables for configuration to make containers adaptable to different environments.

Illustrative Example: Dockerfile for a Machine Learning Model

```
# Use an official Python runtime as a parent image

FROM python:3.9-slim

# Set working directory in the container

WORKDIR /app

# Copy requirements file and install dependencies
```

```
COPY requirements.txt .
RUN pip install --no-cache-dir -r requirements.txt
# Copy the rest of the application code
COPY . .
# Expose port for the model's API server
EXPOSE 8080
# Define environment variable for production mode
ENV ENVIRONMENT production
# Command to run the model server (e.g., using Flask)
CMD ["python", "app.py"]
```

2. Orchestration with Kubernetes

Overview:
Kubernetes is a powerful container orchestration system that automates deployment, scaling, and management of containerized applications. It enables enterprises to efficiently manage large-scale deployments with features like automated rollouts, self-healing, and load balancing.

Best Practices:

- **Resource Management:**
  Define resource requests and limits to ensure optimal scheduling and performance.
- **Health Checks:**
  Implement liveness and readiness probes to monitor container health and ensure smooth rollouts.

- **Scalability:**
  Use Horizontal Pod Autoscaling (HPA) to automatically scale deployments based on load.
- **Configuration Management:**
  Externalize configuration using ConfigMaps and Secrets for secure, dynamic configuration changes.

Illustrative Example: Kubernetes Deployment YAML

```yaml
apiVersion: apps/v1
kind: Deployment
metadata:
  name: ml-model-deployment
  labels:
    app: ml-model
spec:
  replicas: 3
  selector:
    matchLabels:
      app: ml-model
  template:
    metadata:
      labels:
        app: ml-model
    spec:
```

```yaml
containers:
- name: ml-model-container
  image: your-docker-registry/ml-model:latest
  ports:
  - containerPort: 8080
  resources:
    requests:
      memory: "1Gi"
      cpu: "500m"
    limits:
      memory: "2Gi"
      cpu: "1"
  env:
  - name: ENVIRONMENT
    value: "production"
  livenessProbe:
    httpGet:
      path: /health
      port: 8080
    initialDelaySeconds: 30
    periodSeconds: 10
  readinessProbe:
```

```
        httpGet:
          path: /ready
          port: 8080
        initialDelaySeconds: 15
        periodSeconds: 5
---
apiVersion: v1
kind: Service
metadata:
  name: ml-model-service
spec:
  selector:
    app: ml-model
  ports:
  - protocol: TCP
    port: 80
    targetPort: 8080
  type: LoadBalancer
```

3. Serverless Architectures

Overview:

Serverless computing abstracts the underlying infrastructure, allowing developers to focus solely on application logic. With serverless architectures, models can scale automatically in response to demand, optimizing resource utilization and reducing operational costs.

Best Practices:

- **Container Images in Serverless:**
  Many cloud providers support deploying container images in serverless environments (e.g., AWS Lambda with container image support), offering the benefits of Docker packaging with serverless scaling.
- **Cold Start Optimization:**
  Optimize container images and minimize initialization code to reduce cold start latency.
- **Event-Driven Invocation:**
  Leverage event triggers (e.g., HTTP requests, message queues) to invoke serverless functions only when needed, ensuring cost-effective operation.

Illustrative Example: Deploying a Containerized Model on AWS Lambda

AWS Lambda now supports container images up to 10 GB in size, enabling deployment of complex machine learning models. Below is a conceptual outline of steps and a Dockerfile snippet for deploying a model using AWS Lambda:

```
# Use an official AWS Lambda Python base image

FROM public.ecr.aws/lambda/python:3.9

# Copy function code and requirements

COPY app.py ${LAMBDA_TASK_ROOT}

COPY requirements.txt ${LAMBDA_TASK_ROOT}
```

```
# Install dependencies
RUN pip install --no-cache-dir -r requirements.txt
# Set the CMD to your handler (e.g., app.lambda_handler)
CMD ["app.lambda_handler"]
```

Steps for Deployment:

1. **Build the Docker image locally.**
2. **Push the image to Amazon ECR (Elastic Container Registry).**
3. **Create or update an AWS Lambda function with the container image URI.**
4. **Configure triggers (e.g., API Gateway) to invoke the Lambda function.**

In summary, containerization, orchestration, and serverless architectures provide a robust framework for deploying enterprise-grade machine learning models. By utilizing Docker for consistent packaging, Kubernetes for scalable management, and serverless platforms for cost-efficient on-demand execution, organizations can build flexible and resilient infrastructure. These strategies not only streamline deployment workflows but also enhance operational efficiency, enabling rapid scaling and seamless integration with existing enterprise systems. Through careful planning and implementation of best practices, businesses can optimize their infrastructure and cloud strategies to support advanced NLP applications and drive sustainable growth.

Continuous Integration and Delivery (CI/CD)

Automating Testing, Rolling Out Updates, and Minimizing Downtime in Production Systems

In the realm of enterprise solutions, robust CI/CD pipelines are essential for maintaining high-quality, scalable, and resilient applications. By automating the testing, building, and deployment processes, organizations can ensure that updates are delivered seamlessly, with minimal downtime, and that production systems remain stable and secure. This approach not only accelerates innovation but also enhances collaboration among development, operations, and data science teams.

Key Components of CI/CD Pipelines

1. **Automated Testing:**
    - **Unit Testing:** Verifies the functionality of individual components.
    - **Integration Testing:** Ensures that different modules work together as expected.
    - **End-to-End Testing:** Validates the complete workflow in a production-like environment.
    - **Continuous Feedback:** Automated tests provide immediate feedback, allowing developers to detect and address issues early in the development cycle.
2. **Continuous Integration (CI):**
    - **Automated Builds:** Code changes are automatically built and compiled as soon as they are committed.
    - **Version Control Integration:** CI pipelines are typically integrated with version control systems (e.g., Git) to trigger tests and builds upon code commits.
    - **Static Analysis and Linting:** Additional automated checks help maintain code quality and adherence to best practices.

3. **Continuous Delivery/Deployment (CD):**
   - **Automated Deployments:** Successful builds are automatically deployed to staging or production environments.
   - **Rolling Updates:** Deployments are performed incrementally (e.g., using Kubernetes rolling updates) to minimize downtime.
   - **Blue/Green and Canary Deployments:** These strategies allow for safe transitions by routing a fraction of traffic to new releases before full-scale rollout.
4. **Monitoring and Rollback:**
   - **Performance Monitoring:** Continuous monitoring of deployed systems ensures that any performance issues are detected in real time.
   - **Automated Rollbacks:** If an update negatively impacts performance or introduces errors, the system can automatically revert to a previous stable version.

Illustrative Example: CI/CD Pipeline with GitHub Actions and Kubernetes

Below is a simplified example that demonstrates how to set up a CI/CD pipeline using GitHub Actions for automated testing and deployment to a Kubernetes cluster. This pipeline automates the build process, runs tests, builds a Docker image, pushes it to a container registry, and then deploys the update with a rolling update strategy.

GitHub Actions Workflow (ci-cd.yml)

```yaml
name: CI/CD Pipeline
 on:
  push:
    branches:
      - main
jobs:
  build-and-test:
    runs-on: ubuntu-latest
    steps:
    - name: Checkout Code
      uses: actions/checkout@v3
    - name: Set up Python
      uses: actions/setup-python@v3
      with:
        python-version: "3.9"
    - name: Install Dependencies
      run: |
        python -m pip install --upgrade pip
        pip install -r requirements.txt
    - name: Run Unit Tests
```

```
      run: |
        pytest --maxfail=1 --disable-warnings -q
    - name: Build Docker Image
      run: |
        docker build -t your-docker-registry/ml-model:${{
github.sha }} .
    - name: Log in to Docker Hub
      run: echo "${{ secrets.DOCKER_PASSWORD }}" | docker
login -u "${{ secrets.DOCKER_USERNAME }}" --password-
stdin
    - name: Push Docker Image
      run: |
        docker push your-docker-registry/ml-model:${{ github.sha
}}
  deploy:
    runs-on: ubuntu-latest
    needs: build-and-test
    steps:
    - name: Checkout Code
      uses: actions/checkout@v3
    - name: Set up kubectl
      uses: azure/setup-kubectl@v3
      with:
        version: 'latest'
```

```
  - name: Deploy to Kubernetes
    env:
      IMAGE_TAG: ${{ github.sha }}
    run: |
      # Update Kubernetes deployment with new image tag
      kubectl set image deployment/ml-model-deployment ml-model-container=your-docker-registry/ml-model:${IMAGE_TAG} --record
      # Monitor rollout status
      kubectl rollout status deployment/ml-model-deployment
```

Kubernetes Deployment YAML (deployment.yaml)

```
apiVersion: apps/v1
kind: Deployment
metadata:
  name: ml-model-deployment
  labels:
    app: ml-model
spec:
  replicas: 3
  selector:
```

```
    matchLabels:
      app: ml-model
  template:
    metadata:
      labels:
        app: ml-model
    spec:
      containers:
      - name: ml-model-container
        image: your-docker-registry/ml-model:latest
        ports:
        - containerPort: 8080
        resources:
          requests:
            cpu: "500m"
            memory: "1Gi"
          limits:
            cpu: "1"
            memory: "2Gi"
        livenessProbe:
          httpGet:
            path: /health
```

```
      port: 8080
    initialDelaySeconds: 30
    periodSeconds: 10
  readinessProbe:
    httpGet:
      path: /ready
      port: 8080
    initialDelaySeconds: 15
    periodSeconds: 5
```

Explanation:

- **Automated Testing:**
  The GitHub Actions workflow checks out the code, sets up Python, installs dependencies, and runs unit tests using pytest. This ensures that only code that passes all tests proceeds to the build stage.
- **Docker Image Build and Push:**
  After passing tests, the workflow builds a Docker image tagged with the commit SHA, logs in to Docker Hub (or another registry), and pushes the image.
- **Kubernetes Deployment:**
  The deployment job sets up kubectl and updates the Kubernetes deployment with the new image. The kubectl set image command performs a rolling update, ensuring zero downtime by gradually replacing the old pods with the new ones.

- **Health Probes:**
  Liveness and readiness probes in the Kubernetes deployment help maintain stability during updates by ensuring that only healthy pods receive traffic.

Conclusion

Implementing a robust CI/CD pipeline is crucial for the continuous integration, delivery, and maintenance of enterprise NLP and machine learning models. By leveraging containerization with Docker, orchestration with Kubernetes, and automating workflows using tools like GitHub Actions, organizations can minimize downtime, accelerate deployment cycles, and ensure high-quality, reliable updates. This strategic approach not only improves operational efficiency but also supports rapid innovation and scalability in a dynamic production environment.

Chapter 15: Workflow Orchestration and Pipeline Management

Enterprise Data Pipelines

From Ingestion to Insight with ETL Best Practices

In modern enterprises, the journey from raw data to actionable insights is driven by robust data pipelines. These pipelines ensure that data flows seamlessly from various sources, through extraction, transformation, and loading (ETL) processes, to finally deliver insights that inform business decisions. Effective pipeline management is key to maintaining data quality, ensuring compliance, and enabling real-time analytics across the organization.

1. Data Ingestion

Overview:

- **Sources:**
  Data can originate from multiple sources including databases, APIs, logs, IoT devices, and external data feeds.
- **Challenges:**
  Ingestion must handle diverse formats (structured, semi-structured, and unstructured) and ensure that data is captured reliably and in near real-time.
- **Tools:**
  Common tools include Apache Kafka for real-time ingestion, Apache NiFi for data routing and transformation, and cloud-based services like AWS Kinesis or Azure Event Hubs.

Best Practices:

- **Scalability:**
  Use distributed ingestion frameworks that can scale horizontally to handle increasing data volumes.

- **Data Quality Checks:**
  Validate and clean data as it enters the pipeline to prevent downstream issues.
- **Security:**
  Encrypt data in transit and apply strict access controls to ensure compliance with privacy regulations.

2. Data Transformation

Overview:

- **ETL Process:**
  After ingestion, data is transformed into a usable format. This process involves extracting relevant data, transforming it by cleaning, normalizing, aggregating, and enriching, and finally loading it into storage or analytical systems.
- **Transformation Engines:**
  Tools such as Apache Spark, Apache Beam, and cloud services like AWS Glue or Azure Data Factory provide scalable transformation capabilities.

Best Practices:

- **Automation:**
  Automate transformation tasks to ensure consistency and reduce manual errors.
- **Modularity:**
  Design transformation processes as modular components that can be independently updated or reused.
- **Error Handling:**
  Implement robust error detection and logging to ensure that any issues are quickly identified and resolved.

3. Data Loading and Insight Generation

Overview:

- **Storage:**
  Transformed data is loaded into data warehouses, data lakes, or specialized analytics databases (e.g., Amazon Redshift, Google BigQuery, Snowflake).

- **Analytics:**
  Once the data is loaded, it can be used for business intelligence, machine learning models, and real-time dashboards to drive insights and decision-making.

Best Practices:

- **Performance:**
  Optimize loading processes to minimize latency, ensuring that insights are derived from the most current data.

- **Data Governance:**
  Implement data versioning, lineage tracking, and metadata management to maintain high data quality and regulatory compliance.

- **Scalability:**
  Choose storage solutions that scale with data growth and support both batch and streaming analytics.

4. Workflow Orchestration and Pipeline Management

Overview:

- **Workflow Orchestration:**
  Tools like Apache Airflow, Prefect, or cloud-native services (e.g., AWS Step Functions) help automate and manage the complex workflows in data pipelines.

- **Pipeline Management:**
  Monitoring, scheduling, and error recovery are critical for ensuring that data flows smoothly from ingestion to insight. A well-orchestrated pipeline allows teams to focus on analysis rather than operational challenges.

Best Practices:

- **Scheduling:**
  Define clear schedules for data ingestion, transformation, and loading, balancing real-time and batch processing requirements.
- **Monitoring and Alerts:**
  Use monitoring tools and dashboards to track pipeline performance and set up alerts for any failures or performance degradations.
- **Version Control:**
  Maintain version control over pipeline code and configuration to support reproducibility and iterative improvements.

Illustrative Example: A Simple ETL Pipeline in Python

Below is an example of a basic ETL pipeline using Python and Pandas. This pipeline ingests CSV data, performs transformations, and loads the transformed data into a target storage (in this case, another CSV file, which can be substituted with a database or data lake in production).

```
import pandas as pd

import numpy as np

import os

# Step 1: Data Ingestion

def ingest_data(file_path):
```

```
    """
    Reads data from a CSV file into a Pandas DataFrame.
    """
    try:
        df = pd.read_csv(file_path)
        print("Data ingested successfully.")
        return df
    except Exception as e:
        print("Error ingesting data:", e)
        return None
# Step 2: Data Transformation
def transform_data(df):
    """
    Perform data cleaning and transformation:
    - Handle missing values
    - Normalize column names
    - Create new calculated features
    """
    # Remove duplicates and fill missing values
    df = df.drop_duplicates().fillna(method='ffill')
    # Normalize column names
    df.columns = [col.strip().lower().replace(" ", "_") for col in
df.columns]
```

```
    # Create a new feature, e.g., log transformation of a
numerical column
    if 'sales' in df.columns:
        df['log_sales'] = np.log1p(df['sales'])
    print("Data transformation complete.")
    return df
# Step 3: Data Loading
def load_data(df, target_path):
    """
    Load the transformed data into a CSV file (or any target
storage).
    """
    try:
        df.to_csv(target_path, index=False)
        print("Data loaded successfully to", target_path)
    except Exception as e:
        print("Error loading data:", e)

# Main ETL Pipeline Execution
if __name__ == "__main__":
    source_file = "raw_sales_data.csv"  # Example source CSV
file
    target_file = "transformed_sales_data.csv"
```

```
# Ensure the source file exists (for demonstration purposes)
if os.path.exists(source_file):
    # Ingest data
    raw_df = ingest_data(source_file)
    if raw_df is not None:
        # Transform data
        transformed_df = transform_data(raw_df)
        # Load data
        load_data(transformed_df, target_file)
else:
    print(f"Source file '{source_file}' not found.")
```

Explanation:

- **Ingestion:**
  The ingest_data() function reads raw CSV data into a Pandas DataFrame, handling basic file I/O.
- **Transformation:**
  The transform_data() function cleans the data by removing duplicates, filling missing values, normalizing column names, and adding a calculated feature (e.g., log transformation of sales data).
- **Loading:**
  The load_data() function writes the transformed DataFrame to a new CSV file, which can be replaced by database insertion commands or API calls to data lakes in a production scenario.

- **Pipeline Management:**
  This ETL pipeline can be orchestrated using tools like Apache Airflow for scheduling, monitoring, and handling dependencies between tasks in a production environment.

In summary, a well-designed enterprise data pipeline is the backbone of any data-driven organization. By integrating robust ETL processes with effective workflow orchestration and pipeline management, companies can ensure that data flows seamlessly from ingestion to insight. This approach not only optimizes operational efficiency and supports real-time analytics but also facilitates compliance, scalability, and continuous improvement in a rapidly evolving digital landscape. Adopting industry best practices and leveraging modern tools and frameworks will enable enterprises to turn raw data into strategic assets that drive informed decision-making and sustainable growth.

Model Orchestration

Managing Model Ensembles, Parallelized Inference, and Real-Time Decision Frameworks

In enterprise deployments, it's common to rely on multiple machine learning models that complement each other in delivering accurate predictions and robust decision-making. Model orchestration involves managing these model ensembles, coordinating parallelized inference across multiple nodes or containers, and integrating real-time decision frameworks to drive immediate, data-driven actions. This approach ensures scalability, fault tolerance, and efficient use of computational resources.

1. Managing Model Ensembles

Overview:
Model ensembles combine predictions from multiple models to improve overall performance and robustness. Ensemble strategies such as bagging, boosting, and stacking reduce the variance and bias of individual models and often yield superior predictive accuracy.

Best Practices:

- **Diversity of Models:**
  Combine models with different architectures or training methodologies to capture a wider range of patterns.

- **Weighted Averaging or Voting:**
  Aggregate predictions by weighting models based on their performance or using majority voting schemes.

- **Monitoring and Updating:**
  Continuously monitor ensemble performance and update individual models as needed to adapt to new data.

2. Parallelized Inference

Overview:
Parallelized inference involves running multiple models simultaneously on different hardware or within distributed environments. This approach minimizes latency and improves throughput, which is crucial for real-time applications.

Best Practices:

- **Concurrency Frameworks:**
  Utilize Python's concurrency frameworks (e.g., concurrent.futures, asyncio) to dispatch parallel inference tasks.

- **Container Orchestration:**
  Deploy inference services in containers using orchestration tools (e.g., Kubernetes) to ensure efficient resource utilization and scalability.

- **Load Balancing:**
  Distribute incoming requests evenly across available resources to prevent bottlenecks.

3. Real-Time Decision Frameworks

Overview:
Real-time decision frameworks integrate model predictions into business workflows instantly, enabling applications such as fraud detection, dynamic pricing, and personalized recommendations. This requires robust API endpoints, low-latency processing, and integration with event-driven architectures.

Best Practices:

- **API Gateways:**
  Use API gateways to manage and secure access to inference endpoints.
- **Stream Processing:**
  Integrate with real-time data streaming platforms (e.g., Apache Kafka, AWS Kinesis) to trigger model inference on new data events.
- **Fallback Mechanisms:**
  Implement fallback strategies (e.g., reverting to a previous model version) in case of model failures or performance degradation.

Illustrative Example: Parallelized Inference with Model Ensembles

The following Python example demonstrates how to orchestrate multiple models in parallel using the concurrent.futures module. In this example, we simulate three different models (which could represent diverse architectures or ensemble members) and combine their predictions using a simple weighted average.

```
import concurrent.futures

import numpy as np
```

```
# Dummy model prediction functions
def model_predict_1(input_data):
    # Simulate model processing
    return np.array([0.7, 0.3])  # Example: [probability_positive, probability_negative]
def model_predict_2(input_data):
    return np.array([0.6, 0.4])
def model_predict_3(input_data):
    return np.array([0.8, 0.2])
# Function to perform ensemble prediction using parallelized inference
def ensemble_predict(input_data, weights=None):
    # List of model prediction functions
    models = [model_predict_1, model_predict_2, model_predict_3]
    # Default equal weights if none provided
    if weights is None:
        weights = [1/len(models)] * len(models)
    # Use ThreadPoolExecutor to run model predictions in parallel
    with concurrent.futures.ThreadPoolExecutor() as executor:
        # Dispatch each model prediction as a separate task
        future_to_model = {executor.submit(model, input_data): model for model in models}
```

```
        predictions = []
        for future in concurrent.futures.as_completed(future_to_model):
            prediction = future.result()
            predictions.append(prediction)
    # Combine predictions using a weighted average
    predictions = np.array(predictions)
    ensemble_prediction = np.average(predictions, axis=0, weights=weights)
    return ensemble_prediction
# Example input data (could be preprocessed text, embeddings, etc.)
input_data = "Sample input for inference."
# Perform ensemble prediction
final_prediction = ensemble_predict(input_data)
print("Ensemble Prediction (Probabilities):", final_prediction)
print("Predicted Class:", "Positive" if final_prediction[0] > final_prediction[1] else "Negative")
```

Explanation:

- **Model Simulation:**
  Three dummy model functions (model_predict_1, model_predict_2, and model_predict_3) simulate predictions as probability distributions.

- **Parallel Inference:**
  The ensemble_predict function uses ThreadPoolExecutor to run these predictions concurrently, reducing overall inference latency.

- **Weighted Aggregation:**
  The predictions from each model are aggregated using a weighted average (defaulting to equal weights) to form the final ensemble prediction.

- **Real-Time Integration:**
  Such an orchestration framework can be integrated into an API endpoint to deliver real-time decisions in production systems.

In summary, model orchestration, encompassing the management of model ensembles, parallelized inference, and real-time decision frameworks, is a critical aspect of deploying enterprise-level AI solutions. By leveraging containerized environments, concurrency frameworks, and efficient orchestration tools, organizations can achieve high-performance, scalable, and resilient deployments. This approach not only improves response times and operational efficiency but also ensures that decision-making processes are robust, transparent, and adaptable to evolving business needs.

Monitoring and Alerting

Tracking Key Operational Metrics for Robust Performance

In enterprise data pipelines and model deployments, continuous monitoring and alerting are essential to ensure that systems perform reliably under varying loads. Monitoring enables teams to track critical operational metrics such as latency, throughput, error rates, and resource utilization. Effective alerting mechanisms provide early warnings of performance degradation, allowing for proactive intervention before issues impact business operations.

Key Metrics to Monitor

- **Latency:**
  Measures the time taken to process individual requests or tasks. High latency can indicate performance bottlenecks or system overloads.
- **Throughput:**
  Indicates the number of requests or tasks processed per unit time. Consistent throughput levels are crucial for scaling operations, especially in real-time applications.
- **Error Rates:**
  Tracks the frequency of errors or failures in the pipeline. Rising error rates can signal issues in data quality, model performance, or infrastructure reliability.
- **Resource Utilization:**
  Monitors CPU, memory, and network usage to ensure that resources are efficiently allocated and scaled to meet demand.

Best Practices for Monitoring and Alerting

1. **Implement Real-Time Monitoring:**
   Use monitoring frameworks such as Prometheus to collect metrics from your applications and infrastructure in real time.
2. **Set Up Dashboards:**
   Tools like Grafana can visualize key metrics, providing a comprehensive view of system performance at a glance.
3. **Define Alerting Thresholds:**
   Establish thresholds for critical metrics (e.g., latency above a certain value, throughput dropping below expected levels) to trigger alerts.
4. **Automate Alerting:**
   Integrate with notification systems (e.g., Slack, email, PagerDuty)

to ensure that relevant teams are immediately informed of any issues.

5. **Continuous Improvement:**
   Regularly review monitoring data to identify trends and areas for optimization, adjusting thresholds and scaling strategies as necessary.

Illustrative Example: Monitoring with Prometheus in Python

The following Python example demonstrates how to integrate basic monitoring into an application using the prometheus_client library. This script simulates a service processing requests, tracks latency using a histogram, and counts the total number of requests with a counter. The metrics are exposed via an HTTP endpoint that can be scraped by Prometheus.

```
from prometheus_client import start_http_server, Counter, Histogram

import time

import random

# Create a counter for the total number of processed requests

REQUEST_COUNTER = Counter('requests_total', 'Total number of requests processed')

# Create a histogram to measure request latency

REQUEST_LATENCY = Histogram('request_latency_seconds', 'Request latency in seconds')

def process_request():

    """
```

```
    Simulate processing a request by sleeping for a random time.
    """
    processing_time = random.uniform(0.1, 1.0)  # Simulate
latency between 0.1 and 1.0 seconds
    time.sleep(processing_time)
    return processing_time
if __name__ == '__main__':
    # Start the Prometheus HTTP server to expose metrics on
port 8000
    start_http_server(8000)
    print("Prometheus metrics available at
http://localhost:8000")
    # Continuously process requests
    while True:
        start_time = time.time()
        latency = process_request()
        REQUEST_COUNTER.inc()          # Increment the
request counter
        REQUEST_LATENCY.observe(latency)  # Record the
latency of the request
        print(f"Processed request in {latency:.2f} seconds")
```

Explanation:

- **Metrics Collection:**
    - A **counter** (REQUEST_COUNTER) tracks the total number of requests processed.
    - A **histogram** (REQUEST_LATENCY) measures the latency of each request.
- **Simulated Request Processing:**
  The process_request() function simulates processing by sleeping for a random duration, representing variable response times.
- **HTTP Metrics Endpoint:**
  The start_http_server(8000) call starts a lightweight HTTP server that exposes the collected metrics. Prometheus can be configured to scrape this endpoint at regular intervals.
- **Real-Time Monitoring:**
  As the application processes requests, metrics are continuously updated. These metrics can be visualized in dashboards (e.g., Grafana) and used to trigger alerts if thresholds are exceeded.

Conclusion

Continuous monitoring and alerting are vital components of enterprise workflow orchestration and pipeline management. By systematically tracking metrics such as latency and throughput, organizations can detect performance issues early, minimize downtime, and ensure that production systems operate at peak efficiency under load. Integrating monitoring tools like Prometheus with alerting frameworks enables proactive management and rapid response, ultimately driving improved operational resilience and business continuity.

Chapter 16: Scalability and Performance Optimization

High-Performance Hardware

GPU vs. TPU, Memory Constraints, and Distributed Computing for Large-Scale NLP

As enterprises scale their NLP applications to process massive datasets and support real-time decision-making, investing in high-performance hardware becomes imperative. Leveraging GPUs and TPUs, optimizing memory usage, and adopting distributed computing architectures are key strategies to ensure that models are both efficient and scalable.

1. GPUs vs. TPUs

Graphics Processing Units (GPUs):

- **Advantages:**
  - **Flexibility:** GPUs are widely used, supported by numerous deep learning frameworks (e.g., TensorFlow, PyTorch), and excel at handling diverse computational tasks.
  - **Mature Ecosystem:** A rich ecosystem of libraries, tools, and community support makes GPUs a reliable choice.
  - **Cost-Effective:** Often more readily available and less expensive compared to TPUs for many workloads.
- **Considerations:**
  - **Memory Constraints:** GPUs have limited memory capacity, which may necessitate careful batch size management or model parallelism for very large models.
  - **Scalability:** While effective for single-node training, scaling across multiple GPUs requires additional orchestration (e.g., NVIDIA NCCL, Horovod).

Tensor Processing Units (TPUs):

- **Advantages:**
  - **High Throughput:** TPUs are specifically optimized for tensor operations, offering significant speed improvements in training large transformer models.
  - **Scalability:** Designed for massive parallelism, TPUs facilitate distributed training over large clusters, which is ideal for extremely large datasets and models.
- **Considerations:**
  - **Ecosystem:** TPUs are primarily supported within the TensorFlow ecosystem (although frameworks like PyTorch have made strides with XLA support).
  - **Availability:** TPUs are typically accessed via cloud services (e.g., Google Cloud Platform) and may involve higher costs for continuous, large-scale usage.

2. Memory Constraints and Optimization

Managing memory is crucial when deploying large NLP models:

- **Batch Size Tuning:**
  Optimize batch sizes to maximize throughput without exceeding GPU/TPU memory limits.
- **Gradient Accumulation:**
  Use gradient accumulation to simulate larger batch sizes when hardware constraints prevent processing very large batches in a single forward-backward pass.
- **Mixed Precision Training:**
  Leverage mixed precision (e.g., FP16) to reduce memory footprint and accelerate training, while maintaining model accuracy.

3. Distributed Computing for Large-Scale NLP

Distributed computing frameworks enable scaling training and inference across multiple devices:

- **Data Parallelism:**
  Distribute data across multiple GPUs/TPUs, each computing gradients on a subset of data, then aggregate gradients for synchronized updates.
- **Model Parallelism:**
  Split a large model across multiple devices, particularly useful when a single device's memory is insufficient.
- **Frameworks and Tools:**
  - **Horovod:** Simplifies distributed training across multiple GPUs/TPUs.
  - **PyTorch Distributed Data Parallel (DDP):** Offers native support in PyTorch for parallelizing training.
  - **TensorFlow Distributed Strategies:** Provides strategies such as MirroredStrategy and TPUStrategy for scaling training across devices.

Illustrative Example: Distributed Training with PyTorch DDP

Below is an example of using PyTorch's Distributed Data Parallel (DDP) to train a model on multiple GPUs. This example demonstrates setting up a distributed environment and training a simple model in parallel.

```
import os

import torch

import torch.distributed as dist
```

```
import torch.nn as nn
import torch.optim as optim
from torch.nn.parallel import DistributedDataParallel as DDP
from torch.utils.data import DataLoader, TensorDataset
def setup(rank, world_size):
    # Initialize the distributed environment.
    os.environ['MASTER_ADDR'] = 'localhost'
    os.environ['MASTER_PORT'] = '12355'
    dist.init_process_group("nccl", rank=rank,
world_size=world_size)
def cleanup():
    dist.destroy_process_group()
class SimpleModel(nn.Module):
    def __init__(self, input_size, num_classes):
        super(SimpleModel, self).__init__()
        self.fc = nn.Linear(input_size, num_classes)
       def forward(self, x):
        return self.fc(x)
def train(rank, world_size):
    setup(rank, world_size)
    # Create synthetic data
    input_size = 100
    num_classes = 2
```

```
dataset_size = 1000
X = torch.randn(dataset_size, input_size)
y = torch.randint(0, num_classes, (dataset_size,))
dataset = TensorDataset(X, y)
# Create DistributedSampler and DataLoader
sampler =
torch.utils.data.distributed.DistributedSampler(dataset,
num_replicas=world_size, rank=rank)
dataloader = DataLoader(dataset, batch_size=32,
sampler=sampler)
# Set up the model, loss function, and optimizer
model = SimpleModel(input_size, num_classes).to(rank)
ddp_model = DDP(model, device_ids=[rank])
criterion = nn.CrossEntropyLoss()
optimizer = optim.Adam(ddp_model.parameters(), lr=0.001)
# Training loop
num_epochs = 5
for epoch in range(num_epochs):
    sampler.set_epoch(epoch)
    for batch_idx, (data, target) in enumerate(dataloader):
        data, target = data.to(rank), target.to(rank)
        optimizer.zero_grad()
        outputs = ddp_model(data)
```

```
        loss = criterion(outputs, target)
        loss.backward()
        optimizer.step()
        if batch_idx % 10 == 0:
            print(f"Rank {rank}, Epoch [{epoch+1}/{num_epochs}], Batch [{batch_idx}], Loss: {loss.item():.4f}")
    cleanup()
if __name__ == "__main__":
    world_size = 2  # Number of GPUs available
    torch.multiprocessing.spawn(train, args=(world_size,), nprocs=world_size, join=True)
```

Explanation:

- **Distributed Setup:**
  The setup() function initializes the distributed environment using NCCL (recommended for GPUs).
- **Data Preparation:**
  Synthetic data is created and distributed using DistributedSampler, ensuring that each process receives a unique subset of data.
- **Model Definition:**
  A simple linear model is defined and wrapped with DDP to handle gradient synchronization across processes.
- **Training Loop:**
  The model is trained in parallel, with each GPU processing its

subset of data, and gradients aggregated to update the model consistently.

- **Cleanup:**
  After training, the distributed process group is properly destroyed to free resources.

In summary, for enterprise-scale NLP applications, the choice of high-performance hardware - whether GPUs, TPUs, or a combination through distributed computing - directly impacts scalability and performance. By optimizing memory usage, employing distributed training strategies, and leveraging modern hardware accelerators, organizations can significantly reduce training times and support real-time inference at scale. Tools like PyTorch's DDP facilitate the efficient distribution of workloads, ensuring that large-scale NLP deployments are robust, cost-effective, and ready to meet the demands of a dynamic business environment.

Latency Minimization Strategies

Batch Processing vs. Streaming, Caching Mechanisms, and Approximate Nearest-Neighbor Search

In enterprise NLP deployments, minimizing latency is crucial for delivering fast and reliable insights. Optimizing for low-latency environments involves multiple strategies - from choosing the appropriate data processing paradigm to implementing effective caching and leveraging approximate nearest-neighbor (ANN) search for rapid similarity computations. Below, we detail these strategies and provide code examples to illustrate their implementation.

1. Batch Processing vs. Streaming

Batch Processing:

- **Overview:**
  Batch processing involves collecting data over a period and processing it all at once. This approach is typically used for non-

time-sensitive tasks such as offline model training, periodic reporting, or aggregating large datasets.

- **Advantages:**
    - Efficient for processing large volumes of data.
    - Suitable for complex transformations that can be performed offline.
- **Limitations:**
    - Introduces delays as data must be collected before processing.
    - Not ideal for real-time applications where immediate response is required.

Streaming:

- **Overview:**
  Streaming processes data in real-time as it arrives. This paradigm is essential for applications requiring instantaneous insights, such as real-time sentiment analysis, fraud detection, or dynamic pricing.
- **Advantages:**
    - Provides near real-time processing and response.
    - Enables continuous monitoring and immediate decision-making.
- **Limitations:**
    - Requires more sophisticated infrastructure to handle continuous data flows.
    - Often involves trade-offs in terms of processing complexity and state management.

Illustrative Example: Batch vs. Streaming in Python

Below is a simplified demonstration using Python. In a real-world scenario, frameworks such as Apache Spark or Apache Flink would be used, but here we provide a conceptual illustration.

```
# Batch Processing Example: Aggregating Sentiment Scores

import pandas as pd

# Simulate a batch of sentiment scores collected over a day

data = {'timestamp': pd.date_range("2023-01-01", periods=5,
freq='H'),

        'sentiment_score': [0.1, 0.3, 0.2, 0.5, 0.4]}

batch_df = pd.DataFrame(data)

batch_result = batch_df['sentiment_score'].mean()

print("Batch Processing - Average Sentiment Score:",
batch_result)

# Streaming Example: Processing Real-Time Data

import time

import random

def process_stream():

   # Simulate streaming data by generating sentiment scores
every second

   while True:

      sentiment_score = random.uniform(0, 1)
```

```
    print(f"Real-Time Sentiment Score:
{sentiment_score:.2f}")

    time.sleep(1)

# Uncomment the following line to run the streaming example (will run indefinitely)

# process_stream()
```

2. Caching Mechanisms

Overview:
Caching reduces latency by storing frequently accessed data or computation results in fast-access storage (memory). This approach is particularly useful for repeated operations, such as querying precomputed embeddings or model predictions.

Techniques:

- In-Memory Caching:
  Utilize caching libraries (e.g., Python's functools.lru_cache) to cache function outputs.
- Distributed Caching:
  For large-scale systems, use distributed caches (e.g., Redis, Memcached) to store data across multiple nodes.

Illustrative Example: Caching with lru_cache

```
from functools import lru_cache

import time

@lru_cache(maxsize=128)

def compute_heavy_operation(x):
```

```
    # Simulate a heavy computation
    time.sleep(2)
    return x * x
# The first call will take 2 seconds
start = time.time()
print("Result:", compute_heavy_operation(10))
print("Time taken:", time.time() - start, "seconds")
# The second call with the same argument will be almost instantaneous due to caching
start = time.time()
print("Result:", compute_heavy_operation(10))
print("Time taken:", time.time() - start, "seconds")
```

3. Approximate Nearest-Neighbor Search

Overview:
In NLP, tasks such as semantic search or recommendation often require finding the most similar items among large collections of vectors (e.g., word embeddings). Approximate nearest-neighbor (ANN) search algorithms accelerate this process by trading a small amount of accuracy for substantial gains in speed.

Techniques:

- **ANN Libraries:**
  Tools like Facebook's FAISS, Annoy, or HNSWlib are widely used for efficient similarity search.

- **Trade-offs:**
  ANN methods reduce search latency dramatically while maintaining acceptable levels of accuracy, making them suitable for real-time applications.

Illustrative Example: Using FAISS for ANN Search

Below is a basic example using FAISS to perform an approximate nearest-neighbor search on a set of synthetic embeddings.

```
import numpy as np

import faiss

# Generate synthetic embeddings (e.g., 1000 vectors of dimension 128)

d = 128  # dimension

nb = 1000  # number of vectors in the database

np.random.seed(42)

data = np.random.random((nb, d)).astype('float32')

# Build the FAISS index (using IndexFlatL2 for simplicity, though more complex indices exist)

index = faiss.IndexFlatL2(d)

index.add(data)  # add vectors to the index

# Query: Find the 5 nearest neighbors for a random vector

query_vector = np.random.random((1, d)).astype('float32')

k = 5  # number of nearest neighbors

distances, indices = index.search(query_vector, k)
```

```
print("Query Vector:", query_vector)
print("Nearest Neighbors Indices:", indices)
print("Distances:", distances)
```

In summary, latency minimization in enterprise NLP systems is achieved through a combination of data processing paradigms, caching strategies, and efficient search algorithms. Batch processing suits non-real-time applications, while streaming is ideal for instant responses. Caching reduces repeated computation delays, and approximate nearest-neighbor search accelerates similarity-based queries in large datasets. By employing these strategies, organizations can ensure that their systems deliver fast, scalable, and high-performance solutions even under heavy loads.

Cost Management

Balancing Computational Intensity with Corporate Financial Objectives

In large-scale enterprise deployments of NLP and machine learning models, achieving high performance often comes with significant computational costs. Cost management is critical to ensure that technological investments align with corporate financial objectives, maintain scalability, and maximize ROI. This involves careful planning, monitoring, and optimization of resources across hardware, software, and operational processes. Below are key strategies and techniques for effective cost management.

1. Cost Analysis and Budgeting

Overview:
A thorough cost analysis is the foundation of effective cost management. Enterprises need to evaluate both the upfront capital expenditures (CapEx) and ongoing operational expenditures (OpEx)

associated with various deployment strategies—whether on-premises, cloud-based, or hybrid solutions.

- **CapEx vs. OpEx:**
    - **On-Premises:** Requires significant initial investment in hardware and infrastructure, but may lower long-term operational costs.
    - **Cloud-Based:** Uses a pay-as-you-go model, shifting costs to operational expenses that can scale with demand.
    - **Hybrid:** Combines both models to optimize performance and cost based on workload and data sensitivity.
- **Total Cost of Ownership (TCO):**
  Consider all associated costs including maintenance, energy, personnel, and potential downtime.

2. Resource Optimization

Efficient Use of Hardware:
Optimizing the use of high-performance hardware (GPUs, TPUs) and leveraging distributed computing frameworks can drastically reduce computational costs.

- **Mixed Precision Training:**
  Using mixed precision (e.g., FP16) reduces memory usage and speeds up computation without sacrificing accuracy.
- **Dynamic Scaling:**
  Implement auto-scaling policies in cloud environments to match resource usage with demand. Scale down during off-peak times to save costs.
- **Efficient Model Architecture:**
  Choose model architectures that balance performance with computational efficiency. For example, consider lightweight

models or model distillation techniques to reduce resource requirements.

3. Workflow Automation and Cost Tracking

Automated CI/CD and Monitoring:
Integrate cost tracking into your CI/CD pipelines and deployment workflows. Automated testing and deployment systems can be configured to monitor resource usage and provide cost analytics.

- **Cost Estimation Tools:**
  Use cloud cost management tools (e.g., AWS Cost Explorer, Google Cloud's Cost Management) to monitor spending in real time.

- **Custom Metrics and Alerts:**
  Set up custom alerts to notify when spending approaches thresholds or when computational efficiency metrics drop.

4. Example: Cost Estimation and Resource Optimization with Python

The following Python code snippet demonstrates a basic approach to estimating cloud compute costs based on instance type and usage hours. This script can be integrated into a broader cost tracking system to provide real-time estimates and support decision-making.

```
def estimate_compute_costs(instance_hours,
instance_type="standard", region="us-east-1"):

   """

   Estimate the cloud compute costs based on usage hours and
instance type.

   Pricing is illustrative and should be replaced with real pricing
data from your cloud provider.
```

```
    """
    # Example pricing (USD per hour) for demonstration purposes
    pricing = {
        "standard": 0.10,      # Standard instance price per hour
        "high_memory": 0.20,   # High-memory instance price per hour
        "gpu": 0.90,           # GPU-enabled instance price per hour
        "tpu": 4.00            # TPU instance price per hour
    }
    # Retrieve cost per hour for the instance type
    cost_per_hour = pricing.get(instance_type, 0.10)
    # Total estimated cost
    total_cost = instance_hours * cost_per_hour
    return total_cost
# Example usage:
instance_hours = 720  # Example: one month of continuous usage (30 days * 24 hours)
cost_standard = estimate_compute_costs(instance_hours, instance_type="standard")
cost_gpu = estimate_compute_costs(instance_hours, instance_type="gpu")
print("Estimated Monthly Costs:")
print(f"Standard Instance: ${cost_standard:.2f}")
```

```
print(f"GPU-Enabled Instance: ${cost_gpu:.2f}")
```

Explanation:

- **Instance Hours:**
  The function estimate_compute_costs calculates the total cost based on the number of hours an instance is used.
- **Pricing Dictionary:**
  A simple pricing dictionary maps different instance types to their hourly cost. In production, these values should be updated with the latest pricing from your cloud provider.
- **Cost Calculation:**
  The script multiplies instance hours by the cost per hour to provide a cost estimate, helping decision-makers compare different resource configurations.

5. Strategic Considerations

- **Workload Characterization:**
  Understand the specific computational requirements of your NLP workloads. For instance, training large transformer models might justify the higher cost of GPU/TPU resources, whereas inference workloads may be optimized with serverless architectures and auto-scaling.
- **Cost-Performance Trade-offs:**
  Perform regular benchmarking and performance evaluations to ensure that cost reductions do not significantly impact model accuracy or user experience.
- **Vendor Negotiations:**
  Explore options for reserved instances, volume discounts, or long-term contracts with cloud providers to further reduce costs.

- **Continuous Monitoring and Optimization:** Incorporate cost management as part of your continuous improvement process. Regularly review usage data, update resource configurations, and refine scaling policies to ensure optimal spending.

Conclusion

Balancing computational intensity with corporate financial objectives requires a multi-faceted cost management strategy that spans resource optimization, workflow automation, and real-time cost tracking. By employing techniques such as mixed precision training, dynamic scaling, and distributed cost estimation, enterprises can effectively manage expenses while maintaining high performance and scalability in their NLP deployments. This strategic approach ensures that technological advancements align with financial goals, enabling sustainable innovation and competitive advantage.

Chapter 17: Project Management

Building the NLP Center of Excellence

Organizational Structure, Skill Sets, and Team Composition for Sustained NLP Innovation

In today's competitive business environment, establishing an NLP Center of Excellence (CoE) is a strategic imperative for driving innovation, operational efficiency, and data-driven decision-making. A well-structured NLP CoE serves as a centralized hub that fosters collaboration across cross-functional teams, standardizes best practices, and accelerates the deployment of advanced NLP solutions across the enterprise.

1. Organizational Structure

A successful NLP CoE is typically composed of various interconnected teams that work collaboratively to cover the entire lifecycle of NLP initiatives—from research and development to production deployment and continuous improvement. The organizational structure should include:

- **Executive Sponsorship:**
  Senior leadership to champion NLP initiatives and align them with corporate strategy and ROI objectives.
- **NLP CoE Director:**
  A leader responsible for strategic vision, governance, and coordination across teams. This role acts as the liaison between the CoE and business units.
- **Cross-Functional Teams:**
  - **Data Scientists and NLP Researchers:**
    Develop and refine algorithms, conduct experiments, and push the boundaries of state-of-the-art techniques.

  - **NLP Engineers:**
    Focus on model development, integration, and optimization, ensuring that research outputs are translated into scalable production solutions.
  - **Software and DevOps Engineers:**
    Build the underlying infrastructure, manage deployment pipelines, and maintain operational stability.
  - **Product Managers:**
    Align NLP initiatives with business goals, manage project lifecycles, and prioritize features based on stakeholder needs.
  - **Quality Assurance and Compliance Specialists:**
    Ensure models meet ethical, regulatory, and performance standards, focusing on explainability, fairness, and data privacy.

2. Skill Sets and Team Composition

Core Competencies:

- **Technical Expertise:**
  Team members should have strong backgrounds in machine learning, deep learning, and NLP methodologies. Proficiency in programming languages (e.g., Python) and frameworks (e.g., TensorFlow, PyTorch) is essential.
- **Data Engineering and Pipeline Management:**
  Skills in data ingestion, cleaning, transformation, and orchestration (using tools like Apache Spark, Kafka, or cloud services) are critical to support scalable NLP solutions.
- **Model Deployment and Operations:**
  Expertise in containerization (Docker), orchestration (Kubernetes), CI/CD, and monitoring frameworks ensures that NLP models can be reliably deployed and maintained.

- **Business Acumen and Domain Knowledge:**
  Product managers and analysts must understand the business context, user needs, and industry-specific challenges to drive impactful NLP initiatives.

- **Ethical and Regulatory Awareness:**
  Specialists who can ensure that models adhere to legal frameworks (GDPR, CCPA) and ethical guidelines, mitigating risks of bias and ensuring responsible AI practices.

Team Composition Considerations:

- **Diversity and Inclusion:**
  A diverse team enhances creativity and ensures that models are robust and free from bias.

- **Continuous Learning:**
  Encourage ongoing education and training in emerging NLP techniques and technologies to keep the CoE at the cutting edge.

- **Collaboration:**
  Establish regular communication channels and collaborative platforms that foster knowledge sharing across teams.

3. Cross-Functional Alignment and Governance

- **Integrated Roadmap:**
  Develop an enterprise-wide roadmap that aligns NLP initiatives with broader business objectives, ensuring that projects are prioritized based on potential ROI and strategic impact.

- **Governance Framework:**
  Implement governance structures to oversee data quality, model performance, and ethical compliance. Regular audits and review meetings help maintain accountability and transparency.

- **Collaboration Tools:**
  Utilize project management and collaboration tools (e.g., Jira,

Confluence, Slack) to facilitate cross-team coordination, track progress, and manage workflows effectively.

- **Innovation Labs and Pilot Programs:**
  Create dedicated innovation labs to experiment with new NLP techniques and run pilot projects before scaling them across the organization.

Illustrative Example: Visualizing the Organizational Structure Using Graphviz

Below is an example using Python and Graphviz to generate a visual representation of an NLP Center of Excellence's organizational structure:

```
from graphviz import Digraph

# Initialize the directed graph

dot = Digraph(comment='NLP Center of Excellence
Organizational Structure')

# Define nodes for different roles

dot.node('CEO', 'Executive Sponsor')

dot.node('DIR', 'NLP CoE Director')

dot.node('DS', 'Data Scientists & NLP Researchers')

dot.node('NE', 'NLP Engineers')

dot.node('SW', 'Software & DevOps Engineers')

dot.node('PM', 'Product Managers')

dot.node('QA', 'Quality Assurance & Compliance Specialists')

# Define edges representing reporting lines
```

```
dot.edges(['CEDIR'])  # CEO -> NLP CoE Director
dot.edge('DIR', 'DS', label='Leads')
dot.edge('DIR', 'NE', label='Leads')
dot.edge('DIR', 'SW', label='Coordinates')
dot.edge('DIR', 'PM', label='Aligns with')
dot.edge('DIR', 'QA', label='Oversees')
# Optionally, render the graph to a file and view it
dot.render('nlp_coe_structure.gv', view=True)
```

Explanation:

- **Nodes:**
  Each node represents a key role within the NLP Center of Excellence.
- **Edges:**
  Edges indicate reporting lines and relationships, highlighting how the NLP CoE Director connects with various cross-functional teams.
- **Visualization:**
  Rendering the graph provides a clear organizational chart that can be shared with stakeholders to illustrate team composition and reporting structures.

In summary, building an NLP Center of Excellence requires a deliberate and well-structured approach that aligns technical expertise, business acumen, and governance frameworks. By establishing clear organizational structures, fostering cross-functional collaboration, and investing in continuous learning, enterprises can drive sustained innovation in NLP. This strategic alignment not only enhances operational efficiency and model performance but also ensures that NLP initiatives deliver measurable business value while adhering to ethical and regulatory standards.

Stakeholder Engagement

Aligning Executive Leadership, Data Science Teams, and Operational Units Around NLP Goals

In large-scale enterprises, the successful deployment of NLP initiatives hinges not only on technological excellence but also on strong stakeholder engagement. Aligning executive leadership, data science teams, and operational units is essential to ensure that NLP projects deliver measurable business value and integrate seamlessly into existing workflows. A comprehensive stakeholder engagement strategy establishes clear communication channels, fosters cross-functional collaboration, and drives consensus on strategic priorities.

1. Executive Leadership

Role and Responsibilities:

- **Strategic Vision:**
  Executive leadership provides the overarching vision and sets the strategic priorities for NLP initiatives. Their endorsement is crucial for securing the necessary resources and budget.
- **Governance and Oversight:**
  Leaders establish governance frameworks that ensure projects adhere to regulatory, ethical, and performance standards. They are responsible for monitoring ROI and aligning NLP outcomes with overall business goals.
- **Advocacy and Sponsorship:**
  Executives act as champions for NLP projects, communicating their benefits across the organization and ensuring sustained investment in AI capabilities.

Engagement Strategies:

- **Regular Executive Briefings:**
  Hold periodic briefings to update leadership on progress, challenges, and strategic adjustments.
- **Performance Dashboards:**
  Develop dashboards that highlight key performance indicators (KPIs) such as cost savings, operational efficiencies, and revenue growth attributable to NLP initiatives.
- **ROI Reporting:**
  Provide clear, quantitative metrics demonstrating the impact of NLP on business outcomes, thereby reinforcing the value proposition.

2. Data Science Teams

Role and Responsibilities:

- **Innovation and Development:**
  Data science teams are responsible for developing and refining NLP models, experimenting with cutting-edge techniques, and ensuring that solutions meet performance benchmarks.
- **Collaboration and Knowledge Sharing:**
  These teams collaborate closely with domain experts, software engineers, and operational units to translate research into production-ready systems.
- **Model Monitoring and Continuous Improvement:**
  They oversee the lifecycle of NLP models, implementing monitoring systems, conducting regular performance evaluations, and iterating based on feedback.

Engagement Strategies:

- **Collaborative Platforms:**
  Utilize collaborative tools (e.g., GitHub, Confluence, Slack) to

share insights, code, and best practices, ensuring that data scientists remain aligned with business objectives.

- **Cross-Functional Workshops:**
  Organize regular workshops and hackathons to foster innovation, encourage knowledge exchange, and solve domain-specific challenges.

- **Transparent Roadmaps:**
  Develop and maintain clear project roadmaps that detail milestones, resource allocations, and timelines, ensuring that data science efforts are well-integrated with broader business strategies.

3. Operational Units

Role and Responsibilities:

- **Implementation and Integration:**
  Operational teams are on the front lines of deploying NLP solutions into day-to-day business processes. Their feedback is vital for ensuring that models are practical, user-friendly, and aligned with operational realities.

- **Change Management:**
  These units play a critical role in driving user adoption, providing training, and managing the transition from legacy systems to advanced AI-driven processes.

- **Performance and Feedback:**
  Operational teams monitor the real-world performance of NLP solutions, reporting back on issues, user satisfaction, and overall effectiveness in improving processes.

Engagement Strategies:

- **Pilot Programs:**
  Initiate pilot programs to allow operational units to test NLP

solutions in controlled environments, providing valuable feedback and building confidence in the technology.

- **User Training and Support:**
  Implement comprehensive training programs and create support channels to assist staff during the transition to new NLP systems.

- **Feedback Loops:**
  Establish structured mechanisms (e.g., surveys, focus groups, regular review meetings) to gather operational insights and ensure continuous improvement of NLP deployments.

Facilitating Cross-Functional Alignment

A cohesive stakeholder engagement strategy must bridge the communication gaps between executive leadership, data science teams, and operational units. Here are key methods to facilitate alignment:

- **Unified Communication Framework:**
  Develop a centralized communication platform where updates, project milestones, and key decisions are shared transparently. This fosters a culture of openness and ensures that all stakeholders are informed of project progress and challenges.

- **Joint Governance Committees:**
  Establish committees with representatives from all key groups to oversee NLP projects. These committees ensure that technical decisions are balanced with strategic and operational considerations, promoting holistic solutions that drive business value.

- **Iterative Feedback and Improvement Cycles:**
  Encourage a continuous feedback loop where operational insights inform model refinement, and performance improvements are communicated back to leadership. This

iterative process ensures that NLP initiatives remain dynamic and responsive to evolving business needs.

Illustrative Example: Visualizing Stakeholder Alignment Using a Gantt Chart

Below is a conceptual Python example using the plotly library to visualize a project timeline that highlights stakeholder engagement milestones. This can serve as a tool to align executive, data science, and operational teams around NLP project deliverables.

```
import plotly.express as px

import pandas as pd

# Define a sample project timeline with stakeholder milestones

data = {

    "Task": ["Project Kickoff", "Data Collection & Preprocessing", "Model Development", "Pilot Deployment", "Full Rollout", "Performance Review"],

    "Start": ["2023-03-01", "2023-03-15", "2023-04-01", "2023-05-01", "2023-06-01", "2023-07-01"],

    "Finish": ["2023-03-05", "2023-03-31", "2023-04-30", "2023-05-15", "2023-06-30", "2023-07-05"],

    "Stakeholders": ["Executive, Data Science, Ops", "Data Science, Ops", "Data Science", "Ops, Data Science", "Executive, Ops", "All Stakeholders"]

}

df = pd.DataFrame(data)

df['Start'] = pd.to_datetime(df['Start'])
```

```
df['Finish'] = pd.to_datetime(df['Finish'])

# Create a Gantt chart

fig = px.timeline(df, x_start="Start", x_end="Finish",
y="Task", color="Stakeholders", title="NLP Project Timeline
and Stakeholder Engagement")

fig.update_yaxes(autorange="reversed") # Reverse the y-axis
to show tasks in order

fig.show()
```

Explanation:

- **Data Definition:**
  The script defines key project milestones and assigns stakeholder groups responsible for each phase.
- **Gantt Chart Visualization:**
  A Gantt chart is generated to visualize the timeline and engagement of different stakeholder groups, facilitating cross-functional alignment and clear communication of project deliverables.

In summary, effective stakeholder engagement is critical for the successful deployment of NLP initiatives in enterprise settings. By aligning executive leadership, data science teams, and operational units, organizations can ensure that NLP projects are strategically driven, technically robust, and operationally seamless. Leveraging unified communication frameworks, joint governance structures, and continuous feedback loops, enterprises can foster a culture of collaboration and innovation that accelerates the delivery of impactful AI solutions. This cross-functional alignment not only maximizes ROI but also builds a resilient foundation for ongoing digital transformation.

Change Management and User Adoption

Strategies for Training End-Users, Integrating Solutions into Existing Workflows, and Measuring Adoption Rates

Successful deployment of NLP and AI solutions in an enterprise hinges not only on the technical excellence of the models but also on effective change management and user adoption. This involves ensuring that end-users understand, trust, and integrate new technologies into their daily workflows. A comprehensive strategy includes tailored training programs, seamless integration into existing processes, and robust mechanisms to measure adoption and gather feedback.

1. Training End-Users

Overview:
Effective training is critical to overcome resistance to change and build user confidence. Tailored training programs help end-users understand the capabilities and limitations of NLP solutions, enabling them to use these tools to their full potential.

Strategies:

- **Workshops and Seminars:**
  Conduct hands-on workshops and live demonstrations to provide practical experience with the new system.
- **Online Tutorials and Documentation:**
  Develop comprehensive online resources, including video tutorials, user manuals, and FAQs to support self-paced learning.
- **Interactive Demos:**
  Create sandbox environments or interactive demos where users can experiment with the system without affecting live data.
- **Role-Based Training:**
  Customize training sessions to the needs of different user groups

(e.g., data scientists, business analysts, customer support teams) to ensure relevance and higher engagement.

Example:
A training dashboard that tracks user progress and engagement can be built using tools like Plotly Dash to visualize training module completion rates and quiz scores.

```
import dash
from dash import dcc, html
import plotly.express as px
import pandas as pd
# Sample data: user training progress
data = {
    "User": ["Alice", "Bob", "Charlie", "Diana"],
    "Modules_Completed": [5, 3, 4, 6],
    "Total_Modules": [6, 6, 6, 6]
}
df = pd.DataFrame(data)
df["Adoption_Rate"] = df["Modules_Completed"] / df["Total_Modules"]
fig = px.bar(df, x="User", y="Adoption_Rate",
            title="User Training Adoption Rates",
            labels={"Adoption_Rate": "Completion Rate (%)"})
# Initialize Dash app
```

```
app = dash.Dash(__name__)
app.layout = html.Div([
    html.H1("Training Adoption Dashboard"),
    dcc.Graph(figure=fig)
])
if __name__ == '__main__':
    app.run_server(debug=True)
```

2. Integrating Solutions into Existing Workflows

Overview:
For technology adoption to be sustainable, new NLP solutions must seamlessly integrate with existing business processes. This ensures minimal disruption while maximizing the benefits of automation and improved data analytics.

Strategies:

- **Process Mapping and Workflow Analysis:**
  Conduct thorough analysis of current workflows to identify integration points and potential bottlenecks.
- **APIs and Microservices:**
  Develop APIs and microservices that allow NLP solutions to interact with existing enterprise systems (e.g., CRM, ERP, helpdesk software).
- **User Interface (UI) Integration:**
  Embed NLP functionalities directly into the tools that end-users already use, minimizing the need for context switching.

- **Pilot Programs:**
  Implement pilot programs to gather feedback on the integration process and make iterative improvements before full-scale rollout.

Example:
A REST API that serves NLP insights (e.g., sentiment scores) can be integrated with an existing CRM system. Below is a simple Flask-based API example:

```
from flask import Flask, request, jsonify

from transformers import pipeline

# Initialize Flask app and sentiment analysis pipeline

app = Flask(__name__)

sentiment_analyzer = pipeline("sentiment-analysis",
model="distilbert-base-uncased-finetuned-sst-2-english")

@app.route('/analyze', methods=['POST'])

def analyze_sentiment():

    data = request.get_json(force=True)

    text = data.get('text', '')

    result = sentiment_analyzer(text)

    return jsonify(result)

if __name__ == '__main__':

    app.run(debug=True, port=5000)
```

This API can be called by the CRM system to provide real-time sentiment analysis on customer communications, thus integrating NLP insights directly into the existing workflow.

3. Measuring Adoption Rates

Overview:
Quantitative and qualitative metrics are essential for evaluating the success of an NLP deployment. Monitoring adoption rates provides insights into user engagement and helps identify areas for further improvement.

Strategies:

- **Usage Analytics:**
  Track metrics such as frequency of use, number of transactions, and feature utilization to understand how widely and effectively the solution is being used.

- **User Surveys and Feedback:**
  Conduct periodic surveys and interviews to gather qualitative insights on user satisfaction and identify any pain points.

- **Key Performance Indicators (KPIs):**
  Define and monitor KPIs (e.g., reduction in manual tasks, time saved, accuracy improvements) that directly correlate with business outcomes.

- **Dashboards and Reporting:**
  Use business intelligence tools to create dashboards that visualize adoption trends and provide real-time feedback to stakeholders.

Example:
A simple script to log usage data and calculate adoption metrics could be implemented using Python and a database. Below is a conceptual example using SQLite to record and analyze user interactions.

```
import sqlite3
from datetime import datetime
# Connect to (or create) a SQLite database
conn = sqlite3.connect('adoption_metrics.db')
c = conn.cursor()
# Create a table to log usage data if it doesn't exist
c.execute('''
    CREATE TABLE IF NOT EXISTS usage_log (
        id INTEGER PRIMARY KEY AUTOINCREMENT,
        user_id TEXT,
        action TEXT,
        timestamp TEXT
    )
''')
conn.commit()
# Function to log an action
def log_action(user_id, action):
    timestamp = datetime.now().isoformat()
    c.execute('INSERT INTO usage_log (user_id, action,
timestamp) VALUES (?, ?, ?)', (user_id, action, timestamp))
    conn.commit()
# Log some example actions
log_action("user_123", "Completed Training Module 1")
```

```
log_action("user_123", "Used Sentiment Analysis API")
log_action("user_456", "Completed Training Module 2")
# Retrieve and analyze adoption data
def get_adoption_rate():
    c.execute('SELECT user_id, COUNT(*) FROM usage_log GROUP BY user_id')
    data = c.fetchall()
    print("User Adoption Metrics:")
    for user_id, count in data:
        print(f"User: {user_id}, Actions Logged: {count}")
get_adoption_rate()
conn.close()
```

Explanation:

- **Database Logging:**
  The script sets up an SQLite database to log user actions (e.g., training completions, API usage).
- **Logging Function:**
  A function (log_action) records each user action with a timestamp.
- **Adoption Metrics:**
  The get_adoption_rate function aggregates logged actions to provide insights into user engagement levels.

- **Dashboard Integration:**
  In production, this data can be visualized via dashboards in tools like Grafana or Tableau.

Conclusion

Effective change management and user adoption are critical to the successful deployment of NLP solutions in an enterprise. By investing in comprehensive training, seamlessly integrating new tools into existing workflows, and robustly measuring adoption rates, organizations can drive both technological and organizational transformation. These strategies ensure that NLP initiatives deliver tangible business value, enhance operational efficiency, and foster a culture of continuous innovation across the enterprise.

Part VI: Future Outlook and Additional Resources
Chapter 18: Frontiers in NLP Research

Emergent Abilities in Large Language Models

Exploring Unexpected Capabilities and Their Business Implications

Recent breakthroughs in NLP have led to the development of massive pretrained language models (LLMs) that exhibit emergent abilities - capabilities that were not explicitly programmed or observed in smaller models. These emergent abilities include multi-step reasoning, contextual understanding across long documents, few-shot and zero-shot learning, and even rudimentary forms of creativity. Such capabilities are transforming how businesses approach automation, customer engagement, and decision-making.

1. What Are Emergent Abilities?

Emergent abilities refer to advanced functionalities that become apparent only when models reach a certain scale. These functionalities include:

- **Chain-of-Thought Reasoning:**
  LLMs can generate intermediate reasoning steps, enabling them to solve complex problems and answer multi-part questions more effectively.

- **Contextual Adaptation:**
  Massive models can better understand and generate coherent responses over long contexts, maintaining conversation continuity and leveraging prior dialogue effectively.

- **Few-Shot and Zero-Shot Learning:**
  With minimal or no additional training, these models can generalize to new tasks, significantly reducing the need for task-specific fine-tuning.

- **Knowledge Integration:**
  LLMs can synthesize information from various domains, providing insights and answers that span multiple topics, which is particularly useful in complex business environments.

2. Business Implications of Emergent Abilities

The unexpected capabilities of LLMs have significant implications for businesses:

- **Enhanced Customer Support:**
  Chatbots and virtual assistants powered by LLMs can handle complex queries and provide detailed, context-aware responses, improving customer satisfaction.
- **Content Creation and Curation:**
  Automated content generation for marketing, documentation, and reporting can be enhanced through the creative and contextual abilities of large models.
- **Decision Support Systems:**
  LLMs can assist executives by providing detailed analyses, generating summaries of extensive documents, and even offering recommendations based on aggregated data.
- **Innovation in Product Development:**
  The ability to rapidly adapt to new tasks enables businesses to experiment with new services and products, leveraging the model's generalization capabilities.

3. Illustrative Example: Chain-of-Thought Reasoning with an LLM

Below is a simplified example using the Hugging Face Transformers library to illustrate chain-of-thought reasoning with a large language model. This example demonstrates how a model can be prompted to provide intermediate reasoning steps before arriving at a final answer.

```
from transformers import pipeline

# Initialize a text-generation pipeline using a large language model (e.g., GPT-3-like model)

# Note: In practice, you might use a model like GPT-3 or GPT-4 via an API, but here we simulate with a smaller model for demonstration.

generator = pipeline("text-generation", model="gpt2")

# Prompt that encourages chain-of-thought reasoning

prompt = (

    "Question: If a train travels 100 miles in 2 hours and then 150 miles in 3 hours, what is its average speed? "

    "Let's think through this step by step. "

    "Step 1: Calculate the total distance traveled. "

    "Step 2: Calculate the total time taken. "

    "Step 3: Divide the total distance by the total time. "

    "Answer:"

)

# Generate response with chain-of-thought reasoning

response = generator(prompt, max_length=250, num_return_sequences=1)[0]['generated_text']

print("Chain-of-Thought Response:\n", response)
```

Explanation:

- **Prompt Engineering:**
  The prompt is carefully designed to instruct the model to break down the problem into multiple steps (chain-of-thought). This leads to a more transparent reasoning process.
- **Model Response:**
  Although this example uses GPT-2 for illustration, in practice, larger models exhibit more robust chain-of-thought reasoning, providing detailed intermediate steps and ultimately the correct final answer.
- **Business Value:**
  Such reasoning capabilities can enhance decision support systems, where understanding the rationale behind a recommendation is as important as the recommendation itself. It also aids in debugging and refining model behavior.

In summary, emergent abilities in large language models are unlocking unprecedented potentials in NLP applications. By harnessing capabilities such as chain-of-thought reasoning, contextual adaptation, and few-shot learning, businesses can drive significant improvements in customer support, content creation, and strategic decision-making. As these models continue to evolve, enterprises must consider both the technical and ethical dimensions of their deployment to fully capitalize on these transformative capabilities while ensuring transparency and accountability. This frontier in NLP not only represents a leap in computational power but also opens up new avenues for innovation and efficiency in a globalized business landscape.

Low-Resource and Zero-Shot Learning

Handling Scenarios with Scarce or Nonexistent Labeled Data

In many real-world applications, obtaining large amounts of labeled data for training NLP models is a significant challenge - especially for low-resource languages or niche domains. Low-resource and zero-shot learning techniques address this gap by leveraging transfer learning, self-supervised learning, and models pretrained on large, diverse datasets to generalize to new tasks without extensive labeled examples.

1. Low-Resource Learning

Overview:

- **Challenge:**
  Many languages and specialized domains have limited annotated data, making it difficult to train models directly on the target task.
- **Approaches:**
  - **Transfer Learning:**
    Fine-tune a model that has been pretrained on large, diverse datasets (e.g., BERT, GPT, T5) on the small labeled dataset from the target domain. The pretrained model's learned representations often capture universal linguistic features that can be adapted to low-resource tasks.
  - **Data Augmentation:**
    Generate synthetic training examples using techniques like back-translation, paraphrasing, or noise injection to expand the labeled dataset.
  - **Cross-Lingual Transfer:**
    Leverage multilingual models (e.g., mBERT, XLM-R) that have been pretrained on multiple languages. These models can

transfer knowledge from high-resource languages to low-resource ones.

Example Strategy:
Fine-tuning a multilingual BERT variant (e.g., XLM-R) on a small labeled dataset from a low-resource language can significantly boost performance compared to training a model from scratch.

2. Zero-Shot Learning

Overview:

- **Challenge:**
  In some cases, labeled data for a particular task or language may not be available at all.
- **Approaches:**
  Zero-shot learning enables models to perform tasks they were never explicitly trained for by leveraging the generalization capabilities of large pretrained models. These models rely on natural language prompts to frame tasks and generate predictions without task-specific fine-tuning.
- **Techniques:**
  - **Prompt Engineering:**
    Carefully craft input prompts that guide the model to perform the desired task. For instance, using natural language descriptions of classes can allow a model to classify text in a zero-shot manner.
  - **Zero-Shot Classification Pipelines:**
    Frameworks such as Hugging Face's pipeline support zero-shot classification with models like BART or RoBERTa fine-tuned on the MNLI dataset. These models can infer the relevance of predefined labels to the input text without any additional training.

Illustrative Example: Zero-Shot Classification

Below is an example using Hugging Face's Transformers library to perform zero-shot text classification. This approach can be used in scenarios where no labeled data exists for the target task.

```
from transformers import pipeline

# Initialize a zero-shot classification pipeline using a model fine-tuned on MNLI

classifier = pipeline("zero-shot-classification", model="facebook/bart-large-mnli")

# Example input text from a low-resource domain

text = "The recent developments in renewable energy have shown promising results for sustainable power generation."

# Define candidate labels for classification

candidate_labels = ["energy", "finance", "politics", "health"]

# Perform zero-shot classification

result = classifier(text, candidate_labels)

print("Input Text:", text)

print("Candidate Labels:", candidate_labels)

print("Zero-Shot Classification Result:")

print(result)
```

Explanation:

- **Pipeline Initialization:**
  The zero-shot-classification pipeline uses a model like BART-large-mnli to perform classification without additional fine-tuning.

- **Task Framing:**
  The candidate labels provide a natural language description of possible classes. The model evaluates the input text against these labels and assigns a score indicating how well each label describes the text.

- **Output:**
  The output contains the candidate labels, their corresponding scores, and the label with the highest score, allowing for effective classification even in the absence of task-specific labeled data.

3. Business Implications

Enhancing Decision-Making and Automation:

- **Scalability:**
  Zero-shot learning enables rapid deployment across diverse languages and domains without the overhead of extensive data labeling, thereby accelerating time-to-market for new applications.

- **Cost Efficiency:**
  Reducing the dependency on large annotated datasets lowers the costs associated with data collection and labeling, particularly in niche or emerging markets.

- **Innovation:**
  Leveraging low-resource and zero-shot learning techniques allows organizations to experiment with novel applications and pivot quickly in response to market needs, fostering a culture of innovation.

In summary, low-resource and zero-shot learning represent transformative approaches in NLP research and deployment. By leveraging transfer learning, data augmentation, and sophisticated zero-shot classification techniques, enterprises can overcome the challenges of scarce labeled data. These strategies not only unlock the potential of NLP in underrepresented languages and specialized domains but also drive innovation, cost efficiency, and rapid scalability - key factors in maintaining a competitive edge in today's dynamic business landscape.

Integration with Other AI Disciplines

Vision-and-Language Tasks, Robotics Integration, and Real-Time Decision-Making

The frontier of NLP research increasingly focuses on the seamless integration of language understanding with other AI disciplines. Combining NLP with computer vision, robotics, and real-time decision-making not only broadens the scope of intelligent systems but also opens up new avenues for transformative business applications. This integration enables systems to understand multimodal data, execute complex physical tasks based on natural language instructions, and make informed decisions on the fly.

1. Vision-and-Language Tasks

Overview:
Integrating NLP with computer vision empowers applications such as image captioning, visual question answering (VQA), and multimodal search. By bridging the gap between visual inputs and textual understanding, these systems can extract rich contextual information from images and videos, enabling deeper insights and more interactive user experiences.

Key Applications:

- **Visual Question Answering:**
  Answering questions about an image by combining image processing with language understanding.
- **Image Captioning:**
  Automatically generating descriptive captions for images.
- **Multimodal Search:**
  Enhancing search engines by allowing queries that combine text and image inputs.

Illustrative Example with CLIP:

Below is an example using OpenAI's CLIP model via the Hugging Face Transformers library. The code demonstrates how to compare an image against a set of textual descriptions to determine which caption best matches the image.

```
from transformers import CLIPProcessor, CLIPModel

from PIL import Image

import torch

# Load the CLIP model and processor

model = CLIPModel.from_pretrained("openai/clip-vit-base-patch32")

processor = CLIPProcessor.from_pretrained("openai/clip-vit-base-patch32")

# Load an image (replace 'path/to/your/image.jpg' with your image file)

image = Image.open("path/to/your/image.jpg")
```

```
# Define a set of candidate captions

candidate_texts = ["a cat sitting on a sofa", "a dog playing in the park", "a scenic view of mountains"]

# Process the image and texts

inputs = processor(text=candidate_texts, images=image, return_tensors="pt", padding=True)

# Perform inference to get similarity scores

outputs = model(**inputs)

logits_per_image = outputs.logits_per_image  # shape: [1, num_candidate_texts]

probs = logits_per_image.softmax(dim=1)

print("Candidate Texts:", candidate_texts)

print("Probabilities:", probs.detach().numpy())
```

2. Robotics Integration

Overview:
Integrating NLP with robotics enables machines to execute tasks based on natural language commands. This integration is crucial for applications in manufacturing, logistics, and service industries, where robots need to interpret instructions and interact with their environment.

Key Applications:

- **Command and Control:**
  Robots can process natural language commands to perform tasks such as navigation, object manipulation, or process automation.

- **Human-Robot Interaction (HRI):**
  Enhances the usability and effectiveness of robotic systems by providing intuitive interfaces.
- **Adaptive Learning:**
  Robots can learn from contextual language cues and adapt their behavior based on feedback.

Illustrative Example: Simulated Command Processing

Below is a simple example that demonstrates processing a natural language command to control a robot. This script uses a rule-based approach to map text commands to actions. In production, such commands could be integrated with robotics middleware like ROS (Robot Operating System).

```
def process_command(command):
    """
    Simulate processing a natural language command for a robot.
    """
    command = command.lower()
    if "move forward" in command:
        return "Robot is moving forward."
    elif "turn left" in command:
        return "Robot is turning left."
    elif "turn right" in command:
        return "Robot is turning right."
```

```
    elif "stop" in command:
        return "Robot is stopping."
    else:
        return "Command not recognized. Please repeat."
# Example usage
command_input = "Please move forward and then turn left."
action = process_command(command_input)
print("Processed Command:", action)
```

3. Real-Time Decision-Making

Overview:
Real-time decision-making systems integrate NLP with data from various sources (e.g., sensor data, social media, logs) to facilitate instantaneous responses in dynamic environments. Such systems are crucial in applications like financial trading, autonomous vehicles, and emergency response management.

Key Applications:

- **Dynamic Risk Management:**
  Analyze real-time news and social media feeds to adjust trading strategies.
- **Autonomous Systems:**
  Enable self-driving cars and drones to make split-second decisions based on multimodal sensor inputs.
- **Crisis Management:**
  Integrate textual reports with live data streams to coordinate emergency responses.

Illustrative Example: Real-Time Decision-Making with Asynchronous Processing

Below is an example using Python's asyncio to simulate real-time processing of incoming data and making decisions based on NLP analysis.

```
import asyncio

import random

async def process_streaming_data():

    """

    Simulate processing streaming data in real time.

    """

    while True:

        # Simulate receiving a text message from a real-time data
source

        message = random.choice([

            "Market sentiment is positive.",

            "Market sentiment is negative.",

            "Market sentiment is neutral."

        ])

        print("Received message:", message)

            # Process the message (simulate NLP analysis)

        if "positive" in message:

            decision = "Proceed with buying."
```

```
        elif "negative" in message:
            decision = "Consider selling."
        else:
            decision = "Hold position."
        print("Real-Time Decision:", decision)
        await asyncio.sleep(2)  # Simulate a delay for new data
# Run the asynchronous event loop for real-time processing
asyncio.run(process_streaming_data())
```

Explanation:

- **Asynchronous Processing:**
  The example uses asyncio to simulate processing a continuous stream of messages in real time.
- **Decision Logic:**
  Based on the content of the message, the system makes a decision (e.g., "Proceed with buying" or "Consider selling").
- **Real-Time Integration:**
  In production, similar logic would integrate with real-time data feeds (e.g., via Apache Kafka or AWS Kinesis) to support immediate decision-making.

Conclusion

The integration of NLP with other AI disciplines - such as computer vision, robotics, and real-time decision-making - marks a significant frontier in NLP research. By combining the strengths of these diverse technologies, enterprises can create comprehensive systems that not only understand and generate human-like language but also interpret visual data, control robotic actions, and make rapid, informed decisions in dynamic environments. As these technologies continue to evolve, they promise to unlock new opportunities for innovation, efficiency, and competitive advantage across various industries.

Chapter 19: Open Source Ecosystem and Community Projects

Major Open Source Libraries and Frameworks

Empowering NLP Through Community-Driven Innovation

The open source ecosystem has been a critical driver in advancing NLP research and applications. Community-driven projects such as Hugging Face Transformers, spaCy, Stanford CoreNLP, and many others provide powerful, accessible tools that democratize state-of-the-art NLP technology. These frameworks not only enable rapid prototyping and deployment of NLP solutions but also foster a collaborative environment where researchers and practitioners continuously contribute improvements, share insights, and accelerate innovation.

1. Hugging Face Transformers

Overview:
Hugging Face Transformers has become one of the most widely adopted libraries for NLP, offering a vast repository of pretrained models (e.g., BERT, GPT, RoBERTa) that can be easily fine-tuned on a variety of tasks. The library supports multiple frameworks such as PyTorch, TensorFlow, and JAX, making it versatile and accessible.

Key Features:

- **Pretrained Model Hub:**
  Provides thousands of models for tasks ranging from text classification and translation to question answering and summarization.

- **Ease of Use:**
  Simplifies the process of fine-tuning models with high-level pipelines and APIs.

- **Community and Documentation:**
  Robust community support, comprehensive documentation, and tutorials that accelerate learning and implementation.

Illustrative Example: Text Classification Pipeline

```
from transformers import pipeline

# Initialize a text classification pipeline using a pretrained
model (e.g., DistilBERT fine-tuned on SST-2)

classifier = pipeline("sentiment-analysis", model="distilbert-
base-uncased-finetuned-sst-2-english")

# Classify sentiment of a sample text

text = "The new product has exceeded all our expectations!"

result = classifier(text)

print("Sentiment Analysis Result:", result)
```

2. spaCy

Overview:
spaCy is an industrial-strength NLP library designed for production use. It offers fast and accurate NLP pipelines that include tokenization, part-of-speech tagging, named entity recognition, dependency parsing, and more. spaCy's design emphasizes performance and usability, making it ideal for integrating NLP into real-world applications.

Key Features:

- **Speed and Efficiency:**
  Optimized for production with a focus on speed and memory efficiency.
- **Extensibility:**
  Supports custom components and pipelines, allowing for tailored solutions.
- **Pretrained Models:**
  Comes with a variety of pretrained models for different languages and tasks, with straightforward methods to extend or fine-tune these models.

Illustrative Example: Named Entity Recognition

```
import spacy
# Load spaCy's English model
nlp = spacy.load("en_core_web_sm")
# Process a sample text to extract named entities
doc = nlp("Apple is looking at buying U.K. startup for $1
billion")
for ent in doc.ents:
    print(f"Entity: {ent.text}, Label: {ent.label_}")
```

3. Stanford CoreNLP

Overview:
Stanford CoreNLP is a comprehensive suite of NLP tools developed by the Stanford NLP Group. It provides a wide range of

functionalities including tokenization, sentence segmentation, part-of-speech tagging, named entity recognition, coreference resolution, and sentiment analysis. While traditionally implemented in Java, it has APIs for integration with other languages, making it a robust option for academic and industrial applications.

Key Features:

- **Comprehensive NLP Pipeline:**
  Offers one of the most complete sets of NLP tools available, suitable for complex analyses.
- **High Accuracy:**
  Known for its rigorous research foundation and high accuracy in various NLP tasks.
- **Cross-Language Support:**
  Although primarily designed for English, it includes models for other languages and supports custom model training.

Illustrative Example: Using Stanford CoreNLP via Python

```
# Requires installation of the 'stanfordnlp' package and model downloads (for demonstration)

import stanfordnlp

# Set up the Stanford CoreNLP pipeline

stanfordnlp.download('en')  # Download English models if not already done

nlp = stanfordnlp.Pipeline(lang='en', use_gpu=False)

# Process a sample text

doc = nlp("Barack Obama was born in Hawaii.")
```

```
for sentence in doc.sentences:
    for word in sentence.words:
        print(f"Word: {word.text}, POS: {word.pos}")
```

4. Other Community-Driven Projects

Overview:
Beyond these major frameworks, a vibrant ecosystem of open source projects continues to drive innovation in NLP. Some notable mentions include:

- **AllenNLP:**
  Developed by the Allen Institute for AI, AllenNLP provides an extensible platform for deep learning research in NLP, with a focus on interpretability and model analysis.
- **Gensim:**
  Specializes in topic modeling and document similarity analysis, offering efficient implementations of algorithms like Word2Vec, LDA, and TF-IDF.
- **Flair:**
  A simple NLP library from Zalando Research that supports state-of-the-art text embeddings and sequence labeling, allowing for easy stacking of different embeddings for improved performance.

5. Business and Research Implications

- **Accelerated Innovation:**
  Open source libraries allow organizations to rapidly prototype and iterate on NLP models, reducing time-to-market and fostering continuous improvement.
- **Cost Efficiency:**
  Utilizing community-driven tools reduces the need for expensive

proprietary solutions, making advanced NLP accessible to businesses of all sizes.

- **Collaboration and Knowledge Sharing:**
  The open source community encourages collaboration, with contributions and shared resources that benefit both academia and industry. This collective knowledge accelerates the pace of innovation and ensures that the latest research is quickly integrated into practical applications.

In summary, the open source ecosystem, spearheaded by projects like Hugging Face Transformers, spaCy, Stanford CoreNLP, and others, plays a pivotal role in the advancement of NLP technology. These libraries not only provide powerful tools for building state-of-the-art NLP systems but also foster a collaborative environment that drives continuous innovation. By leveraging these community-driven resources, enterprises can achieve high performance, reduce costs, and maintain a competitive edge in the rapidly evolving landscape of NLP research and application.

Contributor Guidelines

Engaging with Open-Source Communities to Accelerate Internal Development and Innovation

Open-source ecosystems are dynamic, collaborative environments that drive rapid technological innovation. By actively engaging with these communities, enterprises can leverage collective expertise, contribute to cutting-edge projects, and accelerate their own internal development efforts. Establishing clear contributor guidelines and fostering a culture of collaboration not only enhances an organization's technical capabilities but also builds valuable relationships with external developers and research institutions.

1. Importance of Contributor Guidelines

Clear Expectations and Consistency:

- **Standardized Practices:** Contributor guidelines ensure that contributions follow consistent coding standards, documentation practices, and testing protocols.
- **Efficient Review Processes:** Clear guidelines streamline code review and integration, reducing friction between internal teams and the open-source community.
- **Quality Assurance:** They set the bar for code quality and project sustainability, ensuring that contributions enhance the overall health and maintainability of the project.

Business Benefits:

- **Accelerated Innovation:** Engagement with open-source projects enables rapid access to state-of-the-art technologies and accelerates internal innovation.
- **Cost Efficiency:** Leveraging and contributing to community-driven projects reduces the need for developing proprietary solutions from scratch.
- **Brand Positioning:** Active participation in open-source communities enhances the enterprise's reputation as a technology leader and fosters long-term partnerships.

2. Key Components of Effective Contributor Guidelines

1. Code Standards and Best Practices:

- **Coding Conventions:** Define language-specific style guides (e.g., PEP 8 for Python) to maintain code consistency.
- **Documentation:** Emphasize the importance of clear documentation for code, APIs, and design decisions.
- **Testing:** Require comprehensive unit and integration tests to ensure contributions do not break existing functionality.

2. Contribution Workflow:

- **Issue Tracking:** Use a robust issue tracking system (e.g., GitHub Issues, JIRA) for bug reports, feature requests, and discussion.
- **Pull Requests (PRs):** Outline the process for submitting PRs, including branching strategies, commit message standards, and review guidelines.
- **Continuous Integration:** Encourage the use of CI pipelines (e.g., GitHub Actions, Travis CI) to automate testing and ensure that new contributions meet quality standards.

3. Communication and Collaboration:

- **Code of Conduct:** Establish a clear code of conduct to create a welcoming and inclusive community.
- **Mentorship Programs:** Pair new contributors with experienced mentors to facilitate onboarding and encourage continued engagement.
- **Community Forums:** Maintain active channels (e.g., Slack, Discord, mailing lists) for real-time collaboration and discussion.

3. Engaging with Open-Source Communities

Strategies for Internal Teams:

- **Allocate Dedicated Resources:**
  Designate a team or individual responsible for managing open-source contributions, tracking community feedback, and integrating external innovations.
- **Incentivize Contributions:**
  Recognize and reward employees who actively contribute to open-source projects, fostering a culture of innovation and continuous learning.

- **Regular Community Participation:**
  Encourage team members to attend open-source conferences, webinars, and meetups to network with other contributors and stay updated on the latest trends.

Example: Creating a CONTRIBUTING.md File for an Open-Source Project

Below is a simplified example of a CONTRIBUTING.md file that outlines guidelines for contributing to an open-source project. This file serves as a reference for both internal teams and external contributors, ensuring clarity and consistency.

```
# Contributing to [Project Name]

Thank you for your interest in contributing to [Project Name]! We welcome contributions from everyone and aim to maintain a collaborative, respectful, and productive community.

## Getting Started

1. **Fork the Repository:**

   Create a personal fork of the repository and clone it to your local machine.

2. **Create a Branch:**

   For every contribution, create a new branch with a descriptive name, e.g., `feature/add-user-auth` or `bugfix/fix-tokenization`.

3. **Code Standards:**
```

- Follow our [coding style guidelines](link-to-style-guide).

- Ensure your code is well-documented and includes comments where necessary.

- Write unit tests for your changes and ensure all tests pass before submitting a pull request.

Submitting a Pull Request

1. **Commit Messages:**

Use clear, concise commit messages that describe your changes.

2. **Pull Request Description:**

Include a detailed description of your changes, why they are needed, and any related issues.

3. **Review Process:**

Your pull request will be reviewed by our maintainers. Be prepared to make adjustments based on feedback.

Reporting Issues

If you encounter any bugs or have feature requests, please open an issue on our GitHub repository. Provide detailed information and steps to reproduce the problem.

Code of Conduct

We expect all contributors to adhere to our [Code of Conduct](link-to-code-of-conduct) to ensure a welcoming and respectful environment.

Getting Help

For any questions or support, please reach out via our [community forum](link-to-forum) or join our Slack channel at [Slack Invite Link].

Thank you for helping us improve [Project Name]!

4. Measuring Impact and Adoption

Metrics to Monitor:

- **Number of Contributions:**
  Track commits, pull requests, and issues from both internal and external contributors.
- **Community Engagement:**
  Monitor activity on community forums, mailing lists, and social media channels.
- **Project Adoption:**
  Evaluate how widely the project is being used, including downloads, forks, and stars on GitHub.
- **Internal Impact:**
  Measure improvements in project velocity, code quality, and innovation metrics as a result of open-source collaboration.

Example: Simple Script to Track GitHub Repository Metrics

Using the GitHub API, the following Python script demonstrates how to retrieve basic repository metrics such as the number of stars, forks, and open issues.

```
import requests
def get_repo_metrics(repo_owner, repo_name):
    url =
f"https://api.github.com/repos/{repo_owner}/{repo_name}"
    response = requests.get(url)
    if response.status_code == 200:
        data = response.json()
        metrics = {
            "stars": data.get("stargazers_count"),
            "forks": data.get("forks_count"),
            "open_issues": data.get("open_issues_count")
        }
        return metrics
    else:
        print("Error fetching repository data:",
response.status_code)
        return None
# Example usage
repo_owner = "huggingface"
repo_name = "transformers"
metrics = get_repo_metrics(repo_owner, repo_name)
if metrics:
    print("Repository Metrics:")
```

```
print(f"Stars: {metrics['stars']}")
print(f"Forks: {metrics['forks']}")
print(f"Open Issues: {metrics['open_issues']}")
```

Explanation:

- **GitHub API Integration:**
  The script fetches repository metrics using the GitHub API, providing a quick snapshot of community engagement.
- **Usage in Reports:**
  These metrics can be incorporated into dashboards and reports to track the impact of open-source contributions and community growth.

In summary, engaging with open-source communities through clear contributor guidelines is a strategic enabler for accelerating internal development and innovation. By establishing structured practices, incentivizing contributions, and fostering a collaborative environment, enterprises can harness the power of community-driven innovation. This not only enhances the quality and reach of NLP projects but also aligns with broader organizational goals of continuous improvement and technological leadership in the rapidly evolving digital landscape.

Keeping Up with Updates

Strategies for Monitoring and Adopting the Latest Breakthroughs in the Fast-Paced NLP Landscape

The rapid evolution of NLP research means that new models, techniques, and tools are continually emerging. For enterprises and research teams to maintain a competitive edge, it is crucial to stay informed and quickly adopt breakthroughs from the open source ecosystem. This involves a proactive strategy that combines automated monitoring of key repositories and publications, active participation in community forums, and the integration of emerging tools into internal workflows.

1. Strategies for Monitoring Updates

- **Automated Repository Monitoring:**
  - **GitHub Notifications and APIs:**
    Utilize GitHub's notification system and API to track new releases, commits, and issues in popular NLP repositories such as Hugging Face Transformers, spaCy, and Stanford CoreNLP.
  - **RSS Feeds:**
    Subscribe to RSS feeds of leading NLP blogs, research journals (e.g., arXiv), and community forums to receive real-time updates.
  - **Email Newsletters:**
    Sign up for newsletters from organizations and communities like Hugging Face, AllenNLP, and AI research institutions.
- **Community Engagement:**
  - **Conferences and Webinars:**
    Attend industry conferences, workshops, and webinars to gain insights into the latest trends and network with experts.
  - **Social Media and Forums:**
    Follow key influencers and join online communities on platforms like Twitter, LinkedIn, Reddit, and specialized Slack or Discord channels.
- **Scheduled Reviews:**
  - **Monthly or Quarterly Reviews:**
    Organize regular internal review sessions to assess the latest

breakthroughs, evaluate their potential business impact, and prioritize adoption strategies.

- **Benchmarking and Prototyping:**
    - **Rapid Prototyping:**
      Maintain a small team dedicated to prototyping emerging technologies. This team can experiment with new models and techniques, assess their performance, and present findings to decision-makers.

2. Automating Update Monitoring with GitHub API

One practical approach to staying updated is to build automated tools that periodically check for new releases or significant commits in key repositories. The following Python example demonstrates how to use the GitHub API to fetch the latest release information from a repository (e.g., Hugging Face Transformers):

```
import requests

import json

from datetime import datetime

def get_latest_release(repo_owner, repo_name):

    """

    Fetches the latest release information for the specified
GitHub repository.

    """

    url =
f"https://api.github.com/repos/{repo_owner}/{repo_name}/r
eleases/latest"
```

```
    response = requests.get(url)
        if response.status_code == 200:
        release_info = response.json()
        release_data = {
            "tag_name": release_info.get("tag_name"),
            "name": release_info.get("name"),
            "published_at": release_info.get("published_at"),
            "body": release_info.get("body")
        }
        return release_data
    else:
        print(f"Failed to fetch release info:
{response.status_code}")
        return None
# Example usage: Checking for the latest release of Hugging
Face Transformers
repo_owner = "huggingface"
repo_name = "transformers"
latest_release = get_latest_release(repo_owner, repo_name)
if latest_release:
    print("Latest Release Information:")
    print(f"Tag Name: {latest_release['tag_name']}")
    print(f"Release Name: {latest_release['name']}")
```

```
    print(f"Published At: {datetime.fromisoformat(latest_release['published_at'][:-1])}")

    print("Release Notes:")

    print(latest_release["body"])
```

Explanation:

- **API Request:**
  The function get_latest_release sends an HTTP GET request to the GitHub API endpoint for the latest release of a repository.
- **Data Extraction:**
  It extracts key details such as the tag name, release name, publication date, and release notes.
- **Automated Alerts:**
  This script can be scheduled (e.g., via cron jobs or CI pipelines) to automatically notify teams when a new release is detected, allowing for timely evaluation and adoption.

3. Integrating Updates into Internal Processes

- **Internal Dashboards:**
  Develop dashboards using tools like Grafana or Tableau that visualize updates from multiple repositories, helping teams quickly assess the relevance and impact of new releases.
- **Collaboration Platforms:**
  Integrate update alerts into collaboration tools like Slack or Microsoft Teams using webhooks or custom bots. This keeps the broader team informed in real time.
- **Documentation and Knowledge Sharing:**
  Maintain an internal knowledge base where updates are

summarized, with clear recommendations on how they might be integrated into current projects.

Conclusion

Staying current in the rapidly evolving field of NLP is essential for maintaining competitive advantage and fostering innovation. By implementing automated monitoring tools, actively engaging with the community, and integrating update reviews into regular workflows, enterprises can efficiently adopt the latest breakthroughs. These strategies not only ensure that technological advancements are leveraged to improve business outcomes but also cultivate a culture of continuous learning and agile adaptation in the face of fast-paced innovation.

Chapter 20: Conclusion: Roadmaps for Corporate Excellence in NLP

A Holistic Recap

The journey from foundational theory to cutting-edge enterprise deployments in NLP is a multifaceted transformation that has redefined how organizations harness language data to drive strategic outcomes. This roadmap encapsulates the evolution from basic linguistic principles and statistical models to advanced deep learning architectures and robust deployment strategies, culminating in solutions that are both innovative and operationally resilient.

From Foundations to Innovation

- **Foundational Theories:**
  The journey begins with a deep understanding of linguistic fundamentals—syntax, semantics, and pragmatics—that underpin all NLP techniques. These core theories provided the groundwork for early rule-based and statistical approaches, establishing the principles that guide modern algorithms.
- **Evolution to Advanced Architectures:**
  With the advent of machine learning and deep learning, approaches such as feedforward networks, CNNs, RNNs, LSTMs, GRUs, and transformers have dramatically improved the capability of NLP systems. Massive pretrained language models, such as BERT, GPT, and their variants, have introduced emergent abilities, few-shot learning, and robust contextual understanding that were previously unimaginable.
- **Enterprise Deployments:**
  Cutting-edge NLP solutions are now integrated into enterprise workflows through containerization, orchestration, and continuous integration/deployment pipelines. These solutions are optimized for scalability and performance using high-

performance hardware, distributed computing, and real-time decision frameworks. They support a wide range of applications—from sentiment analysis in financial services and medical text analysis in healthcare to demand forecasting in manufacturing and multilingual communication across global enterprises.

Strategic Pillars for Corporate Excellence in NLP

- **Infrastructure and Cloud Strategy:**
  Selecting the appropriate mix of on-premises, cloud, and hybrid infrastructures is key to balancing performance, scalability, and cost. Advanced orchestration with Docker, Kubernetes, and serverless architectures ensures robust, efficient deployment pipelines.

- **Workflow Orchestration and Pipeline Management:**
  Efficient data pipelines and model orchestration streamline the flow of information from data ingestion to actionable insights. Monitoring, alerting, and automated CI/CD pipelines maintain system health and responsiveness, ensuring high uptime and performance under load.

- **Project Management and Cross-Functional Alignment:**
  A strong NLP Center of Excellence (CoE) aligns executive leadership, data science teams, and operational units around strategic NLP goals. Effective change management and stakeholder engagement foster a culture of continuous learning, innovation, and adoption.

- **Ethical and Responsible AI:**
  Addressing bias, ensuring fairness, and complying with regulatory standards are fundamental to building trusted and sustainable NLP solutions. Transparent models, rigorous ethical reviews, and compliance with data privacy laws (GDPR, CCPA) are integral components of corporate governance in AI.

- **Continuous Learning and Future-Readiness:**
  Staying at the forefront of NLP requires proactive engagement with the open-source ecosystem, active monitoring of breakthrough research, and a willingness to adopt new techniques—whether it's low-resource learning, zero-shot classification, or the integration of NLP with other AI disciplines like computer vision and robotics.

A Roadmap for Continuous Excellence

The holistic journey in NLP is one of perpetual evolution:

1. **Foundational Mastery:**
   Begin with a strong grasp of linguistic principles and traditional statistical models.

2. **Embrace Innovation:**
   Transition to advanced deep learning architectures, fine-tuning massive pretrained models to solve real-world problems.

3. **Robust Deployment:**
   Develop scalable, resilient infrastructure that supports continuous integration, delivery, and orchestration of NLP solutions.

4. **Strategic Alignment:**
   Establish cross-functional teams and governance structures to ensure alignment between technology, business goals, and ethical standards.

5. **Future-Proofing:**
   Engage with the global open-source community, monitor emerging trends, and iteratively refine your systems to remain agile and competitive.

Illustrative Summary Dashboard (Conceptual Code Example)

While a comprehensive dashboard would typically involve a sophisticated setup with visualization tools like Grafana or Tableau, the following Python example provides a conceptual snapshot of how you might aggregate key metrics from your NLP deployment pipeline into a single summary view using Plotly.

```
import plotly.graph_objects as go
# Example metrics data (values are illustrative)
metrics = {
    "Uptime (%)": 99.8,
    "Average Latency (ms)": 120,
    "Throughput (req/s)": 350,
    "Cost Efficiency (ROI)": 1.75,
    "Adoption Rate (%)": 85
}
# Create a radar chart to visualize key performance metrics
categories = list(metrics.keys())
values = list(metrics.values())
values += values[:1]  # complete the loop
fig = go.Figure(
    data=[
        go.Scatterpolar(
            r=values,
            theta=categories + [categories[0]],
            fill='toself',
```

```
        name='NLP Deployment Metrics'
      )
   ],
   layout=go.Layout(
      title=go.layout.Title(text='Enterprise NLP Performance
Summary'),
      polar={'radialaxis': {'visible': True}},
      showlegend=True
   )
)
fig.show()
```

Explanation:

- **Dashboard Visualization:**
  The code snippet creates a radar chart that aggregates key performance metrics from the NLP deployment, offering a comprehensive, visual summary of operational excellence.
- **Key Metrics:**
  Metrics such as uptime, latency, throughput, ROI, and adoption rate provide an at-a-glance understanding of the system's performance and business impact.
- **Decision Support:**
  Such dashboards help stakeholders quickly assess progress, identify areas for improvement, and align on future strategic initiatives.

In summary, achieving corporate excellence in NLP requires a well-orchestrated roadmap that integrates foundational knowledge, cutting-edge innovation, robust deployment strategies, and continuous stakeholder engagement. As enterprises navigate this complex landscape, a holistic approach - encompassing technical, operational, and ethical dimensions - ensures that NLP initiatives not only drive competitive advantage but also remain agile and responsive to emerging trends and challenges in the digital era.

Strategic Recommendations

Actionable Takeaways for C-Suite Executives, Data Scientists, and Product Managers

As enterprises continue to harness the transformative potential of NLP, a well-defined roadmap for corporate excellence is essential. Strategic recommendations at the executive, technical, and product levels can guide organizations in capitalizing on NLP innovations while mitigating risks and ensuring sustainable growth. Below are actionable takeaways tailored for key stakeholders:

For C-Suite Executives

- **Invest in a Robust NLP Center of Excellence:**
  Establish a dedicated team to drive NLP initiatives, ensuring that AI investments are aligned with corporate strategy and deliver measurable ROI.
- **Adopt a Hybrid Infrastructure Strategy:**
  Balance cost and scalability by leveraging a mix of on-premises, cloud, and hybrid deployments. This approach ensures data security while providing flexibility to scale operations in response to market demands.
- **Focus on Ethical AI and Compliance:**
  Prioritize initiatives that integrate transparency, fairness, and

regulatory compliance. Implement governance frameworks that include regular audits and ethical review boards.

- **Monitor and Measure Impact:**
  Use performance dashboards to track key metrics (e.g., operational efficiency, customer engagement, cost savings) and drive data-driven decision-making at the executive level.

For Data Scientists

- **Leverage Transfer and Zero-Shot Learning:**
  Utilize pretrained models and state-of-the-art techniques to overcome data scarcity. Fine-tuning and prompt-based learning can significantly reduce time-to-market for new applications.
- **Foster Cross-Functional Collaboration:**
  Engage with domain experts and product managers to ensure models are grounded in real business needs and are continuously improved through feedback loops.
- **Embrace Open-Source Ecosystems:**
  Contribute to and integrate with community-driven projects to stay at the forefront of NLP research. Regularly monitor repositories (e.g., Hugging Face Transformers, spaCy) to incorporate the latest advancements.
- **Implement Rigorous Monitoring and Explainability Tools:**
  Use tools like SHAP or LIME to interpret model predictions and ensure transparency. This not only improves model performance but also builds trust with stakeholders.

For Product Managers

- **Align Product Roadmaps with NLP Capabilities:**
  Identify opportunities where NLP can drive competitive advantage—such as personalized customer experiences, real-time decision-making, and automated workflows—and integrate these into your product strategy.

- **Prioritize User Adoption and Change Management:**
  Develop training programs and interactive demos to facilitate user adoption. Gather continuous feedback and adjust your product roadmap accordingly.
- **Establish Clear KPIs and Monitor Performance:**
  Define measurable objectives (e.g., reduction in manual processing time, improvement in customer satisfaction) to evaluate the success of NLP integrations.
- **Ensure Seamless Integration:**
  Work closely with data scientists and operations teams to ensure that NLP solutions are integrated smoothly into existing systems and workflows, minimizing disruption and maximizing utility.

Illustrative Example: A Strategic Dashboard for Stakeholder Alignment

The following Python example uses Plotly to create a radar chart that aggregates key performance indicators (KPIs) relevant to NLP initiatives. This dashboard provides a visual summary that can facilitate strategic discussions among executives, data scientists, and product managers.

```
import plotly.graph_objects as go

# Example KPIs from NLP deployments (illustrative values)

kpi_data = {

    "ROI Improvement (%)": 20,

    "Operational Efficiency Gain (%)": 25,

    "User Adoption Rate (%)": 80,

    "Compliance & Ethical Standards (Score)": 9,
```

```
    "Innovation Impact (Score)": 8,
    "Scalability (Score)": 9,
}
categories = list(kpi_data.keys())
values = list(kpi_data.values())
# Close the radar chart loop by repeating the first value at the end
values += values[:1]
categories += categories[:1]
fig = go.Figure(
    data=[
        go.Scatterpolar(
            r=values,
            theta=categories,
            fill='toself',
            name='NLP Strategic KPIs'
        )
    ],
    layout=go.Layout(
        title=go.layout.Title(text='Strategic Dashboard for NLP Initiatives'),
        polar=dict(
            radialaxis=dict(
```

```
                visible=True,
                range=[0, 10]
            )
        ),
        showlegend=True
    )
)
fig.show()
```

Explanation:

- **Dashboard Visualization:**
  This radar chart aggregates strategic KPIs, providing a snapshot of how NLP initiatives are performing across multiple dimensions critical to enterprise success.
- **Key Metrics:**
  Metrics include ROI improvement, operational efficiency, user adoption, compliance and ethics, innovation impact, and scalability.
- **Stakeholder Alignment:**
  Such a dashboard can be used in strategic meetings to align the perspectives of C-suite executives, data scientists, and product managers, ensuring that all stakeholders are informed and can collaboratively drive continuous improvement.

In summary, achieving corporate excellence in NLP requires a cohesive, multi-disciplinary approach that aligns executive vision, technical innovation, and product strategy. The strategic recommendations outlined above provide actionable takeaways for

C-suite executives, data scientists, and product managers. By investing in robust NLP centers of excellence, leveraging cutting-edge technologies, and integrating continuous feedback mechanisms, enterprises can unlock the full potential of NLP to drive growth, innovation, and competitive advantage. This roadmap not only sets the stage for sustained technological advancement but also ensures that every stakeholder is empowered to contribute to a unified vision for digital transformation.

Vision for the Future

Potential Trajectories of NLP Technologies and Reflections on Sustainable Growth

The future of Natural Language Processing (NLP) promises transformative advancements that will reshape how enterprises interact with data, customers, and the world around them. As we look ahead, several key trajectories and trends are emerging that signal a new era of intelligent, adaptive, and sustainable NLP solutions. This vision for the future is built on three foundational pillars:

1. Evolution of Model Capabilities

- **Multimodal and Cross-Disciplinary Integration:**
  Future NLP systems will increasingly integrate with other AI disciplines, such as computer vision and robotics, to form cohesive multimodal systems. These systems will interpret and generate content that spans text, images, audio, and sensor data, enabling richer interactions and more comprehensive decision-making support.

- **Enhanced Reasoning and Contextual Understanding:**
  As large language models continue to scale, we expect further breakthroughs in emergent abilities, such as improved chain-of-thought reasoning, more effective few-shot and zero-shot learning, and advanced contextual adaptation. This will enable

models to not only respond to queries but also provide detailed, interpretable reasoning that can support critical business decisions.

- **Domain-Specific and Responsible AI:**
  The trend towards specialized, domain-adapted NLP solutions will grow. Enterprises will increasingly leverage transfer learning and continual learning strategies to develop models that are finely tuned to industry-specific language and requirements while adhering to robust ethical standards and regulatory frameworks.

2. Sustainable and Scalable Infrastructure

- **Hardware and Distributed Computing Advances:**
  Advances in high-performance hardware—such as more efficient GPUs, TPUs, and emerging specialized AI chips—will continue to lower the cost and energy consumption of running large-scale NLP models. Combined with advancements in distributed computing frameworks and serverless architectures, these improvements will enable real-time, scalable NLP solutions that are both cost-effective and environmentally sustainable.

- **Automation and Orchestration:**
  The future will see deeper integration of automated CI/CD pipelines, containerization, and orchestration frameworks that facilitate seamless deployment and real-time monitoring. This will ensure that NLP systems remain agile, scalable, and resilient as workloads grow and business requirements evolve.

3. Business and Social Impact

- **Data-Driven Innovation:**
  NLP technologies will increasingly underpin strategic decision-making across industries. By transforming unstructured data into actionable insights, organizations will be empowered to optimize operations, drive personalized customer experiences, and enhance competitive advantage on a global scale.

- **Ethics, Fairness, and Transparency:**
  As NLP becomes more integrated into everyday business processes, a strong emphasis on ethical AI will be crucial. Future developments will focus on building transparent, explainable models that mitigate bias and uphold data privacy, ensuring that technological progress benefits all stakeholders equitably.
- **Sustainable Growth:**
  The continued advancement and adoption of NLP technologies will drive sustainable growth by reducing operational costs, improving process efficiencies, and fostering innovation. Organizations that invest in these capabilities will not only achieve short-term gains but also secure long-term resilience in a rapidly evolving digital landscape.

Illustrative Example: Visualizing Future Trajectories with a Conceptual Dashboard

Below is a conceptual Python example using Plotly to create a radar chart that visualizes potential future trajectories for key NLP capabilities. This dashboard can serve as a strategic tool for stakeholders to monitor progress and guide investment decisions.

```
import plotly.graph_objects as go

# Example future trajectory metrics (scale: 0-10)

future_metrics = {

    "Multimodal Integration": 9,

    "Contextual Reasoning": 8,

    "Domain Specialization": 8,

    "Hardware Efficiency": 9,

    "Scalability": 8,
```

```
    "Ethical & Responsible AI": 10,
    "Business Impact": 9,
    "Sustainability": 8
}
categories = list(future_metrics.keys())
values = list(future_metrics.values())
# Close the radar chart loop by appending the first value to the end
values += values[:1]
categories += categories[:1]
fig = go.Figure(
    data=[
        go.Scatterpolar(
            r=values,
            theta=categories,
            fill='toself',
            name='Future NLP Vision'
        )
    ],
    layout=go.Layout(
        title=go.layout.Title(text='Vision for the Future: NLP Trajectories'),
        polar={'radialaxis': {'visible': True, 'range': [0, 10]}},
```

```
        showlegend=True
    )
)
fig.show()
```

Explanation:

- **Future Metrics:**
  The radar chart visualizes various dimensions that represent the future potential of NLP technologies—from multimodal integration and contextual reasoning to ethical AI and sustainability.
- **Strategic Insights:**
  Such visual tools help stakeholders understand where current investments are paying off and which areas require additional focus or innovation.
- **Decision-Making Support:**
  By aligning these metrics with corporate strategy, executives, data scientists, and product managers can collaboratively steer NLP initiatives toward long-term success.

Final Reflections on Sustainable Growth

The future of NLP is both exciting and challenging, as emerging technologies continue to push the boundaries of what machines can understand and generate. A holistic roadmap for corporate excellence in NLP involves not only technological advancements but also the strategic alignment of resources, ethical considerations, and continuous innovation. Embracing this multifaceted approach ensures that enterprises are well-equipped to leverage NLP for sustainable growth, driving transformative changes that extend well beyond the realm of language processing.

In summary, the vision for the future of NLP is one of integration, innovation, and responsible growth. By investing in cutting-edge models, scalable infrastructure, and robust governance frameworks, organizations can unlock new opportunities, enhance operational efficiency, and create lasting value in an increasingly competitive global landscape.

Appendices

Appendix A: Common NLP Tools and Libraries

This appendix provides a detailed reference guide to popular NLP libraries and tools, including configuration notes, version compatibility, and practical usage tips. These resources are fundamental to both research and production applications, offering extensive functionalities ranging from basic text processing to advanced deep learning models.

1. Hugging Face Transformers

Overview:
Hugging Face Transformers is one of the most widely used libraries for state-of-the-art NLP. It offers a vast collection of pretrained models (e.g., BERT, GPT, RoBERTa, T5) and a unified API that supports PyTorch, TensorFlow, and JAX.

Configuration Notes:

- **Installation:**
  Install via pip:

pip install transformers

- **Version Compatibility:**
- Compatible with Python 3.6 and above.
- Regularly updated; check the GitHub repository for the latest release notes.
- **Dependencies:**
  Requires PyTorch (>=1.0.0) or TensorFlow (>=2.0.0) depending on the backend. Use the command:

pip install torch # or tensorflow

Usage Example:

```
from transformers import pipeline
classifier = pipeline("sentiment-analysis", model="distilbert-base-uncased-finetuned-sst-2-english")
result = classifier("The new update is fantastic!")
print(result)
```

2. spaCy

Overview:
spaCy is a production-ready NLP library designed for efficiency and ease of use. It provides pre-trained models for tokenization, POS tagging, named entity recognition, dependency parsing, and more.

Configuration Notes:

- **Installation:**
  Install via pip:

```
pip install spacy
```

- **Model Downloads:**
  Download language models separately. For example:

```
python -m spacy download en_core_web_sm
```

Version Compatibility:

- Compatible with Python 3.6 and above.
- spaCy 3.x supports pipelines that are fully customizable. Refer to the spaCy documentation for migration guides if using spaCy 2.x.

Usage Example:

```
import spacy

nlp = spacy.load("en_core_web_sm")

doc = nlp("Apple is looking at buying U.K. startup for $1 billion.")

for ent in doc.ents:
    print(ent.text, ent.label_)
```

3. Stanford CoreNLP

Overview:
Stanford CoreNLP is a comprehensive suite of NLP tools that provides robust capabilities for tasks such as tokenization, POS tagging, NER, coreference resolution, and sentiment analysis.

Configuration Notes:

- **Installation:**
  CoreNLP is written in Java. Download the latest version from the Stanford NLP website.
- **Usage in Python:**
  Use the stanfordnlp or stanza library for Python interfaces:

```
pip install stanza
```

Then download models:

```
import stanza

stanza.download('en')

nlp = stanza.Pipeline('en')

doc = nlp("Barack Obama was born in Hawaii.")

for sentence in doc.sentences:
```

```
for word in sentence.words:
    print(word.text, word.pos)
```

- **Version Compatibility:**
  Ensure Java 8 or higher is installed. For Python wrappers, refer to the respective library documentation for compatibility notes.

4. NLTK (Natural Language Toolkit)

Overview:
NLTK is a foundational library for NLP in Python, widely used for educational purposes and prototyping. It provides functionalities for tokenization, stemming, lemmatization, parsing, and more.

Configuration Notes:

- **Installation:**
  Install via pip:

```
pip install nltk
```

Data Downloads:
Download necessary datasets and models:

```
import nltk
nltk.download('punkt')
nltk.download('averaged_perceptron_tagger')
nltk.download('wordnet')
```

- **Version Compatibility:**
  - Compatible with Python 3.6 and above.
  - NLTK is actively maintained; refer to the official website for updates.

Usage Example:

```
import nltk
from nltk.tokenize import word_tokenize
text = "Natural Language Processing is fun and powerful."
tokens = word_tokenize(text)
print(tokens)
```

5. AllenNLP

Overview:
AllenNLP, developed by the Allen Institute for AI, is an extensible library built on PyTorch for deep learning research in NLP. It emphasizes model interpretability and provides tools for a variety of NLP tasks.

Configuration Notes:

- **Installation:**
  Install via pip:

```
pip install allennlp allennlp-models
```

- **Version Compatibility:**
  - Requires Python 3.6 and above.
  - Ensure compatibility with the installed version of PyTorch.

Usage Example:

```
from allennlp.predictors.predictor import Predictor
import allennlp_models.tagging
```

```
predictor =
Predictor.from_path("https://storage.googleapis.com/allennlp
-public-models/ner-model-2020.02.10.tar.gz")

result = predictor.predict(sentence="Barack Obama was born
in Hawaii.")

print(result)
```

6. Gensim

Overview:
Gensim specializes in topic modeling and document similarity analysis. It offers efficient implementations of algorithms such as Word2Vec, LDA, and TF-IDF.

Configuration Notes:

- **Installation:**
  Install via pip:

```
pip install genism
```

- **Version Compatibility:**
  - Compatible with Python 3.6 and above.
  - Works well with Numpy and Scipy; ensure these libraries are up-to-date.

Usage Example:

```
from gensim.models import Word2Vec

sentences = [["this", "is", "a", "sample"], ["we", "are",
"learning", "gensim"]]

model = Word2Vec(sentences, vector_size=100, window=5,
min_count=1, workers=4)

print(model.wv["sample"])
```

7. Flair

Overview:
Flair is an NLP library from Zalando Research that allows users to combine different word embeddings to create powerful text representations. It excels in sequence labeling and text classification tasks.

Configuration Notes:

- **Installation:**
  Install via pip:

```
pip install flair
```

- **Version Compatibility:**
  - Requires Python 3.6 and above.
  - Ensure compatibility with PyTorch; Flair typically uses the latest stable release.

Usage Example:

```
from flair.data import Sentence

from flair.models import SequenceTagger

# Load a pre-trained NER tagger

tagger = SequenceTagger.load("ner")

sentence = Sentence("George Washington went to Washington.")

tagger.predict(sentence)

print(sentence.to_tagged_string())
```

Appendix B: Mathematical Fundamentals

A strong foundation in mathematics is essential for understanding and advancing Natural Language Processing (NLP) models. This appendix covers the key mathematical concepts that underpin many NLP techniques, including linear algebra, optimization methods, and probability theory. These disciplines not only provide the theoretical basis for model design and training but also offer practical tools and methods that are crucial for building, evaluating, and refining NLP systems.

1. Linear Algebra

Overview:

Linear algebra is the backbone of many NLP techniques. It provides the language and tools for representing and manipulating data in high-dimensional spaces. Key concepts include:

- **Vectors and Matrices:**
  Representing text as vectors (e.g., word embeddings) and processing data using matrix operations.
- **Matrix Multiplication:**
  Fundamental for operations such as transforming embeddings, calculating similarities, and propagating information through neural networks.
- **Eigenvalues and Eigenvectors:**
  Useful in dimensionality reduction techniques like Principal Component Analysis (PCA) which can help in visualizing high-dimensional data.

Practical Example: Matrix Multiplication

Below is a Python example using NumPy to perform matrix multiplication, a fundamental operation in neural network computations:

```
import numpy as np
# Define two matrices
A = np.array([[1, 2], [3, 4]])
B = np.array([[5, 6], [7, 8]])
# Perform matrix multiplication
C = np.dot(A, B)
print("Matrix A:")
print(A)
print("\nMatrix B:")
print(B)
print("\nProduct of A and B:")
print(C)
```

2. Optimization Methods

Overview:

Optimization methods are critical in training NLP models. They are used to minimize the loss function, guiding the model to improve its predictions by adjusting its parameters. Key concepts include:

- **Gradient Descent:**
  The most fundamental optimization algorithm that iteratively adjusts parameters by moving in the direction of the negative gradient of the loss function.
- **Stochastic Gradient Descent (SGD):**
  A variant of gradient descent that updates parameters using a

small subset (batch) of the data, improving efficiency for large datasets.

- **Advanced Optimizers:**
  Methods such as Adam, RMSprop, and AdaGrad adapt the learning rate during training, often leading to faster convergence and better performance in deep learning models.

Practical Example: Gradient Descent Simulation

Below is an illustrative example of gradient descent used to minimize a simple quadratic function.

```
import numpy as np

# Define a simple quadratic function: f(x) = (x - 3)^2

def f(x):

    return (x - 3) ** 2

# Its derivative: f'(x) = 2*(x - 3)

def grad_f(x):

    return 2 * (x - 3)

# Gradient Descent parameters

x = 0.0         # Starting point

learning_rate = 0.1

num_iterations = 25

# Perform gradient descent

for i in range(num_iterations):

    grad = grad_f(x)
```

```
    x = x - learning_rate * grad
    print(f"Iteration {i+1}: x = {x:.4f}, f(x) = {f(x):.4f}")
print("Minimum found at x =", x)
```

3. Probability Theory

Overview:

Probability theory provides a framework for modeling uncertainty and making predictions based on incomplete data. It is essential for:

- **Modeling Uncertainty:**
  Understanding how probabilistic models (e.g., Naive Bayes, Hidden Markov Models) work by quantifying the likelihood of various outcomes.
- **Bayesian Inference:**
  Using prior knowledge to update beliefs in the presence of new evidence.
- **Statistical Measures:**
  Calculating expectations, variances, and probability distributions that inform model behavior and performance.

Practical Example: Basic Probability Computation

Below is a simple Python example that computes the probability of an event using basic probability theory.

```
# Define the probability of an event A occurring (e.g., a word appearing in a document)
p_A = 0.3  # 30% chance
```

```
# Define the probability of event B occurring (e.g., another word appearing in the same document)

p_B = 0.5  # 50% chance

# If A and B are independent, the joint probability of both events occurring is:

p_A_and_B = p_A * p_B

print("Probability of both events A and B occurring:", p_A_and_B)

# For conditional probability: P(A|B) = P(A and B) / P(B)

p_A_given_B = p_A_and_B / p_B

print("Probability of A given B:", p_A_given_B)
```

Appendix C: Glossary of Key Terms

This appendix serves as a quick-reference guide to frequently used technical and corporate jargon in the field of Natural Language Processing (NLP) and enterprise AI deployments. The glossary provides concise definitions of key terms, enabling both technical and non-technical stakeholders to navigate the complex landscape of modern AI solutions with ease.

Technical Terms

- **Tokenization:**
  The process of breaking text into smaller units, such as words or subwords, which serve as the basic building blocks for further analysis.
- **Embedding:**
  A numerical vector representation of text (words, phrases, or sentences) that captures semantic relationships in a continuous vector space.
- **Transformer:**
  A deep learning architecture based on self-attention mechanisms, used for processing sequential data in parallel. Notable examples include BERT, GPT, and RoBERTa.
- **Attention Mechanism:**
  A method within neural networks that allows the model to focus on different parts of the input sequence when producing each output element, enabling improved context modeling.
- **Zero-Shot Learning:**
  A learning paradigm where a model can perform a task without having been explicitly trained on it, often by leveraging natural language prompts.

- **Few-Shot Learning:**
  A scenario where a model adapts to a new task with only a small number of labeled examples, leveraging its pretrained knowledge.
- **ETL (Extract, Transform, Load):**
  A process in data engineering that involves extracting data from source systems, transforming it into a suitable format, and loading it into a target system or database.
- **CI/CD (Continuous Integration/Continuous Delivery):**
  Practices that automate testing, integration, and deployment of code to ensure rapid, reliable, and scalable software updates.
- **Model Orchestration:**
  The process of managing multiple machine learning models, including their deployment, scaling, and integration into production systems.
- **Distributed Computing:**
  The use of multiple computing resources (e.g., GPUs, TPUs, or clusters) to perform large-scale processing tasks concurrently, improving speed and scalability.
- **Approximate Nearest-Neighbor (ANN) Search:**
  Algorithms that quickly find the closest vectors in high-dimensional space, trading off a small amount of accuracy for significant gains in search speed.
- **Mixed Precision Training:**
  A technique that uses lower-precision arithmetic (e.g., FP16) during training to reduce memory usage and increase computational speed without significant loss in accuracy.

Corporate and Deployment Terms

- **Center of Excellence (CoE):**
  A dedicated team or unit within an organization that drives innovation, best practices, and governance in a specific domain—in this case, NLP and AI.

- **Operational Efficiency:**
  Measures of how effectively an organization uses resources (time, money, human capital) to achieve its objectives, often improved by automation and data-driven insights.

- **Scalability:**
  The ability of a system to handle growing amounts of work or to be readily enlarged to accommodate that growth, both in terms of processing power and data volume.

- **Cost Management:**
  Strategies and practices to balance computational and operational costs with business objectives, ensuring that investments in technology yield a high return on investment (ROI).

- **Hybrid Infrastructure:**
  A mix of on-premises, cloud-based, and edge computing resources used to optimize performance, security, and cost-effectiveness.

- **Workflow Orchestration:**
  The coordination and management of complex processes across multiple systems and teams to ensure smooth and efficient operations.

- **Ethical AI:**
  The practice of developing and deploying AI systems in a manner that is fair, transparent, and accountable, minimizing bias and ensuring compliance with regulations.

- **Data Governance:**
  Policies, procedures, and standards that ensure data is managed properly, securely, and in compliance with regulatory requirements.
- **Change Management:**
  The structured approach to transitioning individuals, teams, and organizations from a current state to a desired future state, ensuring smooth adoption of new technologies and processes.
- **User Adoption:**
  The process by which end-users embrace and effectively utilize new technologies, often measured by metrics such as usage rates, feedback, and productivity improvements.

Usage and Integration

This glossary is designed to be a living document. As the field of NLP and enterprise AI continues to evolve, new terms and concepts will emerge. Organizations should periodically update this glossary to reflect the latest developments and ensure that all stakeholders remain aligned on terminology and strategic objectives.

By establishing a common vocabulary, this glossary helps bridge the gap between technical teams and corporate leadership, fostering clearer communication and more effective collaboration across the organization.

www.ingramcontent.com/pod-product-compliance
Lightning Source LLC
LaVergne TN
LVHW032223200926
848481LV00001B/221